OECD Insurance Statistics 2017

OECD
BETTER POLICIES FOR BETTER LIVES

This work is published under the responsibility of the Secretary-General of the OECD. The opinions expressed and arguments employed herein do not necessarily reflect the official views of OECD member countries.

This document, as well as any data and any map included herein, are without prejudice to the status of or sovereignty over any territory, to the delimitation of international frontiers and boundaries and to the name of any territory, city or area.

Please cite this publication as:
OECD (2018), *OECD Insurance Statistics 2017*, OECD Publishing, Paris.
https://doi.org/10.1787/ins_stats-2017-en

ISBN 978-92-64-30342-3 (print)
ISBN 978-92-64-30343-0 (PDF)

Series: OECD Insurance Statistics
ISSN 2307-8421 (print)
ISSN 2307-843X (online)

The statistical data for Israel are supplied by and under the responsibility of the relevant Israeli authorities. The use of such data by the OECD is without prejudice to the status of the Golan Heights, East Jerusalem and Israeli settlements in the West Bank under the terms of international law.

Corrigenda to OECD publications may be found on line at: *www.oecd.org/publishing/corrigenda*.

Table of contents

Conventional signs and abbreviations

Signs and abbreviations

c	Confidential.
..	Not available.
.	Decimal point.
|	Break in series.

ISO country codes and abbreviations for currency

	ISO code	Currency	Abbreviation
Australia	AUS	dollar	AUD
Austria	AUT	euro	EUR
Belgium	BEL	euro	EUR
Canada	CAN	dollar	CAD
Chile	CHL	peso	CLP
Czech Republic	CZE	koruna	CZK
Denmark	DNK	krone	DKK
Estonia	EST	euro	EUR
Finland	FIN	euro	EUR
France	FRA	euro	EUR
Germany	DEU	euro	EUR
Greece	GRC	euro	EUR
Hungary	HUN	forint	HUF
Iceland	ISL	króna	ISK
Ireland	IRL	euro	EUR
Israel	ISR	sheqel	ILS
Italy	ITA	euro	EUR
Japan	JPN	yen	JPY
Korea	KOR	won	KRW
Latvia	LVA	euro	EUR
Luxembourg	LUX	euro	EUR
Mexico	MEX	peso	MXN
Netherlands	NLD	euro	EUR
New Zealand	NZL	dollar	NZD
Norway	NOR	krone	NOK
Poland	POL	zloty	PLN
Portugal	PRT	euro	EUR
Slovak Republic	SVK	euro	EUR
Slovenia	SVN	euro	EUR
Spain	ESP	euro	EUR
Sweden	SWE	krona	SEK
Switzerland	CHE	franc	CHF
Turkey	TUR	lira	TRY
United Kingdom	GBR	pound	GBP
United States	USA	dollar	USD

Common definitions and notes

Notes on data sources

All the data in the statistical tables of each country have been reported by the relevant national insurance authorities. Regarding comparative tables of indicators, the data are mainly drawn from the tables by country. The economic data on exchange rates, population and GDP are taken from the OECD publication *Main Economic Indicators*.

To achieve greater clarity, the number of variables selected and displayed in this publication has been limited. Data have been extracted from the Global Insurance Statistics Database. *The complete database can be accessed online at the following link:*

OECD Insurance Statistics, *http://dx.doi.org/10.1787/ins-data-en.*

A significant effort has been made to achieve comparability among countries. Definitions, classifications, calculation methods, and units have been standardised as far as possible.

General notes

a) Life and non life categories follow the definitions used in national law. However, the premiums for accident and sickness insurance underwritten by life companies should be included in non life figures.

b) Up until 2008, the insurance business is broken down between life and non-life business. As of 2009, the insurance business is broken down between the business of pure life, pure non-life and composite undertakings and composite undertakings' business is further broken down between life and non-life business. Some countries do not allow for insurance undertakings to be active in both life and non-life insurance business and therefore composite insurance undertakings do not exist in these countries. In other countries (e.g., Austria, Belgium, Hungary, Italy, Mexico, Portugal, Spain) however, the share of employment in composite insurance undertakings accounts for more than half of the whole domestic insurance sector. Therefore, to have comparable data across years for life business data (respectively non-life), one has to sum up the life (respectively non-life) business of pure life (respectively non-life) undertakings and the life (respectively non-life) business of composite undertakings as of 2009.

c) Figures provided for the number of companies and for insurance premiums should include all insurance companies licensed or authorised in the reporting country, *including* professional reinsurers, whether or not these are controlled, but *excluding* any statutory system of social security administered by the State.

d) *Domestic companies* means those companies incorporated under national law, together with those companies in the reporting country which are unincorporated, but excluding the branches and agencies of foreign companies.

e) *Foreign controlled companies* means those domestic companies controlled by foreign interests, such "control" being defined according to national law (see the definition of foreign controlled companies in notes by country). The data of *foreign controlled companies* are part of those of *Domestic companies*.

f) *Foreign companies* means companies incorporated outside the reporting country.

International comparisons

Detailed metadata at: *http://metalinks.oecd.org/ins/20180621/57fd*.

Country tables

In this part, the main insurance statistics are presented through separate tables for each OECD member country. Figures refer to the calendar year. The premiums and other amounts are described in millions of the national currency unit.

OECD Insurance Statistics 2017

PART I
International comparisons

Table 1. Balance sheet and income, direct insurance (All insurance companies)

2016

Million US dollars

	Gross claims payments	Gross operating expenses	Commissions	Outstanding claims provision (changes)	Total assets	Gross technical provisions	Gross technical provisions unit-linked	Shareholders' equity	Net income
Argentina	6 550	3 050	1 772	2 713	22 342	6 157	..	4 735	1 352
Australia	63 523	10 907	3 454	..	229 940	52 618	..	31 812	3 596
Austria	16 787	971	3 509	294	133 533	92 247	18 621	..	..
Belgium	31 420	3 326	3 668	582	300 273	256 480	33 562	14 307	1 467
Bolivia	304	179	46	..	1 006	474	..	1 494	27
Brazil	13 157	11 430	4 818	725	268 991	180 701	149 492	24 902	5 108
Canada	..	..	..	..	..	..	..	..	..
Chile	7 141	1 658	931	3 298	60 964	52 740	4 901	6 086	736
Colombia	304	179	46	..	1 006	474	..	1 494	27
Costa Rica	658	231	165	52	3 837	1 492	0	1 542	100
Czech Republic	3 734	1 075	299	93	18 178	13 184	3 439	2 968	489
Denmark	23 765	2 498	321	22 266	447 735	350 608	134 264	28 332	2 959
Ecuador	920	272	274	614	2 321	895	..	617	2 135
El Salvador	37	13	9	11	93	23	..	42	5
Estonia	408	167	..	..	1 917	1 209	597	421	56
Finland	8 215	1 346	371	-189	82 266	69 232	36 285	5 735	911
France	..	..	..	..	2 803 040	2 266 271	322 510	183 314	12 862
Germany	173 314	16 271	18 700	3 391	1 592 396	1 433 410	106 390	58 648	2 177
Greece	..	1 087	..	..	16 839	12 382	2 509	3 271	..
Guatemala	477	244	85	..	1 210	657	..	439	86
Honduras	..	..	..	..	..	..	..	..	..
Hong Kong, China	2 413	570	798	..	..	..	..	..	..
Hungary	1 956	829	487	23	8 596	7 181	3 847	903	185
India	40 598	9 228	3 455	53 359	406 387	392 011	46 680	10 704	1 585
Indonesia	9 207	2 180	2 109	10	43 139	29 558	12 463	10 033	1 268
Iceland	359	68	..	414	1 295	656	47	509	89
Ireland	37 797	2 940	5 199	..	306 344	267 570	208 093	23 827	..
Israel[1]	8 870	1 678	1 827	498	121 078	106 547	69 904	5 869	374
Italy	97 937	14 809	11 751	-2 804	854 075	731 451	131 191	69 951	6 306
Japan	314 319	72 561	12 268	20 250	3 480 991	2 748 475	..	121 185	18 604
Korea	92 051	36 760	..	..	846 833	603 972	81 080	78 937	4 797
Latvia	346	102	36	26	634	438	52	145	116
Lithuania	264	151	4	-10	1 474	1 076	492	296	8
Luxembourg	16 040	2 224	1 341	-226	194 688	176 705	120 464	5 050	430
Malaysia	8 631	2 240	1 283	6	59 699	48 861	8 253	6 019	1 114
Mexico	11 939	1 541	3 548	..	63 905	49 242	..	8 889	2 087
Netherlands	..	..	..	..	..	..	..	..	..
New Zealand	4 498	6 519	929	..	20 631	..	..	5 634	1 002
Nicaragua	82	22	20	31	316	161	15	93	21
Norway	12 248	2 323	452	-291	187 868	158 232	27 663	19 811	2 226
Paraguay	..	115	50	..	..	..	..	..	..
Peru	1 658	829	315	15	12 571	8 179	..	2 125	304
Poland	9 302	3 741	348	130	44 353	34 151	13 626	8 182	1 061
Portugal	13 780	1 635	685	86	54 253	46 440	12 212	5 112	176
Puerto Rico	10 650	2 253	386	-53	8 200	5 709	..	2 492	156
Russia	7 787	4 831	2 591	3 079	30 869	18 752	..	7 608	1 213
Singapore	14 236	1 748	2 212	..	141 853	112 198	..	19 735	1 976
Slovak Republic	2 740	..	..	..	6 941	4 602	1 164	..	..
Slovenia	1 444	482	106	-11	7 341	5 166	1 272	1 488	154
South Africa	35 822	4 001	2 676	2 304	204 941	174 452	93 201	15 562	813
Spain	47 545	9 517	5 767	714	317 923	224 888	14 749	43 525	4 786
Sweden	16 680	3 317	952	29 642	478 202	331 091	137 902	114 955	11 319
Switzerland	51 448	4 346	5 073	1 105	460 598	340 183	..	47 115	7 499
Tunisia	540	240	..	..	..	..	..	..	..
Turkey	6 002	2 508	1 949	1 363	33 859	13 148	..	4 204	818
United Kingdom	245 985	50 904	..	..	2 891 206	2 426 743	1 478 729	..	..
United States	1 315 527	301 877	97 002	83 959	5 764 873	814 039	..	1 164 337	89 565

.. Not available

Note: Detailed metadata at: http://metalinks.oecd.org/ins/20180621/caf9.

Disclaimer: http://oe.cd/disclaimer

1. Information on data for Israel: http://oe.cd/israel-disclaimer.

Source: Balance sheet and income, OECD Insurance Statistics (database)

Table 2. Balance sheet and income, direct insurance (Life insurance companies)
2016

Million US dollars

	Gross claims payments	Gross operating expenses	Commissions	Outstanding claims provision (changes)	Total assets	Gross technical provisions	Gross technical provisions unit-linked	Shareholders' equity	Net income
Argentina	243	129	18	3	3 850	3 137	..	425	168
Australia	41 560	5 334	2 326	..	150 180	..	..	13 738	1 414
Austria	1 047	41	89	4	11 655	10 390	3 647	..	..
Belgium	689	46	28	9	9 763	8 306	959	448	8
Bolivia	89	65	19	..	636	392	..	468	10
Brazil	466	1 537	530	71	..	101 338	98 793	8 623	2 055
Canada	..	..	..	..	..	..	..	..	..
Chile	4 938	981	470	3 292	54 869	48 192	4 901	4 978	625
Colombia	89	65	19	..	636	392	..	468	10
Costa Rica	0	0	0	0	0	0	0	..	..
Czech Republic	264	103	2	0	1 934	1 735	804	140	33
Denmark	17 123	711	51	21 492	423 158	336 241	134 264	20 906	1 662
Ecuador	63	33	35	4	144	68	..	40	27
El Salvador	17	6	3	7	33	10	..	12	1
Estonia	96	16	..	..	776	557	538	49	16
Finland	4 783	377	152	49	62 139	56 181	36 285	2 440	262
France	..	..	..	..	568 686	492 739	68 386	31 730	1 805
Germany	86 939	4 316	5 591	572	1 087 851	1 004 209	106 343	16 249	373
Greece	..	39	..	..	2 515	2 225	219	225	..
Guatemala	0	..	..	..	..	..	..	..	..
Honduras	..	..	..	..	..	..	..	..	..
Hong Kong, China	..	..	..	..	..	..	..	..	..
Hungary	551	124	59	1	2 903	2 652	1 354	167	21
India	30 188	5 772	3 012	40 908	394 147	369 639	46 680	3 928	1 103
Indonesia	7 113	1 301	1 408	30	33 569	25 582	12 463	6 280	889
Iceland	14	10	..	18	146	60	47	55	11
Ireland	26 607	1 271	2 511	..	259 431	237 850	208 093	13 218	..
Israel[1]	2	8	5	1	305	258	255	31	-6
Italy	23 835	1 066	693	-419	219 981	206 377	72 341	8 168	730
Japan	266 691	43 446	..	20 044	3 214 941	2 748 475	..	91 474	12 840
Korea	67 704	24 989	..	..	647 635	453 911	81 080	54 452	2 086
Latvia	0	0	0	0	0	0	0	..	0
Lithuania	28	16	0	0	271	235	208	31	14
Luxembourg	13 615	1 258	683	25	181 648	167 750	120 464	3 164	236
Malaysia	2 388	454	510	0	25 882	21 312	2 746	974	212
Mexico	795	91	64	..	13 441	12 063	..	1 209	170
Netherlands	..	..	..	..	..	..	..	..	..
New Zealand	1 112	1 733	395	..	9 372	..	..	2 453	611
Nicaragua	..	..	..	..	..	..	..	..	..
Norway	6 171	941	106	..	160 139	143 870	27 663	10 926	794
Paraguay	..	0	0	..	..	..	..	..	..
Peru	477	175	36	10	5 059	4 102	..	641	102
Poland	4 637	1 432	56	69	24 691	20 903	13 626	2 929	570
Portugal	7 265	332	116	-15	30 739	27 855	11 587	1 841	32
Puerto Rico	970	306	117	73	3 425	2 721	..	704	83
Russia	593	934	709	25	7 435	6 111	..	998	378
Singapore	5 557	500	1 181	..	68 310	57 815	..	4 749	742
Slovak Republic	205	..	..	..	674	433	335	..	..
Slovenia	56	13	4	1	890	538	167	302	15
South Africa	30 357	2 610	1 615	..	193 813	173 786	93 201	11 238	1
Spain	3 395	470	275	76	31 376	23 744	3 421	3 088	352
Sweden	8 978	1 474	358	4 261	413 630	299 603	137 902	101 825	9 264
Switzerland	29 522	1 102	911	94	323 820	278 951	..	15 102	1 070
Tunisia	34	22	..	..	..	..	..	..	..
Turkey	979	652	435	41	21 730	2 268	..	1 621	438
United Kingdom	161 448	11 320	..	..	2 158 979	1 886 609	1 376 121	..	..
United States	353 883	67 975	46 930	40 670	4 161 570	18 118	..	443 631	51 450

.. Not available

Note: Detailed metadata at: http://metalinks.oecd.org/ins/20180621/caf9.

Disclaimer: http://oe.cd/disclaimer

1. Information on data for Israel: http://oe.cd/israel-disclaimer.

Source: Balance sheet and income, OECD Insurance Statistics (database)

Table 3. Balance sheet and income, direct insurance (Non-life insurance companies)
2016

Million US dollars

	Gross claims payments	Gross operating expenses	Commissions	Outstanding claims provision (changes)	Total assets	Gross technical provisions	Gross technical provisions unit-linked	Shareholders' equity	Net income
Argentina	2 731	671	324	1 460	6 406	426	..	1 229	267
Australia	21 963	5 573	1 128	..	79 760	52 618	..	18 075	2 182
Austria	1 979	154	744	52	14 067	2 669	40	..	..
Belgium	2 805	709	790	55	13 929	8 282	..	2 353	-256
Bolivia	215	113	26	..	370	82	..	1 026	17
Brazil	2 751	1 684	786	-16	..	4 710	0	1 658	196
Canada	..	..	..	..	..	..	..	..	..
Chile	2 204	676	461	6	6 095	4 548	0	1 108	111
Colombia	215	113	26	..	370	82	..	1 026	17
Costa Rica	25	10	9	2	61	37	0	17	-4
Czech Republic	155	99	23	16	533	255	..	177	17
Denmark	6 642	1 787	270	774	24 577	14 367	..	7 425	1 297
Ecuador	683	201	169	573	1 920	769	..	438	1 633
El Salvador	6	3	2	2	21	3	..	13	0
Estonia	269	128	..	..	714	322	0	319	35
Finland	3 432	969	219	-238	20 127	13 051	..	3 295	649
France	..	..	..	..	291 844	135 047	0	58 799	3 743
Germany	86 375	11 955	13 108	2 819	504 546	429 201	47	42 399	1 804
Greece	..	274	..	..	2 302	1 344	..	741	..
Guatemala	3	16	3	..	116	23	..	68	10
Honduras	..	..	..	..	..	..	..	..	..
Hong Kong, China	2 413	570	798	..	..	..	..	..	..
Hungary	121	78	37	22	314	140	0	110	18
India	10 410	3 457	442	12 450	12 240	22 372	..	6 776	482
Indonesia	2 053	816	695	-23	9 466	3 949	..	3 685	374
Iceland	345	57	..	396	1 150	596	0	454	78
Ireland	11 190	1 669	2 688	..	46 913	29 719	..	10 608	..
Israel[1]	568	99	76	-194	3 811	2 772	0	381	23
Italy	5 584	2 837	2 197	106	22 980	14 919	0	5 769	501
Japan	47 628	29 115	12 268	206	266 050	..	..	29 712	5 764
Korea	24 347	11 771	..	..	199 198	150 061	..	24 484	2 711
Latvia	265	97	36	26	437	263	0	125	114
Lithuania	191	113	3	-11	571	327	0	159	-14
Luxembourg	2 425	966	658	-251	13 040	8 955	0	1 885	193
Malaysia	2 090	648	274	29	6 418	3 376	0	2 967	389
Mexico	1 276	312	491	..	5 399	3 326	..	959	148
Netherlands	..	..	..	..	..	..	..	..	..
New Zealand	3 386	4 786	534	..	11 259	..	..	3 181	391
Nicaragua	..	..	..	..	..	..	..	..	..
Norway	6 077	1 381	346	-291	27 729	14 362	..	8 886	1 432
Paraguay	..	69	25	..	..	..	..	..	..
Peru	501	318	145	0	1 993	406	..	804	112
Poland	4 665	2 309	292	61	19 662	13 248	0	5 253	491
Portugal	1 477	516	248	34	3 327	2 076	..	764	-19
Puerto Rico	9 680	1 947	269	-126	4 775	2 988	..	1 788	73
Russia	6 498	3 512	1 675	2 825	21 344	11 540	..	6 039	680
Singapore	2 743	778	302	..	14 091	4 512	..	7 199	656
Slovak Republic	..	..	..	..	..	..	..	..	..
Slovenia	389	52	7	0	272	79	0	157	4
South Africa	4 945	1 359	940	2 279	10 068	142	0	4 078	812
Spain	10 456	3 181	1 770	111	29 122	15 111	..	9 674	1 062
Sweden	7 702	1 843	594	25 381	64 571	31 489	..	13 129	2 055
Switzerland	21 927	3 244	4 161	1 011	136 778	61 232	..	32 013	6 429
Tunisia	53	28	..	..	..	..	..	..	..
Turkey	5 022	1 856	1 514	1 321	12 129	10 880	..	2 583	381
United Kingdom	37 703	21 563	..	..	171 965	99 380	..	..	..
United States	961 644	233 902	50 072	43 289	1 603 303	795 921	..	720 706	38 115

.. Not available

Note: Detailed metadata at: http://metalinks.oecd.org/ins/20180621/caf9.

Disclaimer: http://oe.cd/disclaimer

1. Information on data for Israel: http://oe.cd/israel-disclaimer.

Source: Balance sheet and income, OECD Insurance Statistics (database)

Table 4. Portfolio allocation, direct insurance (All insurance companies)

2016

Million US dollars

	Cash and deposits	Land and buildings	Equity	Bills and bonds	Loans	Collective investment schemes	Private equity funds	Hedge funds	Structured products	Assets for unit-linked contracts	Total investments
Argentina	268	264	847	9 052	30	4 255	0	0	0	0	17 195
Australia	..	..	7 375	47 996	3 617	..	..	..	..	101 801	174 875
Austria	3 862	8 214	14 551	51 636	3 661	21 790	101	..	2 211	20 607	126 749
Belgium	8 968	9 236	16 076	212 521	28 915	14 274	706	..	2 904	33 121	327 480
Bolivia	29	52	9	343	2	0	53	0	0	0	618
Brazil	360	584	881	24 428	113	27 786	7 450	598	0	186 132	248 404
Canada	..	..	..	..	..	..	..	..	..	..	..
Chile	1 893	8 173	552	30 655	6 120	2 123	0	0	0	4 983	54 791
Colombia	29	52	9	343	2	0	53	0	0	0	618
Costa Rica	180	59	139	2 260	437	142	0	0	0	0	3 216
Czech Republic	754	121	96	9 994	90	799	0	..	231	2 738	14 830
Denmark	10 441	1 755	102 235	105 779	6 521	44 210	..	..	..	143 740	447 748
Ecuador	50	49	22	375	..	..	165	..	..	..	1 416
El Salvador	6	1	7	40	5	..	..	..	..	..	68
Estonia	186	0	2	875	6	77	0	0	6	665	1 828
Finland	3 232	2 312	3 214	21 417	2 081	7 498	..	..	..	36 285	77 458
France	55 839	44 392	184 707	1 500 232	29 620	372 001	16 091	..	65 877	333 148	2 610 579
Germany	13 796	26 964	103 703	641 020	305 618	518 015	4 467	..	..	105 614	1 729 850
Greece	910	662	108	9 363	147	1 204	..	..	0	2 400	15 134
Guatemala	85	37	15	596	57	..	..	..	..	..	798
Honduras	..	..	..	..	..	..	..	..	..	..	..
Hong Kong, China	..	..	..	..	..	..	..	..	..	..	..
Hungary	233	86	46	3 787	14	417	..	..	..	3 846	8 587
India	..	..	..	..	..	..	..	..	..	..	..
Indonesia	4 740	790	3 830	6 762	18	5 464	..	..	..	12 420	34 174
Iceland	44	11	312	470	14	183	0	0	0	47	1 081
Ireland	8 516	1 105	3 189	38 762	2 571	3 577	..	..	1 327	208 959	269 223
Israel[1]	3 591	1 519	1 115	25 392	3 961	1 585	964	75	83	70 035	110 008
Italy	11 238	6 589	59 882	489 711	3 436	..	..	..	..	131 491	792 092
Japan	77 618	58 975	244 055	2 281 273	307 893	..	..	..	..	..	3 399 465
Korea	17 585	17 169	31 493	330 521	145 275	..	..	..	..	81 875	803 841
Latvia	147	16	9	281	5	52	0	3	0	53	574
Lithuania	79	6	14	570	7	85	0	0	5	488	1 273
Luxembourg	1 759	88	849	30 550	56	2 637	..	..	..	120 841	181 706
Malaysia	4 634	1 015	6 570	31 597	2 928	..	..	..	..	0	55 107
Mexico	..	704	5 859	37 902	1 388	..	..	..	..	..	48 657
Netherlands	..	..	..	..	..	..	..	..	..	..	..
New Zealand	..	..	..	4 212	..	2 554	..	..	..	..	6 766
Nicaragua	3	6	0	194	7	..	..	..	..	..	232
Norway	1 778	14 421	22 610	94 545	13 528	803	..	..	..	27 613	178 235
Paraguay	52	12	2	183	0	0	0	0	0	0	248
Peru	350	609	372	7 512	78	267	0	0	0	0	10 071
Poland	1 447	83	79	16 771	682	4 199	..	..	23	12 867	40 162
Portugal	1 965	929	3 328	28 122	66	2 030	72	31	396	12 257	49 213
Puerto Rico	75 394	23 737	223 889	2 017 857	358 623	..	..	..	..	..	2 923 715
Russia	..	1 397	2 255	9 619	260	..	..	..	..	..	35 485
Singapore	6 642	2 654	26 617	74 073	3 766	10 676	..	..	-1 175	21 327	133 905
Slovak Republic	..	..	..	..	..	..	..	..	..	..	..
Slovenia	237	252	560	4 008	83	342	..	..	37	1 430	6 952
South Africa	..	3 278	123 541	41 286	13 988	..	..	..	..	..	202 029
Spain	23 421	10 979	15 027	219 226	2 079	11 393	365	..	4 445	16 029	297 245
Sweden	8 784	9 883	124 893	132 976	9 493	50 820	..	..	..	119 778	470 745
Switzerland	16 403	45 747	14 747	216 326	48 939	18 379	2 377	4 842	630	18 334	436 291
Tunisia	..	..	..	..	..	..	..	..	..	..	..
Turkey	7 338	85	4 204	3 969	44	194	..	..	..	1 075	11 669
United Kingdom	10 938	27 144	88 578	666 119	..	109 994	..	..	..	1 361 286	2 451 450
United States	196 790	38 064	511 209	3 821 675	574 047	..	..	22 018	-563	..	5 405 584

.. Not available

Note: Detailed metadata at: http://metalinks.oecd.org/ins/20180621/60aa.

Disclaimer: http://oe.cd/disclaimer

1. Information on data for Israel: http://oe.cd/israel-disclaimer.

Source: Outstanding investment by direct insurance companies, OECD Insurance Statistics (database)

Table 5. Portfolio allocation, direct insurance (Life insurance companies)
2016

Million US dollars

	Cash and deposits	Land and buildings	Equity	Bills and bonds	Loans	Collective investment schemes	Private equity funds	Hedge funds	Structured products	Assets for unit-linked contracts	Total investments
Argentina	21	39	30	2 619	2	687	0	0	0	0	3 699
Australia	.. c	.. c	6 216	19 966	746	..	..	..	..	101 801	131 171
Austria	66	9	35	2 999	138	4 163	24	..	172	3 834	11 440
Belgium	574	288	459	5 142	1 799	477	0	..	570	861	10 261
Bolivia	21	34	5	286	2	0	43	0	0	0	447
Brazil	63	21	314	4 870	73	6 632	4 838	160	0	123 426	140 405
Canada	..	..	..	..	..	..	..	..	..	..	..
Chile	1 343	8 077	549	29 455	6 117	2 042	0	0	0	4 983	52 817
Colombia	21	34	5	286	2	0	43	0	0	0	447
Costa Rica	..	..	..	..	..	..	..	..	..	..	..
Czech Republic	14	0	0	23	0	1	0	..	0	88	126
Denmark	7 077	1 475	99 467	90 623	6 034	42 268	..	..	..	143 740	423 171
Ecuador	1	5	2	37	..	..	29	..	..	..	235
El Salvador	2	1	0	19	0	..	..	..	..	..	27
Estonia	47	0	0	151	0	11	0	0	0	570	779
Finland	1 835	1 259	1 832	13 078	880	4 274	..	..	..	36 285	59 816
France	9 959	8 697	33 796	335 549	4 644	60 799	1 528	..	9 775	70 438	538 820
Germany	5 658	18 150	49 047	426 641	217 327	362 075	2 168	..	..	105 567	1 194 301
Greece	59	2	17	2 091	0	22	..	..	0	222	2 436
Guatemala	..	..	..	..	..	..	..	..	..	..	..
Honduras	..	..	..	..	..	..	..	..	..	..	..
Hong Kong, China	..	..	..	..	..	..	..	..	..	..	..
Hungary	93	5	0	1 366	4	138	..	..	..	1 354	2 969
India	..	..	..	..	..	..	..	..	..	..	..
Indonesia	2 871	738	3 078	5 573	15	4 694	..	..	..	12 420	29 501
Iceland	11	0	7	49	0	15	0	0	0	47	129
Ireland	3 964	144	2 418	21 682	433	2 231	..	..	118	208 959	241 154
Israel[1]	8	0	0	28	0	0	0	0	0	255	290
Italy	3 193	334	3 345	117 354	93	..	..	..	..	72 446	210 698
Japan	64 512	51 006	184 201	2 211 368	291 708	..	..	..	..	..	3 155 920
Korea	12 546	11 941	26 252	269 833	97 485	..	..	..	..	81 875	624 787
Latvia	..	..	..	..	..	..	..	..	..	..	..
Lithuania	11	0	0	45	0	2	0	0	0	208	267
Luxembourg	1 315	8	573	26 079	56	2 347	..	..	..	120 841	172 486
Malaysia	1 269	400	4 314	14 414	1 723	..	..	..	..	0	26 321
Mexico	..	28	4	12 474	156	..	..	..	..	..	12 921
Netherlands	..	..	..	..	..	..	..	..	..	..	..
New Zealand	..	..	..	2 260	..	1 817	..	..	..	..	4 078
Nicaragua	..	..	..	..	..	..	..	..	..	..	..
Norway	847	13 969	19 091	81 538	13 312	691	..	..	..	27 613	159 434
Paraguay	..	..	..	..	..	..	..	..	..	..	..
Peru	97	318	136	3 860	77	116	0	0	0	0	4 695
Poland	563	25	13	7 682	144	2 105	..	..	5	12 867	23 678
Portugal	496	107	226	15 098	52	966	19	24	251	11 666	28 932
Puerto Rico	52 051	18 119	90 725	1 669 782	350 354	..	..	..	..	..	2 356 997
Russia	..	67	222	5 280	14	..	..	..	..	..	8 821
Singapore	2 065	1 178	13 392	31 556	1 426	7 063	..	..	-473	14 978	64 120
Slovak Republic	..	..	..	..	..	..	..	..	..	..	..
Slovenia	47	0	108	459	0	112	0	0	1	167	895
South Africa	..	3 170	120 714	38 091	13 162	..	..	..	..	..	190 434
Spain	1 420	214	749	21 892	57	737	82	..	1 053	3 419	29 712
Sweden	7 199	7 528	108 652	112 652	7 274	42 900	..	..	..	116 441	414 825
Switzerland	6 454	38 659	9 809	174 135	38 680	8 789	1 710	3 506	553	18 324	313 428
Tunisia	..	..	..	..	..	..	..	..	..	..	..
Turkey	1 938	44	1 621	1 378	44	39	..	..	..	1 074	3 443
United Kingdom	4 769	11 352	30 127	310 340	..	49 695	..	..	..	1 285 890	1 838 112
United States	95 985	24 680	162 574	2 949 159	568 452	..	..	21 966	-544	..	4 007 549

.. Not available; c Confidential data

Note: Detailed metadata at: http://metalinks.oecd.org/ins/20180621/60aa.

Disclaimer: http://oe.cd/disclaimer

1. Information on data for Israel: http://oe.cd/israel-disclaimer.

Source: Outstanding investment by direct insurance companies, OECD Insurance Statistics (database)

Table 6. Portfolio allocation, direct insurance (Non-life insurance companies)

2016

Million US dollars

	Cash and deposits	Land and buildings	Equity	Bills and bonds	Loans	Collective investment schemes	Private equity funds	Hedge funds	Structured products	Assets for unit-linked contracts	Total investments
Argentina	85	64	102	2 482	4	1 610	0	0	0	0	5 367
Australia	3 545	96	1 158	28 029	2 871	7 570	..	..	..	..	43 703
Austria	1 527	634	7 335	1 533	185	1 852	0	..	5	0	13 071
Belgium	844	300	848	6 226	257	1 616	2	..	108	..	10 244
Bolivia	8	18	4	57	0	0	10	0	0	0	171
Brazil	62	0	1	1 600	0	1 859	3	157	0	0	3 691
Canada	..	..	..	..	..	..	..	..	..	..	..
Chile	550	96	2	1 200	3	81	0	0	0	0	1 974
Colombia	8	18	4	57	0	0	10	0	0	0	171
Costa Rica	11	0	0	23	15	0	0	0	0	0	50
Czech Republic	98	18	1	104	5	12	0	..	0	0	240
Denmark	3 364	280	2 768	15 156	486	1 942	..	..	..	..	24 577
Ecuador	41	34	18	250	..	..	119	..	..	..	958
El Salvador	1	0	7	6	0	..	..	..	..	..	15
Estonia	114	0	1	467	2	30	0	0	6	0	625
Finland	1 397	1 053	1 382	8 339	1 201	3 223	..	..	..	..	17 642
France	11 676	6 717	62 756	108 688	6 937	42 496	1 346	..	2 259	..	243 887
Germany	8 138	8 814	54 657	214 380	88 291	155 940	2 299	..	..	47	535 550
Greece	277	173	20	1 116	42	303	..	..	0	0	1 979
Guatemala	9	3	1	73	1	..	..	..	..	..	88
Honduras	..	..	..	..	..	..	..	..	..	..	..
Hong Kong, China	..	..	..	..	..	..	..	..	..	..	..
Hungary	50	2	0	186	0	21	..	..	..	0	271
India	..	..	..	..	..	..	..	..	..	..	..
Indonesia	1 869	52	753	1 188	3	769	..	..	..	0	4 674
Iceland	33	11	305	421	14	167	0	0	0	0	952
Ireland	4 552	962	772	17 081	2 138	1 346	..	..	1 209	0	28 069
Israel[1]	432	34	58	2 077	140	365	26	1	8	0	3 168
Italy	1 111	683	1 732	11 943	28	..	..	..	..	..	17 330
Japan	13 106	7 968	59 854	69 905	16 185	..	..	..	..	..	243 545
Korea	5 038	5 228	5 241	60 687	47 789	..	..	..	..	..	179 054
Latvia	135	16	9	207	5	5	0	0	0	0	378
Lithuania	46	6	6	269	1	51	0	0	0	0	396
Luxembourg	444	80	276	4 471	0	290	..	..	..	..	9 221
Malaysia	1 662	107	150	1 897	12	..	..	..	..	0	5 644
Mexico	..	111	225	1 718	35	..	..	..	..	..	2 243
Netherlands	..	..	..	..	..	..	..	..	..	..	..
New Zealand	..	..	..	1 952	..	737	..	..	..	..	2 688
Nicaragua	..	..	..	..	..	..	..	..	..	..	..
Norway	931	453	3 519	13 006	216	112	..	..	..	..	18 801
Paraguay	24	7	2	81	0	0	0	0	0	0	114
Peru	88	112	36	373	0	23	0	0	0	0	953
Poland	884	58	66	9 089	538	2 093	..	..	19	0	16 484
Portugal	184	232	81	2 050	4	252	0	7	22	0	2 832
Puerto Rico	23 343	5 618	133 164	348 075	8 269	..	..	..	..	..	566 718
Russia	..	1 136	1 676	3 874	191	..	..	..	..	..	22 513
Singapore	3 409	362	1 718	4 530	1 329	188	..	..	-1	0	11 347
Slovak Republic	..	..	..	..	..	..	..	..	..	..	..
Slovenia	38	21	0	158	0	6	0	0	0	0	224
South Africa	..	105	2 809	2 531	757	..	..	..	..	..	10 550
Spain	3 535	1 907	2 751	9 382	548	2 899	146	..	85	0	21 368
Sweden	1 585	2 355	16 240	20 324	2 219	7 920	..	..	..	3 338	55 920
Switzerland	9 949	7 088	4 937	42 191	10 258	9 590	667	1 336	77	10	122 863
Tunisia	..	..	..	..	..	..	..	..	..	..	..
Turkey	5 428	41	2 602	2 602	0	155	..	..	..	1	8 227
United Kingdom	2 313	1 525	2 155	80 191	..	10 979	..	..	..	88	114 107
United States	100 805	13 384	348 635	873 242	5 595	..	..	52	-19	..	1 398 761

.. Not available

Note: Detailed metadata at: http://metalinks.oecd.org/ins/20180621/60aa.

Disclaimer: http://oe.cd/disclaimer

1. Information on data for Israel: http://oe.cd/israel-disclaimer.

Source: Outstanding investment by direct insurance companies, OECD Insurance Statistics (database)

Table 7. Total gross premiums (Life and Non-life)

Million US dollars

	2009	2010	2011	2012	2013	2014	2015	2016
Argentina	..	..	..	13 157	14 819	14 534	17 851	15 334
Australia	57 732	70 793	84 541	85 880	87 591	97 011	78 796	74 145
Austria	..	..	..	..	25 077	25 069	21 082	20 633
Belgium	39 575	39 170	40 818	41 938	37 510	38 294	30 734	30 415
Bolivia	..	..	..	316	..	..	..	468
Brazil	..	..	..	..	..	69 867	55 519	58 914
Canada	75 424	85 752	93 998	97 037	98 545	93 075	83 591	..
Chile	6 248	8 309	9 699	11 298	11 776	10 976	11 413	12 401
Colombia	..	..	..	316	..	..	..	468
Costa Rica	..	718	793	927	1 036	1 157	1 049	1 212
Czech Republic	7 562	8 167	8 764	7 846	7 998	7 608	6 173	6 002
Denmark	..	..	33 844	32 745	225 775	37 098	31 997	33 498
Ecuador	..	..	..	..	..	..	2 316	2 135
El Salvador	..	..	55	57	62	65	70	71
Estonia	343	565	560	617	774	838	764	815
Finland	9 470	11 615	10 119	9 353	13 057	14 106	11 912	10 005
France	300 973	297 035	288 704	258 656	275 671	293 642	250 772	327 320
Germany	246 786	240 817	255 374	302 757	333 618	338 313	292 969	294 460
Greece	7 215	6 948	6 884	5 781	5 405	5 049	3 963	3 906
Guatemala	..	..	..	611	683	749	804	856
Honduras	..	..	..	..	368	379	398	..
Hong Kong, China	24 153	26 903	29 268	33 191	37 856	43 121	47 901	59 301
Hungary	4 081	4 053	4 054	3 377	3 582	3 584	2 991	3 146
India	..	..	73 109	..	..	..	..	69 847
Indonesia	..	..	..	16 249	15 782	14 325	14 629	17 290
Iceland	277	382	415	404	419	444	420	487
Ireland	46 659	45 269	44 533	45 589	45 301	52 487	48 782	54 145
Israel[1]	10 253	11 234	12 665	12 471	13 941	14 366	14 117	15 142
Italy	166 837	169 745	156 776	138 240	161 115	193 198	165 787	151 321
Japan	471 373	498 713	568 376	465 476	355 940	351 337	311 854	407 370
Korea	98 989	120 803	137 828	163 065	169 186	187 068	183 642	185 646
Latvia	512	434	555	574	625	686	589	581
Lithuania	..	596	685	665	753	797	715	785
Luxembourg	23 063	27 438	19 151	25 169	24 698	28 907	21 270	20 275
Malaysia	9 540	13 242	14 878	16 338	16 974	17 588	15 346	15 100
Mexico	17 528	19 548	22 683	23 596	27 184	27 349	24 929	24 150
Netherlands	67 166	52 399	58 577	51 270	51 127	48 539	37 384	..
New Zealand	2 948	3 372	..	4 590	5 139	5 359	4 657	4 753
Nicaragua	..	..	..	138	157	178	191	204
Norway	9 289	20 570	23 794	25 748	25 536	26 461	20 647	20 210
Paraguay	..	..	..	227	360	..	381	377
Peru	..	..	2 660	3 041	3 392	3 602	3 709	3 354
Poland	16 475	17 963	19 289	19 231	18 307	17 412	14 539	14 213
Portugal	19 727	21 046	15 622	13 560	16 998	18 642	13 939	12 071
Puerto Rico	..	..	..	..	9 610	9 108	11 145	14 563
Russia	17 583	..	23 718	..	..	26 658	17 299	18 218
Singapore	8 664	20 231	23 470	24 947	27 186	30 379	30 331	33 160
Slovak Republic	2 887	2 813	2 994	2 772	2 958	2 982	2 399	..
Slovenia	3 021	2 885	3 035	2 816	2 807	2 779	2 385	2 414
South Africa	..	50 272	56 005	51 452	54 268	51 527	47 054	42 473
Spain	85 164	76 313	86 265	72 884	77 155	76 502	65 488	73 605
Sweden	25 465	25 624	28 062	24 669	27 203	49 890	40 254	39 107
Switzerland	57 191	61 637	71 482	70 214	74 264	74 480	70 367	67 493
Tunisia	..	..	..	..	..	..	..	864
Turkey	8 455	9 971	10 247	11 399	13 212	12 314	11 775	13 718
United Kingdom	342 609	325 141	339 365	368 525	340 385	365 688	336 743	389 353
United States	2 029 504	2 035 562	2 154 851	2 279 817	2 289 921	2 431 323	2 621 083	2 703 793

.. Not available

Note: Detailed metadata at: http://metalinks.oecd.org/ins/20180621/57fd.

Disclaimer: http://oe.cd/disclaimer

1. Information on data for Israel: http://oe.cd/israel-disclaimer.

Source: Insurance activity indicators, OECD Insurance Statistics (database)

Table 8. Total gross premiums (Life)

Million US dollars

	2009	2010	2011	2012	2013	2014	2015	2016
Argentina	..	..	..	2 720	2 644	2 401	2 733	2 452
Australia	32 297	40 318	47 949	46 069	48 122	59 315	46 633	41 066
Austria	..	..	..	..	8 554	8 890	7 437	6 696
Belgium	25 649	25 465	25 795	27 142	21 645	21 635	17 038	16 543
Bolivia	..	..	..	69	..	..	..	157
Brazil	..	..	..	..	..	42 061	34 819	38 935
Canada	26 843	30 491	32 005	31 148	32 390	26 679	23 996	..
Chile	4 067	5 484	6 067	7 400	7 830	7 224	7 795	8 726
Colombia	..	..	..	69	..	..	..	157
Costa Rica	..	63	84	110	139	142	133	187
Czech Republic	3 160	3 757	4 069	3 680	3 657	3 429	2 537	2 435
Denmark	..	..	23 069	22 489	215 331	25 124	22 055	23 001
Ecuador	..	..	..	..	..	..	453	471
El Salvador	..	..	11	13	17	17	18	18
Estonia	..	229	223	209	227	254	238	245
Finland	4 653	6 914	5 179	4 786	7 421	8 097	6 941	5 060
France	50 761	51 003	184 360	160 628	172 138	188 383	160 881	196 502
Germany	113 997	115 270	116 636	107 431	120 258	121 584	99 588	97 584
Greece	3 315	3 005	3 008	2 497	2 237	2 497	1 999	1 844
Guatemala	..	..	..	124	136	156	156	170
Honduras	..	..	..	..	114	134	145	..
Hong Kong, China	20 470	22 867	24 808	28 123	32 425	37 459	41 972	53 421
Hungary	2 054	2 155	2 212	1 790	1 951	1 965	1 529	1 559
India	..	..	62 483	..	..	..	..	54 608
Indonesia	..	..	..	11 465	10 720	9 490	10 093	12 560
Iceland	26	29	30	29	33	36	35	43
Ireland	37 757	36 342	35 275	36 586	36 514	43 164	38 837	37 101
Israel[1]	5 031	5 792	6 682	6 602	7 374	7 426	7 568	7 986
Italy	115 091	121 811	105 179	91 863	115 115	148 447	129 025	114 701
Japan	376 888	399 898	458 422	465 476	355 940	351 337	311 854	307 549
Korea	61 419	71 964	79 314	96 195	100 261	106 188	104 801	104 560
Latvia	81	100	102	101	118	141	127	130
Lithuania	..	207	226	213	241	285	262	273
Luxembourg	21 501	25 870	17 309	23 499	22 705	27 130	19 633	18 556
Malaysia	5 801	8 090	8 976	9 907	10 200	10 594	9 306	9 317
Mexico	7 714	9 016	10 143	10 900	12 523	12 812	11 530	11 266
Netherlands	34 141	26 774	30 133	24 393	24 256	23 171	16 300	..
New Zealand	..	..	..	..	..	..	..	..
Nicaragua	..	..	..	22	27	32	33	38
Norway	..	11 017	12 771	14 051	13 838	14 629	11 383	11 202
Paraguay	..	..	..	..	44	..	50	1
Peru	..	..	1 276	1 435	1 587	1 768	1 794	1 519
Poland	9 705	10 421	10 749	11 170	9 802	9 087	7 302	6 051
Portugal	13 957	15 703	10 030	8 582	11 981	13 599	9 407	7 195
Puerto Rico	..	..	..	..	411	570	542	1 977
Russia	21	..	1 777	..	..	3 353	2 408	3 721
Singapore	7 508	13 828	15 723	16 402	18 449	20 808	21 033	23 739
Slovak Republic	1 486	1 492	1 592	1 403	1 641	1 610	1 229	..
Slovenia	663	645	669	623	629	636	552	544
South Africa	..	39 453	43 695	40 746	42 679	41 476	37 576	33 870
Spain	40 561	36 291	40 499	33 822	34 387	33 567	28 520	34 672
Sweden	12 931	12 510	13 923	13 311	14 190	34 734	29 507	29 302
Switzerland	27 290	29 210	34 589	33 598	35 791	36 140	34 407	31 677
Tunisia	..	..	..	..	..	..	..	175
Turkey	1 436	1 743	1 880	1 758	2 072	1 510	1 390	2 048
United Kingdom	260 293	239 465	249 303	277 966	246 475	268 267	246 702	258 821
United States	798 795	799 066	864 830	919 547	881 541	880 040	973 634	970 503

.. Not available

Note: Detailed metadata at: http://metalinks.oecd.org/ins/20180621/57fd.

Disclaimer: http://oe.cd/disclaimer

1. Information on data for Israel: http://oe.cd/israel-disclaimer.

Source: Insurance activity indicators, OECD Insurance Statistics (database)

Table 9. Total gross premiums (Non-life)

Million US dollars

	2009	2010	2011	2012	2013	2014	2015	2016
Argentina	..	..	..	10 437	12 175	12 133	15 118	12 882
Australia	25 435	30 475	36 592	39 812	39 469	37 695	32 163	33 079
Austria	..	..	..	..	16 523	16 179	13 645	13 937
Belgium	13 927	13 705	15 023	14 797	15 865	16 658	13 696	13 873
Bolivia	..	..	..	248	..	..	..	312
Brazil	..	..	..	..	..	27 806	20 699	19 979
Canada	48 581	55 261	61 993	65 889	66 155	66 396	59 596	..
Chile	2 181	2 825	3 633	3 898	3 946	3 751	3 619	3 676
Colombia	..	..	..	248	..	..	..	312
Costa Rica	..	655	709	816	897	1 014	916	1 024
Czech Republic	4 403	4 410	4 695	4 165	4 341	4 179	3 636	3 566
Denmark	..	..	10 775	10 256	10 445	11 974	9 943	10 497
Ecuador	..	..	..	..	..	..	1 864	1 665
El Salvador	..	..	43	44	46	47	50	51
Estonia	343	336	337	408	547	584	526	570
Finland	4 816	4 701	4 941	4 567	5 636	6 009	4 972	4 946
France	95 772	94 470	104 344	98 028	103 533	105 258	89 891	130 818
Germany	132 789	125 547	138 738	195 326	213 359	216 729	193 381	196 876
Greece	3 900	3 943	3 876	3 284	3 168	2 552	1 963	2 062
Guatemala	..	..	..	487	547	593	648	685
Honduras	..	..	..	..	254	246	253	..
Hong Kong, China	3 683	4 037	4 460	5 068	5 431	5 661	5 929	5 880
Hungary	2 027	1 898	1 842	1 587	1 631	1 619	1 462	1 588
India	..	..	10 627	..	..	..	..	15 239
Indonesia	..	..	..	4 784	5 062	4 835	4 537	4 730
Iceland	251	353	385	374	385	408	384	444
Ireland	8 902	8 927	9 258	9 003	8 787	9 323	9 945	17 044
Israel[1]	5 222	5 442	5 983	5 868	6 567	6 940	6 548	7 156
Italy	51 746	47 934	51 598	46 377	46 000	44 751	36 762	36 620
Japan	94 485	98 815	109 954	..	..	..	..	99 821
Korea	37 571	48 839	58 515	66 870	68 925	80 880	78 841	81 086
Latvia	431	334	452	473	507	545	462	451
Lithuania	..	389	459	452	512	512	454	513
Luxembourg	1 562	1 568	1 842	1 671	1 993	1 777	1 637	1 719
Malaysia	3 739	5 152	5 902	6 431	6 773	6 994	6 041	5 782
Mexico	9 814	10 532	12 540	12 696	14 661	14 536	13 399	12 884
Netherlands	33 025	25 625	28 445	26 877	26 871	25 367	21 084	..
New Zealand	2 948	3 372	..	4 590	5 139	5 359	4 657	4 753
Nicaragua	..	..	..	116	130	146	158	166
Norway	9 289	9 553	11 023	11 697	11 697	11 833	9 264	9 008
Paraguay	..	..	..	161	316	..	330	376
Peru	..	..	1 384	1 605	1 805	1 834	1 916	1 835
Poland	6 770	7 542	8 540	8 061	8 416	8 325	7 237	8 162
Portugal	5 770	5 342	5 592	4 977	5 017	5 044	4 532	4 876
Puerto Rico	..	..	..	..	9 199	8 538	10 603	12 586
Russia	11 136	..	20 193	..	..	16 937	14 891	14 497
Singapore	1 156	6 403	7 748	8 544	8 737	9 571	9 298	9 421
Slovak Republic	1 401	1 321	1 403	1 279	1 317	1 364	1 170	..
Slovenia	2 358	2 240	2 367	2 193	2 178	2 143	1 833	1 870
South Africa	..	10 819	12 310	10 706	11 589	10 051	9 478	8 602
Spain	44 603	40 023	45 766	39 062	42 767	42 935	36 967	38 933
Sweden	12 534	13 114	14 140	11 357	13 013	15 156	10 746	9 805
Switzerland	29 901	32 428	36 893	36 616	38 474	38 340	35 959	35 817
Tunisia	..	..	..	..	..	..	..	689
Turkey	7 018	8 228	8 367	9 641	11 140	10 804	10 386	11 670
United Kingdom	82 316	85 677	90 062	90 559	93 910	97 421	90 041	130 531
United States	1 230 709	1 236 495	1 290 021	1 360 270	1 408 380	1 551 283	1 647 449	1 733 290

.. Not available

Note: Detailed metadata at: http://metalinks.oecd.org/ins/20180621/57fd.

Disclaimer: http://oe.cd/disclaimer

1. Information on data for Israel: http://oe.cd/israel-disclaimer.

Source: Insurance activity indicators, OECD Insurance Statistics (database)

Table 10. Market share in OECD (Life and Non-life)

Per cent

	2009	2010	2011	2012	2013	2014	2015	2016
Australia	1.4	1.6	1.8	1.8	1.8	2.0	1.6	1.5
Austria	..	..	..	..	0.5	0.5	0.4	0.4
Belgium	0.9	0.9	0.9	0.9	0.8	0.8	0.6	0.6
Canada	1.8	2.0	2.0	2.1	2.0	1.9	1.7	..
Chile	0.1	0.2	0.2	0.2	0.2	0.2	0.2	0.2
Czech Republic	0.2	0.2	0.2	0.2	0.2	0.2	0.1	0.1
Denmark	..	..	0.7	0.7	4.6	0.7	0.7	0.7
Estonia	0.0	0.0	0.0	0.0	0.0	0.0	0.0	0.0
Finland	0.2	0.3	0.2	0.2	0.3	0.3	0.2	0.2
France	7.1	6.9	6.3	5.5	5.7	5.9	5.2	6.5
Germany	5.8	5.6	5.5	6.5	6.9	6.8	6.1	5.9
Greece	0.2	0.2	0.1	0.1	0.1	0.1	0.1	0.1
Hungary	0.1	0.1	0.1	0.1	0.1	0.1	0.1	0.1
Iceland	0.0	0.0	0.0	0.0	0.0	0.0	0.0	0.0
Ireland	1.1	1.0	1.0	1.0	0.9	1.1	1.0	1.1
Israel	0.2	0.3	0.3	0.3	0.3	0.3	0.3	0.3
Italy	3.9	3.9	3.4	3.0	3.3	3.9	3.4	3.0
Japan	11.1	11.5	12.3	9.9	7.3	7.1	6.4	8.1
Korea	2.3	2.8	3.0	3.5	3.5	3.8	3.8	3.7
Latvia	0.0	0.0	0.0	0.0	0.0	0.0	0.0	0.0
Luxembourg	0.5	0.6	0.4	0.5	0.5	0.6	0.4	0.4
Mexico	0.4	0.5	0.5	0.5	0.6	0.6	0.5	0.5
Netherlands	1.6	1.2	1.3	1.1	1.1	1.0	0.8	..
New Zealand	0.1	0.1	..	0.1	0.1	0.1	0.1	0.1
Norway	0.2	0.5	0.5	0.6	0.5	0.5	0.4	0.4
Poland	0.4	0.4	0.4	0.4	0.4	0.4	0.3	0.3
Portugal	0.5	0.5	0.3	0.3	0.3	0.4	0.3	0.2
Slovak Republic	0.1	0.1	0.1	0.1	0.1	0.1	0.1	..
Slovenia	0.1	0.1	0.1	0.1	0.1	0.1	0.0	0.0
Spain	2.0	1.8	1.9	1.6	1.6	1.5	1.4	1.5
Sweden	0.6	0.6	0.6	0.5	0.6	1.0	0.8	0.8
Switzerland	1.3	1.4	1.5	1.5	1.5	1.5	1.5	1.3
Turkey	0.2	0.2	0.2	0.2	0.3	0.2	0.2	0.3
United Kingdom	8.0	7.5	7.4	7.9	7.0	7.4	7.0	7.8
United States	47.6	47.1	46.7	48.7	47.0	49.1	54.2	53.9

.. Not available

Note: Detailed metadata at: http://metalinks.oecd.org/ins/20180621/57fd.

Disclaimer: http://oe.cd/disclaimer

Source: Insurance activity indicators, OECD Insurance Statistics (database)

Table 11. Market share in OECD (Life)

Per cent

	2009	2010	2011	2012	2013	2014	2015	2016
Australia	1.5	1.9	2.0	1.9	1.9	2.4	2.0	1.7
Austria	..	..	..	..	0.3	0.4	0.3	0.3
Belgium	1.2	1.2	1.1	1.1	0.8	0.9	0.7	0.7
Canada	1.3	1.4	1.3	1.3	1.3	1.1	1.0	..
Chile	0.2	0.3	0.2	0.3	0.3	0.3	0.3	0.4
Czech Republic	0.2	0.2	0.2	0.1	0.1	0.1	0.1	0.1
Denmark	..	..	0.9	0.9	8.4	1.0	0.9	1.0
Estonia	..	0.0	0.0	0.0	0.0	0.0	0.0	0.0
Finland	0.2	0.3	0.2	0.2	0.3	0.3	0.3	0.2
France	2.4	2.4	7.6	6.5	6.7	7.6	6.8	8.3
Germany	5.4	5.4	4.8	4.3	4.7	4.9	4.2	4.1
Greece	0.2	0.1	0.1	0.1	0.1	0.1	0.1	0.1
Hungary	0.1	0.1	0.1	0.1	0.1	0.1	0.1	0.1
Iceland	0.0	0.0	0.0	0.0	0.0	0.0	0.0	0.0
Ireland	1.8	1.7	1.4	1.5	1.4	1.7	1.6	1.6
Israel	0.2	0.3	0.3	0.3	0.3	0.3	0.3	0.3
Italy	5.5	5.7	4.3	3.7	4.5	6.0	5.4	4.9
Japan	18.0	18.7	18.8	18.7	13.9	14.1	13.1	13.1
Korea	2.9	3.4	3.3	3.9	3.9	4.3	4.4	4.4
Latvia	0.0	0.0	0.0	0.0	0.0	0.0	0.0	0.0
Luxembourg	1.0	1.2	0.7	0.9	0.9	1.1	0.8	0.8
Mexico	0.4	0.4	0.4	0.4	0.5	0.5	0.5	0.5
Netherlands	1.6	1.3	1.2	1.0	0.9	0.9	0.7	..
New Zealand	..	..	..	..	..	..	..	..
Norway	..	0.5	0.5	0.6	0.5	0.6	0.5	0.5
Poland	0.5	0.5	0.4	0.4	0.4	0.4	0.3	0.3
Portugal	0.7	0.7	0.4	0.3	0.5	0.5	0.4	0.3
Slovak Republic	0.1	0.1	0.1	0.1	0.1	0.1	0.1	..
Slovenia	0.0	0.0	0.0	0.0	0.0	0.0	0.0	0.0
Spain	1.9	1.7	1.7	1.4	1.3	1.3	1.2	1.5
Sweden	0.6	0.6	0.6	0.5	0.6	1.4	1.2	1.2
Switzerland	1.3	1.4	1.4	1.4	1.4	1.5	1.4	1.3
Turkey	0.1	0.1	0.1	0.1	0.1	0.1	0.1	0.1
United Kingdom	12.4	11.2	10.2	11.2	9.6	10.8	10.4	11.0
United States	38.2	37.4	35.5	37.0	34.3	35.4	40.9	41.2

.. Not available

Note: Detailed metadata at: http://metalinks.oecd.org/ins/20180621/57fd.

Disclaimer: http://oe.cd/disclaimer

Source: Insurance activity indicators, OECD Insurance Statistics (database)

Table 12. Market share in OECD (Non-life)

Per cent

	2009	2010	2011	2012	2013	2014	2015	2016
Australia	1.3	1.5	1.7	1.8	1.7	1.5	1.3	1.2
Austria	..	..	..	..	0.7	0.7	0.6	0.5
Belgium	0.7	0.7	0.7	0.7	0.7	0.7	0.6	0.5
Canada	2.4	2.7	2.8	3.0	2.9	2.7	2.4	..
Chile	0.1	0.1	0.2	0.2	0.2	0.2	0.1	0.1
Czech Republic	0.2	0.2	0.2	0.2	0.2	0.2	0.1	0.1
Denmark	..	..	0.5	0.5	0.5	0.5	0.4	0.4
Estonia	0.0	0.0	0.0	0.0	0.0	0.0	0.0	0.0
Finland	0.2	0.2	0.2	0.2	0.2	0.2	0.2	0.2
France	4.8	4.7	4.8	4.5	4.5	4.3	3.7	4.9
Germany	6.6	6.2	6.4	8.9	9.3	8.8	7.9	7.4
Greece	0.2	0.2	0.2	0.2	0.1	0.1	0.1	0.1
Hungary	0.1	0.1	0.1	0.1	0.1	0.1	0.1	0.1
Iceland	0.0	0.0	0.0	0.0	0.0	0.0	0.0	0.0
Ireland	0.4	0.4	0.4	0.4	0.4	0.4	0.4	0.6
Israel	0.3	0.3	0.3	0.3	0.3	0.3	0.3	0.3
Italy	2.6	2.4	2.4	2.1	2.0	1.8	1.5	1.4
Japan	4.7	4.9	5.0	..	..	..	..	3.8
Korea	1.9	2.4	2.7	3.1	3.0	3.3	3.2	3.0
Latvia	0.0	0.0	0.0	0.0	0.0	0.0	0.0	0.0
Luxembourg	0.1	0.1	0.1	0.1	0.1	0.1	0.1	0.1
Mexico	0.5	0.5	0.6	0.6	0.6	0.6	0.5	0.5
Netherlands	1.6	1.3	1.3	1.2	1.2	1.0	0.9	..
New Zealand	0.1	0.2	..	0.2	0.2	0.2	0.2	0.2
Norway	0.5	0.5	0.5	0.5	0.5	0.5	0.4	0.3
Poland	0.3	0.4	0.4	0.4	0.4	0.3	0.3	0.3
Portugal	0.3	0.3	0.3	0.2	0.2	0.2	0.2	0.2
Slovak Republic	0.1	0.1	0.1	0.1	0.1	0.1	0.0	..
Slovenia	0.1	0.1	0.1	0.1	0.1	0.1	0.1	0.1
Spain	2.2	2.0	2.1	1.8	1.9	1.7	1.5	1.5
Sweden	0.6	0.6	0.6	0.5	0.6	0.6	0.4	0.4
Switzerland	1.5	1.6	1.7	1.7	1.7	1.6	1.5	1.3
Turkey	0.3	0.4	0.4	0.4	0.5	0.4	0.4	0.4
United Kingdom	4.1	4.2	4.1	4.1	4.1	4.0	3.7	4.9
United States	61.1	60.9	59.2	62.0	61.2	63.0	67.0	65.1

.. Not available

Note: Detailed metadata at: http://metalinks.oecd.org/ins/20180621/57fd.

Disclaimer: http://oe.cd/disclaimer

Source: Insurance activity indicators, OECD Insurance Statistics (database)

Table 13. Density (Life and Non-life)

US dollar per inhabitant

	2009	2010	2011	2012	2013	2014	2015	2016
Argentina	..	..	..	314	350	316	385	328
Australia	2 396	2 901	3 378	3 329	3 352	3 691	2 931	2 672
Austria	2 723	2 638	2 740	2 492	2 602	2 653	2 228	2 153
Belgium	3 613	3 510	3 596	3 678	3 252	3 304	2 652	2 613
Bolivia	..	..	..	31	..	..	..	43
Brazil	..	..	318	333	335	344	271	286
Canada	2 050	2 331	2 516	2 560	2 534	2 159	1 922	..
Chile	369	486	560	645	664	612	629	674
Colombia	..	..	..	31	..	..	..	43
Costa Rica	..	158	173	199	219	241	216	246
Czech Republic	719	770	822	733	747	712	574	555
Denmark	..	..	6 069	5 823	6 079	6 543	5 610	5 699
Ecuador	..	..	..	..	..	..	139	127
El Salvador	..	..	..	..	..	..	..	..
Estonia	257	424	421	466	586	636	582	621
Finland	1 743	2 139	1 847	1 699	2 370	2 552	2 149	1 796
France	4 420	4 310	4 181	3 645	3 892	4 105	3 550	4 205
Germany	..	..	..	2 890	3 111	3 127	2 596	2 588
Greece	..	618	608	511	480	457	361	356
Guatemala	..	..	41	39	43	46	48	50
Honduras	..	..	..	46	47	48	49	..
Hong Kong, China	3 316	3 648	3 917	4 403	5 003	5 658	6 259	7 662
Hungary	405	402	403	336	357	360	300	317
India	..	..	59	..	..	..	..	53
Indonesia	..	..	60	63	60	55	56	65
Iceland	864	1 190	1 273	1 224	1 254	1 316	1 230	1 423
Ireland	10 152	9 791	9 572	9 721	9 649	11 147	10 280	11 284
Israel[1]	1 370	1 474	1 631	1 577	1 731	1 749	1 685	1 772
Italy	2 768	2 808	2 575	2 268	2 636	3 121	2 677	2 443
Japan	3 501	3 745	4 252	3 287	2 589	2 611	2 355	3 001
Korea	1 865	2 290	2 612	3 090	3 182	3 502	3 417	3 436
Latvia	236	203	263	277	309	343	297	295
Lithuania	..	192	226	222	254	272	246	273
Luxembourg	46 639	54 276	36 701	47 317	45 556	51 926	37 491	35 079
Malaysia	321	433	478	514	520	530	454	440
Mexico	153	168	192	198	226	224	203	194
Netherlands	3 776	2 930	3 483	3 019	2 997	2 836	2 171	..
New Zealand	666	759	..	1 024	1 141	1 169	964	983
Nicaragua	..	..	21	24	26	30	31	33
Norway	4 385	4 191	4 785	5 111	5 011	5 132	3 967	3 840
Paraguay	..	..	..	46	54	..	56	54
Peru	..	..	88	100	110	116	118	106
Poland	427	467	502	500	475	453	372	361
Portugal	1 814	1 936	1 425	1 237	1 569	1 732	1 292	1 109
Puerto Rico	..	..	..	..	2 661	2 552	3 182	4 247
Russia	113	..	159	..	..	179	117	123
Singapore	1 659	2 989	3 391	3 728	4 047	4 489	4 400	4 631
Slovak Republic	533	519	550	508	542	543	434	..
Slovenia	1 308	1 239	1 303	1 202	1 209	1 196	1 011	1 028
South Africa	..	986	1 083	..	995	930	836	738
Spain	1 801	1 605	1 735	1 518	1 529	1 519	1 295	1 459
Sweden	2 502	2 525	2 781	2 376	2 644	4 908	3 961	3 796
Switzerland	6 397	6 755	7 969	7 634	7 898	7 892	7 456	7 027
Tunisia	..	..	..	..	..	..	..	76
Turkey	..	130	133	146	168	151	145	162
United Kingdom	5 195	4 885	4 937	5 316	4 793	5 098	4 598	3 725
United States	5 221	5 228	5 492	5 750	5 684	5 967	6 302	6 498

.. Not available

Note: Detailed metadata at: http://metalinks.oecd.org/ins/20180621/57fd.

Disclaimer: http://oe.cd/disclaimer

1. Information on data for Israel: http://oe.cd/israel-disclaimer.

Source: Insurance activity indicators, OECD Insurance Statistics (database)

Table 14. Density (Life)

US dollar per inhabitant

	2009	2010	2011	2012	2013	2014	2015	2016
Argentina	..	..	..	64	62	55	62	55
Australia	1 396	1 713	1 993	1 856	1 899	2 323	1 785	1 527
Austria	1 219	1 178	1 143	981	1 007	1 038	861	769
Belgium	2 381	2 339	2 334	2 441	1 932	1 928	1 511	1 456
Bolivia	..	..	..	7	..	..	..	14
Brazil	..	..	189	209	203	207	170	189
Canada	767	836	856	819	833	627	553	..
Chile	241	321	351	424	444	405	431	475
Colombia	..	..	..	7	..	..	..	14
Costa Rica	..	14	18	24	30	30	27	38
Czech Republic	303	359	388	350	348	326	241	229
Denmark	..	..	4 147	4 005	4 236	4 443	3 878	4 006
Ecuador	..	..	..	..	..	..	28	28
El Salvador	..	..	..	..	..	..	..	..
Estonia	..	172	168	158	172	193	181	186
Finland	872	1 291	962	885	1 365	1 483	1 268	922
France	721	715	2 758	2 305	2 485	2 680	2 342	2 544
Germany	..	..	..	1 326	1 444	1 454	1 179	1 142
Greece	..	269	267	225	203	228	184	170
Guatemala	..	..	8	8	9	10	9	10
Honduras	..	..	..	22	23	17	18	..
Hong Kong, China	2 897	3 208	3 454	3 882	4 446	5 082	5 644	7 050
Hungary	205	215	221	180	197	199	155	158
India	..	..	51	..	..	..	..	42
Indonesia	..	..	44	47	43	38	40	49
Iceland	83	90	94	91	102	110	106	127
Ireland	8 234	7 883	7 635	7 867	7 838	9 237	8 242	7 852
Israel[1]	672	760	861	835	915	904	903	935
Italy	1 909	2 015	1 728	1 506	1 891	2 410	2 095	1 863
Japan	2 859	3 076	3 515	3 287	2 589	2 611	2 355	2 340
Korea	1 198	1 413	1 566	1 894	1 966	2 069	2 031	2 015
Latvia	38	47	49	49	59	71	64	66
Lithuania	..	67	75	71	81	97	90	95
Luxembourg	43 488	51 162	33 174	44 176	41 856	48 703	34 590	32 101
Malaysia	205	280	305	332	333	340	294	290
Mexico	68	78	87	93	105	106	95	92
Netherlands	1 835	1 431	1 804	1 455	1 444	1 374	962	..
New Zealand	..	..	..	..	..	..	..	..
Nicaragua	..	..	3	4	5	5	5	6
Norway	2 471	2 245	2 568	2 789	2 715	2 837	2 187	2 128
Paraguay	..	..	..	..	7	..	7	0
Peru	..	..	42	47	51	57	57	48
Poland	254	273	282	293	260	239	192	160
Portugal	1 320	1 483	950	816	1 146	1 307	908	697
Puerto Rico	..	..	..	..	114	161	156	578
Russia	0	..	12	..	..	23	17	26
Singapore	1 473	2 390	2 723	2 725	3 045	3 392	3 404	3 611
Slovak Republic	276	277	295	276	303	200	227	..
Slovenia	326	315	326	303	305	309	268	264
South Africa	..	774	845	..	801	766	683	606
Spain	873	778	857	722	729	711	605	737
Sweden	1 380	1 325	1 466	1 362	1 469	3 562	2 994	2 931
Switzerland	3 511	3 715	4 372	4 177	4 385	4 378	4 113	3 740
Tunisia	..	..	..	..	..	..	..	15
Turkey	..	23	25	23	26	19	17	25
United Kingdom	4 049	3 687	3 670	4 054	3 488	3 781	3 411	2 218
United States	2 381	2 364	2 517	2 640	2 471	2 474	2 574	2 587

.. Not available

Note: Detailed metadata at: http://metalinks.oecd.org/ins/20180621/57fd.

Disclaimer: http://oe.cd/disclaimer

1. Information on data for Israel: http://oe.cd/israel-disclaimer.

Source: Insurance activity indicators, OECD Insurance Statistics (database)

Table 15. Density (Non-life)

US dollar per inhabitant

	2009	2010	2011	2012	2013	2014	2015	2016
Argentina	..	..	..	249	288	262	323	273
Australia	1 000	1 188	1 385	1 473	1 454	1 368	1 147	1 145
Austria	1 504	1 460	1 597	1 511	1 595	1 615	1 368	1 384
Belgium	1 232	1 171	1 263	1 237	1 320	1 376	1 141	1 157
Bolivia	..	..	..	24	..	..	..	28
Brazil	..	..	129	123	132	137	101	97
Canada	1 284	1 495	1 660	1 741	1 701	1 532	1 369	..
Chile	128	165	209	221	221	207	198	199
Colombia	..	..	..	24	..	..	..	28
Costa Rica	..	144	154	175	190	211	188	208
Czech Republic	416	411	434	383	399	386	333	325
Denmark	..	..	1 923	1 818	1 843	2 101	1 732	1 692
Ecuador	..	..	..	..	..	..	112	98
El Salvador	..	..	..	..	..	..	..	..
Estonia	257	252	253	308	414	444	401	434
Finland	871	848	885	814	1 005	1 069	881	874
France	1 340	1 307	1 422	1 340	1 407	1 425	1 208	1 662
Germany	..	..	..	1 564	1 667	1 672	1 416	1 446
Greece	..	348	341	286	277	228	177	187
Guatemala	..	..	33	31	34	36	38	40
Honduras	..	..	..	24	24	31	31	..
Hong Kong, China	419	440	463	521	557	577	615	612
Hungary	200	187	182	156	160	161	145	158
India	..	..	8	..	..	..	..	11
Indonesia	..	..	16	17	17	18	17	17
Iceland	780	1 100	1 178	1 133	1 152	1 206	1 124	1 296
Ireland	1 918	1 908	1 938	1 854	1 811	1 910	2 038	3 432
Israel[1]	698	714	771	742	815	845	782	838
Italy	859	792	847	762	745	711	582	580
Japan	643	668	737	..	..	..	..	661
Korea	667	877	1 046	1 196	1 215	1 433	1 386	1 421
Latvia	198	156	214	228	250	272	232	229
Lithuania	..	125	151	151	173	175	156	178
Luxembourg	3 151	3 114	3 526	3 141	3 699	3 223	2 901	2 978
Malaysia	117	153	173	182	187	190	160	150
Mexico	85	90	105	105	121	118	108	103
Netherlands	1 941	1 499	1 679	1 564	1 553	1 462	1 209	..
New Zealand	666	759	..	1 024	1 141	1 169	964	983
Nicaragua	..	..	18	20	22	24	26	27
Norway	1 914	1 946	2 217	2 322	2 295	2 295	1 780	1 712
Paraguay	..	..	..	27	47	..	48	54
Peru	..	..	46	53	59	59	61	58
Poland	173	194	220	207	216	214	180	202
Portugal	495	453	475	421	423	425	384	413
Puerto Rico	..	..	..	..	2 546	2 391	3 026	3 670
Russia	69	..	135	..	..	112	100	97
Singapore	185	599	668	1 004	1 001	1 098	996	1 021
Slovak Republic	257	242	255	232	238	244	207	..
Slovenia	982	924	977	899	904	888	744	764
South Africa	..	212	238	..	194	164	153	132
Spain	927	827	878	796	800	808	689	722
Sweden	1 122	1 200	1 315	1 015	1 175	1 346	967	865
Switzerland	2 886	3 040	3 597	3 458	3 513	3 514	3 343	3 286
Tunisia	..	..	..	..	..	..	..	61
Turkey	..	107	108	123	141	131	128	137
United Kingdom	1 146	1 198	1 267	1 262	1 306	1 317	1 188	1 507
United States	2 840	2 864	2 975	3 110	3 212	3 493	3 728	3 912

.. Not available

Note: Detailed metadata at: http://metalinks.oecd.org/ins/20180621/57fd.

Disclaimer: http://oe.cd/disclaimer

1. Information on data for Israel: http://oe.cd/israel-disclaimer.

Source: Insurance activity indicators, OECD Insurance Statistics (database)

Table 16. Penetration (Life and Non-life)

Per cent

	2009	2010	2011	2012	2013	2014	2015	2016
Argentina	..	..	..	2.3	2.4	2.4	2.6	2.6
Australia	5.2	5.0	4.9	4.8	5.1	6.0	5.6	5.0
Austria	5.7	5.6	5.3	5.1	5.1	5.1	5.0	4.8
Belgium	8.0	7.9	7.5	8.2	7.0	7.0	6.5	6.3
Bolivia	..	..	..	1.2	..	..	..	1.3
Brazil	..	..	2.4	2.7	2.7	2.8	3.1	3.3
Canada	5.0	4.9	4.8	4.9	4.8	4.3	4.4	..
Chile	3.6	3.8	3.8	4.2	4.2	4.2	4.7	5.0
Colombia	..	..	..	1.2	..	..	..	1.3
Costa Rica	..	1.9	1.9	2.0	2.1	2.3	1.9	2.1
Czech Republic	3.6	3.9	3.8	3.7	3.8	3.6	3.2	3.0
Denmark	..	..	9.8	9.9	9.9	10.4	10.5	10.6
Ecuador	..	..	..	..	..	..	2.3	2.1
El Salvador	..	..	..	..	..	..	..	..
Estonia	1.7	2.9	2.4	2.7	3.1	3.2	3.4	3.5
Finland	3.7	4.6	3.6	3.6	4.8	5.1	5.1	4.1
France	10.2	10.2	9.2	8.6	8.8	9.2	9.4	11.0
Germany	..	..	..	6.6	6.7	6.5	6.3	6.2
Greece	..	2.3	2.4	2.3	2.2	2.1	2.0	2.0
Guatemala	..	..	1.3	1.2	1.2	1.2	1.2	1.2
Honduras	..	..	..	1.9	2.0	1.9	1.9	..
Hong Kong, China	10.8	11.3	11.2	12.0	13.1	14.1	14.8	17.6
Hungary	3.1	3.1	2.9	2.6	2.6	2.5	2.4	2.5
India	..	..	3.8	..	..	..	..	3.1
Indonesia	..	..	1.6	1.7	1.6	1.6	1.7	1.8
Iceland	2.1	2.9	2.8	2.8	2.6	2.5	2.4	2.4
Ireland	19.5	20.2	18.3	19.8	18.6	20.0	16.5	17.4
Israel[1]	4.9	4.8	4.8	4.8	4.8	4.7	4.7	4.8
Italy	7.5	7.8	6.7	6.5	7.4	8.8	8.9	8.0
Japan	8.5	8.4	8.8	6.8	6.4	6.8	6.8	7.7
Korea	10.2	10.4	10.8	12.7	12.3	12.6	12.6	12.5
Latvia	1.9	1.8	1.9	2.0	2.1	2.2	2.2	2.1
Lithuania	..	1.6	1.6	1.6	1.6	1.6	1.7	1.8
Luxembourg	44.9	51.2	31.3	43.8	39.6	43.1	36.5	34.5
Malaysia	4.3	4.9	4.7	4.8	4.9	4.8	4.8	4.7
Mexico	1.9	1.8	1.9	1.9	2.1	2.0	2.1	2.2
Netherlands	7.3	5.8	6.5	6.1	5.8	5.4	4.9	..
New Zealand	2.4	2.3	..	2.6	2.7	2.7	2.6	2.5
Nicaragua	..	..	1.3	1.3	1.4	1.5	1.5	1.6
Norway	5.5	4.8	4.8	5.0	4.9	5.3	5.3	5.4
Paraguay	..	..	..	1.2	1.2	..	1.4	1.4
Peru	..	..	1.6	1.6	1.7	1.8	1.9	1.7
Poland	3.7	3.7	3.6	3.8	3.5	3.2	3.0	2.9
Portugal	7.9	8.6	6.1	6.0	7.3	7.8	6.7	5.6
Puerto Rico	..	..	..	..	9.3	8.8	10.7	14.3
Russia	1.2	..	1.1	..	..	1.2	1.2	1.4
Singapore	4.3	6.4	6.4	6.8	7.2	8.0	8.2	8.7
Slovak Republic	3.2	3.1	3.0	2.0	3.0	2.9	2.7	..
Slovenia	5.3	5.3	5.2	5.3	5.2	4.9	4.8	4.7
South Africa	..	13.4	13.4	..	14.4	14.3	14.6	14.0
Spain	5.6	5.2	5.5	5.3	5.2	5.1	5.0	5.5
Sweden	5.4	4.9	4.7	4.2	4.4	8.3	7.8	7.4
Switzerland	9.1	9.0	9.0	9.1	9.2	9.1	9.0	8.7
Tunisia	..	..	..	..	..	..	..	2.0
Turkey	..	1.2	1.2	1.3	1.4	1.3	1.3	1.5
United Kingdom	13.6	12.6	11.9	12.7	11.2	10.9	10.4	9.2
United States	11.1	10.8	11.0	11.2	10.8	10.9	11.2	11.3

.. Not available

Note: Detailed metadata at: http://metalinks.oecd.org/ins/20180621/57fd.

Disclaimer: http://oe.cd/disclaimer

1. Information on data for Israel: http://oe.cd/israel-disclaimer.

Source: Insurance activity indicators, OECD Insurance Statistics (database)

Table 17. Penetration (Life)

Per cent

	2009	2010	2011	2012	2013	2014	2015	2016
Argentina	..	..	..	0.5	0.4	0.4	0.4	0.4
Australia	3.0	2.9	2.9	2.7	2.9	3.8	3.4	2.8
Austria	2.5	2.5	2.2	2.0	2.0	2.0	1.9	1.7
Belgium	5.3	5.2	4.9	5.4	4.1	4.1	3.7	3.5
Bolivia	..	..	..	0.3	..	..	..	0.5
Brazil	..	..	1.4	1.7	1.7	1.7	1.9	2.2
Canada	1.9	1.8	1.6	1.6	1.6	1.2	1.3	..
Chile	2.4	2.5	2.4	2.8	2.8	2.8	3.2	3.5
Colombia	..	..	..	0.3	..	..	..	0.5
Costa Rica	..	0.2	0.2	0.2	0.3	0.3	0.2	0.3
Czech Republic	1.5	1.8	1.8	1.8	1.7	1.7	1.4	1.2
Denmark	..	..	6.7	6.8	6.9	7.1	7.3	7.5
Ecuador	..	..	..	..	..	..	0.4	0.5
El Salvador	..	..	..	..	..	..	..	..
Estonia	..	1.2	1.0	0.9	0.9	1.0	1.1	1.0
Finland	1.8	2.8	1.9	1.9	2.7	3.0	3.0	2.1
France	1.7	1.7	6.1	5.4	5.6	6.0	6.2	6.7
Germany	..	..	..	3.0	3.1	3.0	2.9	2.7
Greece	..	1.0	1.0	1.0	0.9	1.1	1.0	1.0
Guatemala	..	..	0.2	0.2	0.3	0.3	0.2	0.2
Honduras	..	..	..	0.9	1.0	0.7	0.7	..
Hong Kong, China	9.5	9.9	9.9	10.6	11.6	12.6	13.3	16.2
Hungary	1.6	1.6	1.6	1.4	1.4	1.4	1.2	1.2
India	..	..	3.3	..	..	..	..	2.4
Indonesia	..	..	1.2	1.2	1.2	1.1	1.2	1.3
Iceland	0.2	0.2	0.2	0.2	0.2	0.2	0.2	0.2
Ireland	15.8	16.2	14.6	16.0	15.1	16.5	13.2	12.1
Israel[1]	2.4	2.5	2.6	2.6	2.5	2.4	2.5	2.5
Italy	5.2	5.6	4.5	4.3	5.3	6.8	7.0	6.1
Japan	7.0	6.9	7.3	6.8	6.4	6.8	6.8	6.0
Korea	6.6	6.4	6.5	7.8	7.6	7.4	7.5	7.3
Latvia	0.3	0.4	0.4	0.4	0.4	0.5	0.5	0.5
Lithuania	..	0.6	0.5	0.5	0.5	0.6	0.6	0.6
Luxembourg	41.8	48.3	28.3	40.9	36.4	40.4	33.7	31.5
Malaysia	2.8	3.1	3.0	3.1	3.1	3.1	3.1	3.1
Mexico	0.9	0.8	0.9	0.9	1.0	1.0	1.0	1.0
Netherlands	3.5	2.8	3.4	2.9	2.8	2.6	2.1	..
New Zealand	..	..	..	..	..	..	..	..
Nicaragua	..	..	0.2	0.2	0.2	0.3	0.3	0.3
Norway	3.1	2.6	2.6	2.8	2.6	2.9	2.9	3.0
Paraguay	..	..	..	..	0.2	..	0.2	0.0
Peru	..	..	0.7	0.7	0.8	0.9	0.9	0.8
Poland	2.2	2.2	2.0	2.2	1.9	1.7	1.5	1.3
Portugal	5.7	6.6	4.1	4.0	5.3	5.9	4.7	3.5
Puerto Rico	..	..	..	..	0.4	0.6	0.5	1.9
Russia	0.0	..	0.1	..	..	0.2	0.2	0.3
Singapore	3.8	5.1	5.1	5.0	5.4	6.0	6.3	6.8
Slovak Republic	1.7	1.7	1.6	1.6	1.7	1.6	1.4	..
Slovenia	1.3	1.3	1.3	1.3	1.3	1.3	1.3	1.2
South Africa	..	10.5	10.5	..	11.6	11.8	11.9	11.5
Spain	2.7	2.5	2.7	2.5	2.5	2.4	2.3	2.8
Sweden	3.0	2.6	2.5	2.4	2.4	6.1	5.9	5.7
Switzerland	5.0	5.0	4.9	5.0	5.1	5.0	5.0	4.7
Tunisia	..	..	..	..	..	..	..	0.4
Turkey	..	0.2	0.2	0.2	0.2	0.2	0.2	0.2
United Kingdom	10.6	9.5	8.9	9.7	8.2	8.1	7.7	5.5
United States	5.1	4.9	5.1	5.1	4.7	4.5	4.6	4.5

.. Not available

Note: Detailed metadata at: http://metalinks.oecd.org/ins/20180621/57fd.

Disclaimer: http://oe.cd/disclaimer

1. Information on data for Israel: http://oe.cd/israel-disclaimer.

Source: Insurance activity indicators, OECD Insurance Statistics (database)

Table 18. Penetration (Non-life)

Per cent

	2009	2010	2011	2012	2013	2014	2015	2016
Argentina	..	..	..	1.8	2.0	2.0	2.2	2.2
Australia	2.2	2.0	2.0	2.1	2.2	2.2	2.2	2.1
Austria	3.1	3.1	3.1	3.1	3.1	3.1	3.1	3.1
Belgium	2.7	2.6	2.6	2.8	2.8	2.9	2.8	2.8
Bolivia	..	..	..	0.9	..	..	..	0.9
Brazil	..	..	1.0	1.0	1.1	1.1	1.1	1.1
Canada	3.1	3.1	3.2	3.3	3.2	3.0	3.1	..
Chile	1.3	1.3	1.4	1.4	1.4	1.4	1.5	1.5
Colombia	..	..	..	0.9	..	..	..	0.9
Costa Rica	..	1.8	1.7	1.8	1.8	2.0	1.7	1.8
Czech Republic	2.1	2.1	2.0	1.9	2.0	2.0	1.9	1.8
Denmark	..	..	3.1	3.1	3.0	3.3	3.3	3.1
Ecuador	..	..	..	..	..	..	1.8	1.7
El Salvador	..	..	..	..	..	..	..	..
Estonia	1.7	1.7	1.5	1.8	2.2	2.2	2.3	2.4
Finland	1.8	1.8	1.7	1.7	2.0	2.1	2.1	2.0
France	3.1	3.1	3.1	3.2	3.2	3.2	3.2	4.4
Germany	..	..	..	3.6	3.6	3.5	3.4	3.4
Greece	..	1.3	1.3	1.3	1.3	1.1	1.0	1.1
Guatemala	..	..	1.0	0.9	1.0	1.0	1.0	1.0
Honduras	..	..	..	1.0	1.0	1.2	1.2	..
Hong Kong, China	1.4	1.4	1.3	1.4	1.5	1.4	1.5	1.4
Hungary	1.5	1.4	1.3	1.2	1.2	1.1	1.2	1.2
India	..	..	0.5	..	..	..	..	0.7
Indonesia	..	..	0.4	0.4	0.5	0.5	0.5	0.5
Iceland	1.9	2.6	2.6	2.6	2.4	2.3	2.2	2.2
Ireland	3.7	3.9	3.7	3.8	3.5	3.4	3.3	5.3
Israel[1]	2.5	2.3	2.3	2.3	2.2	2.3	2.2	2.3
Italy	2.3	2.2	2.2	2.2	2.1	2.0	1.9	1.9
Japan	1.6	1.5	1.5	..	..	..	..	1.7
Korea	3.6	4.0	4.3	4.9	4.7	5.2	5.1	5.2
Latvia	1.6	1.4	1.6	1.7	1.7	1.7	1.7	1.6
Lithuania	..	1.0	1.1	1.1	1.1	1.1	1.1	1.2
Luxembourg	3.0	2.9	3.0	2.9	3.2	2.7	2.8	2.9
Malaysia	1.6	1.7	1.7	1.7	1.7	1.7	1.7	1.6
Mexico	1.1	1.0	1.0	1.0	1.1	1.1	1.1	1.2
Netherlands	3.7	3.0	3.1	3.2	3.0	2.8	2.7	..
New Zealand	2.4	2.3	..	2.6	2.7	2.7	2.6	2.5
Nicaragua	..	..	1.1	1.1	1.2	1.2	1.2	1.3
Norway	2.4	2.2	2.2	2.3	2.2	2.4	2.4	2.4
Paraguay	..	..	..	0.7	1.1	..	1.2	1.4
Peru	..	..	0.8	0.8	0.9	0.9	1.0	0.9
Poland	1.5	1.5	1.6	1.6	1.6	1.5	1.4	1.6
Portugal	2.1	2.0	2.0	2.0	2.0	1.9	2.0	2.1
Puerto Rico	..	..	..	..	8.9	8.3	10.2	12.4
Russia	0.8	..	0.9	..	..	0.8	1.1	1.1
Singapore	0.5	1.3	1.3	1.8	1.8	1.9	1.9	1.9
Slovak Republic	1.6	1.5	1.4	1.3	1.3	1.3	1.3	..
Slovenia	4.0	3.9	3.9	4.0	3.9	3.7	3.6	3.5
South Africa	..	2.9	3.0	..	2.8	2.5	2.7	2.5
Spain	2.9	2.7	2.8	2.8	2.7	2.7	2.7	2.7
Sweden	2.4	2.3	2.2	1.8	2.0	2.3	1.9	1.7
Switzerland	4.1	4.1	4.0	4.1	4.1	4.0	4.1	4.1
Tunisia	..	..	..	..	..	..	..	1.6
Turkey	..	1.0	1.0	1.1	1.1	1.1	1.2	1.3
United Kingdom	3.0	3.1	3.1	3.0	3.1	2.8	2.7	3.7
United States	6.1	5.9	6.0	6.0	6.1	6.4	6.6	6.8

.. Not available

Note: Detailed metadata at: http://metalinks.oecd.org/ins/20180621/57fd.

Disclaimer: http://oe.cd/disclaimer

1. Information on data for Israel: http://oe.cd/israel-disclaimer.

Source: Insurance activity indicators, OECD Insurance Statistics (database)

Table 19. Life insurance share
Percentage of total insurance

Per cent

	2009	2010	2011	2012	2013	2014	2015	2016
Argentina	..	..	..	20.7	17.8	16.5	15.3	16.0
Australia	55.9	57.0	56.7	53.6	54.9	61.1	59.2	55.4
Austria	..	..	..	..	34.1	35.5	35.3	32.5
Belgium	64.8	65.0	63.2	64.7	57.7	56.5	55.4	54.4
Bolivia	..	..	..	21.8	..	..	..	33.5
Brazil	..	..	..	..	..	60.2	62.7	66.1
Canada	35.6	35.6	34.0	32.1	32.9	28.7	28.7	..
Chile	65.1	66.0	62.5	65.5	66.5	65.8	68.3	70.4
Colombia	..	..	..	21.8	..	..	..	33.5
Costa Rica	..	8.8	10.6	11.9	13.4	12.3	12.7	15.4
Czech Republic	41.8	46.0	46.4	46.9	45.7	45.1	41.1	40.6
Denmark	..	..	68.2	68.7	95.4	67.7	68.9	68.7
Ecuador	..	..	..	..	..	..	19.5	22.0
El Salvador	..	..	20.7	22.7	26.7	25.7	25.6	24.7
Estonia	..	40.6	39.8	33.9	29.3	30.3	31.2	30.0
Finland	49.1	59.5	51.2	51.2	56.8	57.4	58.3	50.6
France	16.9	17.2	63.9	62.1	62.4	64.2	64.2	60.0
Germany	46.2	47.9	45.7	35.5	36.0	35.9	34.0	33.1
Greece	46.0	43.3	43.7	43.2	41.4	49.5	50.5	47.2
Guatemala	..	..	..	20.3	19.9	20.8	19.4	19.9
Honduras	..	..	..	..	30.9	35.3	36.4	..
Hong Kong, China	84.8	85.0	84.8	84.7	85.7	86.9	87.6	90.1
Hungary	50.3	53.2	54.6	53.0	54.5	54.8	51.1	49.5
India	..	..	85.5	..	..	..	..	78.2
Indonesia	..	..	..	70.6	67.9	66.2	69.0	72.6
Iceland	9.5	7.5	7.3	7.3	7.9	8.2	8.4	8.8
Ireland	80.9	80.3	79.2	80.3	80.6	82.2	79.6	68.5
Israel[1]	49.1	51.6	52.8	52.9	52.9	51.7	53.6	52.7
Italy	69.0	71.8	67.1	66.5	71.4	76.8	77.8	75.8
Japan	80.0	80.2	80.7	100.0	100.0	100.0	100.0	75.5
Korea	62.0	59.6	57.5	59.0	59.3	56.8	57.1	56.3
Latvia	15.9	23.0	18.4	17.6	18.9	20.6	21.6	22.3
Lithuania	..	34.7	33.0	32.0	32.0	35.8	36.6	34.7
Luxembourg	93.2	94.3	90.4	93.4	91.9	93.9	92.3	91.5
Malaysia	60.8	61.1	60.3	60.6	60.1	60.2	60.6	61.7
Mexico	44.0	46.1	44.7	46.2	46.1	46.8	46.3	46.7
Netherlands	50.8	51.1	51.4	47.6	47.4	47.7	43.6	..
New Zealand	..	..	..	..	..	..	..	..
Nicaragua	..	..	..	15.8	17.2	17.8	17.4	18.6
Norway	..	53.6	53.7	54.6	54.2	55.3	55.1	55.4
Paraguay	..	..	..	..	12.2	..	13.3	0.2
Peru	..	..	48.0	47.2	46.8	49.1	48.4	45.3
Poland	58.9	58.0	55.7	58.1	54.0	52.2	50.2	42.6
Portugal	70.8	74.6	64.2	63.3	70.5	72.9	67.5	59.6
Puerto Rico	..	..	..	..	4.3	6.3	4.9	13.6
Russia	0.1	..	7.5	..	..	12.6	13.9	20.4
Singapore	86.7	68.4	67.0	65.8	67.9	68.5	69.3	71.6
Slovak Republic	51.5	53.0	53.2	53.9	55.5	54.3	51.2	..
Slovenia	21.9	22.4	22.0	22.1	22.4	22.9	23.1	22.5
South Africa	..	78.5	78.0	79.2	78.6	80.5	79.9	79.7
Spain	47.6	47.6	46.9	46.4	44.6	43.9	43.6	47.1
Sweden	50.8	48.8	49.6	54.0	52.2	69.6	73.3	74.9
Switzerland	47.7	47.4	48.4	47.9	48.2	48.5	48.9	46.9
Tunisia	..	..	..	..	..	..	..	20.3
Turkey	17.0	17.5	18.3	15.4	15.7	12.3	11.8	14.9
United Kingdom	76.0	73.6	73.5	75.4	72.4	73.4	73.3	66.5
United States	39.4	39.3	40.1	40.3	38.5	36.2	37.1	35.9

.. Not available

Note: Detailed metadata at: http://metalinks.oecd.org/ins/20180621/57fd.

Disclaimer: http://oe.cd/disclaimer

1. Information on data for Israel: http://oe.cd/israel-disclaimer.

Source: Insurance activity indicators, OECD Insurance Statistics (database)

Table 20. Direct total gross premiums per insurance company employee

US dollars

	2009	2010	2011	2012	2013	2014	2015	2016
Argentina	..	..	..	..	257 394	231 152	267 706	..
Australia	..	..	..	..	..	..	..	..
Austria	814 159	794 659	830 770	765 436	795 141	815 630	688 309	660 435
Belgium	873 393	907 893	..	..	..	..	..	..
Bolivia	..	..	..	..	..	..	..	112 942
Brazil	..	..	..	..	..	..	..	..
Canada	..	..	..	..	..	..	..	..
Chile	315 541	406 570	448 189	486 192	493 638	454 677	495 261	510 666
Colombia	..	..	..	..	..	..	..	112 942
Costa Rica	..	..	..	..	..	..	..	..
Czech Republic	67 190	..	..	..	..	..	..	..
Denmark	..	..	2 092 465	2 052 306	2 215 121	2 158 639	1 927 585	2 018 459
Ecuador	..	..	..	..	..	..	2 202 989	292 344
El Salvador	..	..	..	..	..	..	..	..
Estonia	197 403	..	208 774	224 249	200 167	221 703	200 336	..
Finland	962 386	1 198 102	1 027 920	949 685	1 363 348	1 512 846	1 310 951	1 087 714
France	..	..	..	..	..	..	..	..
Germany	..	..	..	1 508 982	1 607 329	1 646 967	1 370 540	1 366 726
Greece	..	..	..	..	..	..	..	..
Guatemala	..	..	..	137 904	..	159 900	..	181 604
Honduras	..	..	..	..	267 721	183 148	217 165	..
Hong Kong, China	..	..	..	..	..	..	..	..
Hungary	..	145 931	151 723	143 598	157 425	161 509	147 122	169 626
India	..	..	..	..	..	..	..	..
Indonesia	..	..	..	23 320	..	..	..	..
Iceland	445 140	613 285	624 626	..	665 881	731 603	703 782	..
Ireland	..	..	4 521 646	5 146 079	5 004 239	..	..	..
Israel[1]	..	..	..	..	..	..	..	..
Italy	622 200	632 728	572 450	516 329	588 438	728 137	622 467	584 701
Japan	..	..	..	..	131 616	131 735	143 752	..
Korea	326 451	347 369	387 679	442 588	466 477	580 301	590 964	611 062
Latvia	107 551	104 420	134 363	144 568	198 707	237 130	301 704	..
Lithuania	..	118 376	131 547	116 324	128 811	136 338	120 793	129 952
Luxembourg	1 743 713	1 972 257	1 408 398	1 776 286	1 555 995	4 322 564	2 996 082	2 884 045
Malaysia	..	482 196	492 814	567 984	651 774	650 745	461 454	465 847
Mexico	364 757	397 414	447 668	457 259	436 528	403 458	330 532	410 335
Netherlands	..	..	..	..	..	..	..	..
New Zealand	302 172	343 870	..	425 805	473 708	..	..	..
Nicaragua	..	..	..	..	1 704 849	119 312	2 050 664	..
Norway	..	2 109 103	..	..	..	..	..	..
Paraguay	..	..	..	104 627	379 327	..	110 593	..
Peru	..	..	257 668	251 417	285 142	301 442	290 594	..
Poland	166 861	181 086	181 330	198 127	169 341	183 450	167 678	..
Portugal	512 137	561 280	414 091	389 160	490 832	550 771	416 110	371 730
Puerto Rico	..	..	..	..	780 437	704 962	856 812	1 128 095
Russia	..	..	51 053	..	..	73 609	..	61 185
Singapore	..	..	..	..	..	..	..	..
Slovak Republic	376 284	380 861	417 623	378 475	..	400 070	..	..
Slovenia	212 028	..	..	..	..	..	..	..
South Africa	..	..	..	..	..	..	..	..
Spain	1 630 315	1 462 199	..	..	424 580	402 914	..	..
Sweden	1 065 209	1 131 069	1 264 886	1 073 328	1 210 867	2 042 276	1 771 433	..
Switzerland	1 197 915	..	..	..	..	..	..	..
Tunisia	..	..	..	..	..	..	..	173 680
Turkey	..	301 983	369 673	322 731	379 315	335 385	298 749	233 812
United Kingdom	..	..	..	..	..	..	..	..
United States	..	..	..	..	..	..	..	..

.. Not available

Note: Detailed metadata at: http://metalinks.oecd.org/ins/20180621/57fd.

Disclaimer: http://oe.cd/disclaimer

1. Information on data for Israel: http://oe.cd/israel-disclaimer.

Source: Insurance activity indicators, OECD Insurance Statistics (database)

Table 21. Retention ratio (Life and Non-life)

Per cent

	2009	2010	2011	2012	2013	2014	2015	2016
Argentina	..	..	..	88.9	90.6	86.5	87.5	88.4
Australia	85.7	85.2	84.5	84.1	84.5	86.0	83.8	80.4
Austria	..	..	..	..	81.3	83.6	84.2	81.1
Belgium	94.2	94.0	95.1	92.6	91.2	88.7	88.5	87.2
Bolivia	..	..	..	50.3	..	..	..	49.8
Brazil	..	..	..	..	..	95.2	95.4	95.8
Canada	78.4	78.9	75.2	73.3	73.1	73.5	71.4	..
Chile	81.6	..	80.6	83.1	84.4	84.0	84.8	84.4
Colombia	..	..	..	50.3	..	..	..	49.8
Costa Rica	..	79.4	81.1	80.9	78.6	80.2	77.9	78.9
Czech Republic	83.2	82.4	81.5	81.3	80.6	80.3	79.3	78.9
Denmark	..	..	95.8	96.3	99.4	97.2	97.1	96.9
Ecuador	..	..	..	..	..	..	72.4	72.3
El Salvador	..	..	61.0	62.0	66.6	66.6	66.5	64.2
Estonia	..	95.2	95.1	..	..	..	..	..
Finland	99.5	97.2	96.7	96.7	97.4	97.6	97.7	97.3
France	91.7	91.4	89.9	89.2	89.3	91.0	88.6	84.7
Germany	..	..	..	90.2	89.7	89.0	87.7	87.9
Greece	48.6	88.2	83.3	88.1	79.8	87.6	87.2	88.8
Guatemala	..	..	..	68.0	66.3	64.2	64.9	67.8
Honduras	..	..	..	..	55.7	54.4	53.0	..
Hong Kong, China	89.9	89.0	86.0	87.6	87.0	87.7	88.3	90.4
Hungary	84.1	84.0	83.9	83.3	86.1	86.1	86.1	86.7
India	..	..	95.5	..	..	..	..	95.2
Indonesia	..	..	..	86.2	85.5	83.8	84.8	86.0
Iceland	92.6	92.2	92.9	93.3	93.9	94.4	94.8	95.4
Ireland	90.0	89.0	86.7	88.4	87.8	89.2	88.0	79.6
Israel[1]	84.2	86.0	85.6	85.7	87.3	88.5	88.4	84.9
Italy	95.4	95.9	95.5	95.1	96.2	97.1	97.2	96.4
Japan	93.9	94.1	93.3	94.1	94.9	94.3	94.6	89.5
Korea	92.9	93.8	94.6	95.0	94.7	94.7	94.7	94.7
Latvia	91.7	93.1	94.0	94.2	96.3	96.3	95.9	95.2
Lithuania	..	..	..	..	..	95.2	95.1	95.0
Luxembourg	73.1	73.9	78.4	68.6	74.9	71.8	84.1	82.2
Malaysia	86.9	87.1	86.5	86.9	87.8	87.8	87.9	88.3
Mexico	81.9	85.4	82.3	83.8	82.6	83.9	83.0	84.4
Netherlands	92.4	91.3	86.2	92.0	92.3	89.4	91.7	..
New Zealand	..	..	..	..	..	..	..	..
Nicaragua	..	..	..	62.0	63.8	63.3	65.7	66.7
Norway	85.4	..	..	93.0	92.9	93.1	92.2	92.7
Paraguay	..	..	..	..	79.1	..	79.6	78.0
Peru	..	..	78.0	76.7	76.7	75.5	74.5	73.3
Poland	95.3	93.7	93.3	92.7	92.7	92.4	90.5	87.9
Portugal	51.0	93.5	91.1	89.6	91.1	92.0	90.5	88.9
Puerto Rico	..	..	..	..	99.6	98.6	92.9	94.3
Russia	82.4	..	97.7	..	..	86.9	88.6	88.9
Singapore	65.0	87.3	86.9	85.5	85.9	86.8	79.2	77.6
Slovak Republic	87.5	86.9	85.5	85.6	85.8	85.3	84.5	..
Slovenia	86.5	87.3	87.2	87.1	87.8	86.9	88.1	87.7
South Africa	..	..	85.1	90.9	87.6	88.2	89.7	88.9
Spain	92.0	92.4	93.0	92.5	90.0	91.3	91.3	91.0
Sweden	92.3	92.6	92.9	92.2	92.7	95.6	97.0	97.3
Switzerland	93.2	91.8	93.0	92.5	92.6	92.9	93.1	93.7
Tunisia	..	..	..	..	..	..	..	80.9
Turkey	73.9	76.9	74.9	77.9	75.6	75.0	74.8	76.1
United Kingdom	90.3	89.6	88.4	87.7	87.4	84.8	89.0	75.8
United States	70.2	73.9	74.0	73.6	71.3	74.9	72.8	72.5

.. Not available

Note: Detailed metadata at: http://metalinks.oecd.org/ins/20180621/57fd.

Disclaimer: http://oe.cd/disclaimer

1. Information on data for Israel: http://oe.cd/israel-disclaimer.

Source: Insurance activity indicators, OECD Insurance Statistics (database)

Table 22. Retention ratio (Life)

Per cent

	2009	2010	2011	2012	2013	2014	2015	2016
Argentina	..	..	..	92.7	96.6	97.1	97.2	96.7
Australia	92.3	91.8	91.9	92.1	92.3	92.5	91.3	89.3
Austria	..	..	..	..	96.7	97.4	97.6	97.4
Belgium	97.8	97.8	97.6	97.7	97.0	97.6	97.9	96.7
Bolivia	..	..	..	79.5	..	..	..	64.6
Brazil	..	..	..	..	..	99.6	99.5	99.6
Canada	79.4	78.5	75.6	73.9	75.2	69.5	67.6	..
Chile	96.0	..	96.3	97.4	98.0	97.7	97.5	95.0
Colombia	..	..	..	79.5	..	..	..	64.6
Costa Rica	..	93.0	93.3	90.8	84.7	87.4	81.4	82.9
Czech Republic	97.5	97.8	96.1	95.0	93.9	93.0	92.4	92.3
Denmark	..	..	99.7	99.7	..	99.8	99.8	99.8
Ecuador	..	..	..	..	..	..	81.6	99.2
El Salvador	..	..	78.4	81.1	95.0	87.3	81.6	80.8
Estonia	..	99.1	98.9	..	..	..	..	..
Finland	99.0	99.3	99.0	99.0	99.4	99.5	99.5	99.3
France	92.1	89.2	93.1	92.9	92.5	94.1	90.7	86.4
Germany	..	..	..	96.9	96.8	97.0	97.0	96.6
Greece	94.9	94.8	84.8	95.1	94.8	95.6	95.9	96.2
Guatemala	..	..	..	76.6	75.3	76.6	76.9	80.9
Honduras	..	..	..	..	61.1	45.4	56.1	..
Hong Kong, China	93.1	92.4	89.2	91.0	90.0	90.5	91.0	92.8
Hungary	91.4	92.8	93.1	93.6	95.0	96.3	96.8	97.3
India	..	..	99.8	..	..	..	..	99.6
Indonesia	..	..	..	97.3	97.2	96.7	96.8	97.3
Iceland	81.1	84.2	82.0	82.5	83.9	82.3	83.7	85.2
Ireland	93.8	93.5	91.3	94.4	93.7	94.0	94.1	94.9
Israel[1]	94.6	95.0	95.0	95.2	95.3	95.2	95.5	95.1
Italy	98.2	98.4	98.2	98.3	98.8	99.0	99.1	99.1
Japan	97.0	97.2	96.4	94.1	94.9	94.3	94.6	93.1
Korea	96.1	97.2	98.5	98.8	98.8	98.8	98.7	98.6
Latvia	99.1	99.3	99.7	99.7	99.8	99.8	99.8	99.8
Lithuania	..	..	..	..	..	98.5	98.0	98.5
Luxembourg	73.6	74.1	80.0	68.9	76.4	72.1	85.3	83.6
Malaysia	97.0	96.8	96.8	96.7	97.3	96.9	96.7	96.6
Mexico	97.3	97.4	94.6	94.8	95.3	96.6	96.4	96.2
Netherlands	95.8	95.8	94.6	94.9	95.4	89.6	94.0	..
New Zealand	..	..	..	..	..	..	..	..
Nicaragua	..	..	..	63.7	60.3	55.3	59.2	58.2
Norway	..	..	..	98.6	98.8	98.9	98.7	98.9
Paraguay	..	..	..	..	80.7	..	81.7	41.0
Peru	..	..	90.8	88.8	89.5	84.4	84.7	82.4
Poland	98.1	98.2	99.1	97.6	98.6	98.5	98.2	98.3
Portugal	39.3	98.5	97.9	96.4	97.0	97.7	97.2	96.5
Puerto Rico	..	..	..	..	..	..	56.0	85.7
Russia	..	..	..	..	..	98.4	98.6	98.8
Singapore	64.0	95.3	96.3	96.6	95.1	96.1	88.4	84.3
Slovak Republic	99.2	99.2	98.3	98.4	98.4	98.2	97.0	..
Slovenia	98.0	98.1	97.6	97.5	97.2	96.9	96.7	96.3
South Africa	..	..	89.4	94.9	92.5	93.2	95.2	94.6
Spain	98.3	98.1	98.0	94.7	93.9	96.4	96.8	97.3
Sweden	97.4	98.0	98.0	99.1	98.7	99.6	99.8	99.9
Switzerland	99.2	99.3	99.3	99.4	99.3	99.4	99.4	99.3
Tunisia	..	..	..	..	..	..	..	90.4
Turkey	89.3	89.3	90.5	95.1	95.7	94.8	95.1	95.8
United Kingdom	93.7	92.7	90.4	89.0	88.9	85.4	91.2	78.9
United States	76.9	84.7	84.3	83.5	77.4	88.3	80.4	80.0

.. Not available

Note: Detailed metadata at: http://metalinks.oecd.org/ins/20180621/57fd.

Disclaimer: http://oe.cd/disclaimer

1. Information on data for Israel: http://oe.cd/israel-disclaimer.

Source: Insurance activity indicators, OECD Insurance Statistics (database)

Table 23. Retention ratio (Non-life)

Per cent

	2009	2010	2011	2012	2013	2014	2015	2016
Argentina	..	..	..	87.9	89.3	84.4	85.7	86.8
Australia	77.2	76.6	74.9	74.9	75.0	75.7	73.0	69.3
Austria	..	..	..	..	73.2	76.0	77.0	73.3
Belgium	87.7	83.2	87.0	83.2	83.4	77.2	76.8	75.9
Bolivia	..	..	..	42.2	..	..	..	42.4
Brazil	..	..	..	..	..	88.5	88.5	88.4
Canada	77.8	79.1	75.0	73.0	72.1	75.2	72.9	..
Chile	54.8	..	54.4	55.9	57.6	57.7	57.4	59.1
Colombia	..	..	..	42.2	..	..	..	42.4
Costa Rica	..	78.1	79.7	79.5	77.6	79.2	77.3	78.2
Czech Republic	72.9	69.2	68.8	69.2	69.4	69.8	70.2	69.8
Denmark	..	..	87.3	88.9	88.1	91.7	91.1	90.6
Ecuador	..	..	..	..	..	..	70.1	64.7
El Salvador	..	..	56.4	56.3	56.2	58.4	60.1	57.1
Estonia	..	92.6	92.5	..	..	..	..	..
Finland	..	94.2	94.3	94.3	94.7	95.0	95.2	95.3
France	85.2	84.9	84.2	83.2	84.1	85.3	84.8	82.2
Germany	..	..	..	86.5	85.7	84.6	82.9	83.7
Greece	81.7	83.2	82.2	82.9	69.1	79.8	78.3	82.2
Guatemala	..	..	..	65.9	64.0	61.0	62.0	64.5
Honduras	..	..	..	..	53.3	59.3	51.3	..
Hong Kong, China	71.8	69.9	68.5	68.7	69.3	69.0	69.8	68.9
Hungary	76.7	74.1	72.9	71.6	75.3	73.6	75.0	76.2
India	..	..	70.4	..	..	..	..	79.5
Indonesia	..	..	..	59.4	60.8	58.4	58.3	55.7
Iceland	93.8	92.9	93.7	94.2	94.7	95.5	95.8	96.3
Ireland	74.2	70.9	69.3	64.1	63.1	67.1	64.1	46.3
Israel[1]	74.2	76.4	75.1	75.0	78.2	81.2	80.2	73.6
Italy	89.2	89.4	90.0	89.0	89.9	90.5	90.6	87.9
Japan	81.7	81.4	80.2	..	..	..	..	78.4
Korea	87.5	88.8	89.4	89.5	88.6	89.5	89.4	89.8
Latvia	90.3	91.3	92.7	93.0	95.5	95.4	94.8	93.9
Lithuania	..	..	..	..	..	93.3	93.4	93.0
Luxembourg	67.4	70.7	64.1	64.3	58.5	65.9	68.9	66.7
Malaysia	71.2	71.8	70.9	71.8	73.6	74.0	74.4	74.9
Mexico	69.9	75.1	72.5	74.4	71.7	72.8	71.5	74.0
Netherlands	89.0	86.6	77.2	89.4	89.5	89.2	89.9	..
New Zealand	87.1	87.0	..	78.7	77.5	80.0	80.5	73.8
Nicaragua	..	..	..	61.7	64.6	65.0	67.0	68.7
Norway	85.4	..	..	86.2	85.9	85.9	84.3	85.0
Paraguay	..	..	..	71.2	78.9	..	79.3	78.0
Peru	..	..	66.1	65.8	65.5	67.0	65.0	65.7
Poland	91.3	87.6	85.9	85.9	85.8	85.8	82.8	80.2
Portugal	79.4	78.6	78.8	77.9	76.9	76.8	76.6	77.7
Puerto Rico	..	..	..	..	99.5	98.5	94.8	95.7
Russia	77.0	..	84.3	..	..	82.0	87.0	86.4
Singapore	71.2	70.0	67.9	64.2	66.5	66.5	58.4	60.9
Slovak Republic	75.2	73.0	71.0	70.7	70.1	69.9	70.4	..
Slovenia	83.2	84.2	84.3	84.2	85.1	84.0	85.5	85.2
South Africa	..	..	69.5	75.7	69.8	67.7	68.0	66.8
Spain	86.2	87.3	88.5	90.5	86.8	87.3	87.0	85.3
Sweden	87.0	87.4	87.9	84.0	86.1	86.5	89.3	89.5
Switzerland	87.7	85.2	87.0	86.1	86.4	86.7	87.0	88.8
Tunisia	..	..	..	..	..	..	..	78.6
Turkey	70.8	74.3	71.4	74.8	71.9	72.2	72.1	72.7
United Kingdom	79.8	81.0	82.8	83.8	83.4	83.2	82.8	69.5
United States	65.9	66.9	67.1	66.9	67.4	67.3	68.2	68.3

.. Not available

Note: Detailed metadata at: http://metalinks.oecd.org/ins/20180621/57fd.

Disclaimer: http://oe.cd/disclaimer

1. Information on data for Israel: http://oe.cd/israel-disclaimer.

Source: Insurance activity indicators, OECD Insurance Statistics (database)

Table 24. Ratio of reinsurance accepted (Life and Non-life)

Per cent

	2009	2010	2011	2012	2013	2014	2015	2016
Argentina	..	..	..	0.5	0.3	7.2	7.0	6.7
Australia	9.3	9.1	10.0	11.1	10.9	10.1	10.9	12.5
Austria	..	..	..	..	12.0	9.6	8.9	9.3
Belgium	1.8	2.9	3.1	2.7	3.2	3.5	3.0	2.8
Bolivia	..	..	..	0.6	..	..	..	1.0
Brazil	..	..	..	..	..	0.0	0.0	0.0
Canada	8.7	7.7	8.2	8.5	9.7	17.7	17.6	..
Chile	0.4	0.3	0.3	0.5	0.5	0.6	0.8	1.1
Colombia	..	..	..	0.6	..	..	..	1.0
Costa Rica	..	0.1	0.1	0.2	0.3	0.3	0.3	0.3
Czech Republic	0.9	1.4	1.7	1.9	1.8	1.6	2.0	2.4
Denmark	..	..	0.3	0.8	..	0.8	0.8	2.9
Ecuador	..	..	..	..	..	..	2.0	1.7
El Salvador	..	..	..	..	..	..	..	..
Estonia	0.1	0.0	0.1	..	..	..	..	..
Finland	2.0	1.5	1.9	1.9	1.5	1.4	1.3	1.5
France	8.3	8.9	8.7	10.7	10.1	10.5	8.9	17.0
Germany	..	..	..	23.2	22.4	22.4	24.6	24.5
Greece	..	1.2	1.7	2.0	2.3	1.2	1.1	1.0
Guatemala	..	..	..	2.9	2.7	2.7	3.1	2.9
Honduras	..	..	..	..	0.0	0.0	0.0	..
Hong Kong, China	3.9	4.4	4.8	4.9	4.7	4.8	4.5	4.8
Hungary	0.5	0.6	0.7	1.0	1.3	0.9	1.0	1.0
India	..	..	1.7	..	..	..	..	0.7
Indonesia	..	..	..	4.2	4.9	2.5	2.1	2.0
Iceland	1.0	0.8	1.9	2.3	2.3	2.5	2.4	1.7
Ireland	1.1	1.2	1.6	2.0	1.8	1.9	1.9	2.2
Israel[1]	0.0	0.0	0.0	..	..	..	..	0.0
Italy	2.1	2.1	2.5	2.5	2.4	1.8	1.8	2.1
Japan	5.2	4.2	4.4	9.9	7.4	5.5	4.1	6.5
Korea	7.1	6.1	5.4	4.9	5.2	5.0	5.1	5.2
Latvia	0.4	0.6	1.5	1.4	0.0	0.0	0.0	0.0
Lithuania	..	0.1	0.1	0.1	0.1	0.0	0.0	0.0
Luxembourg	0.1	0.7	1.9	1.3	0.9	1.2	0.8	0.3
Malaysia	5.5	6.5	6.5	7.1	7.4	7.5	7.7	7.7
Mexico	1.7	1.6	2.0	1.8	1.7	1.8	1.7	1.6
Netherlands	7.1	7.1	0.7	1.4	1.5	1.5	1.7	
New Zealand	2.1	1.6	..	1.3	0.6	0.6	3.8	1.8
Nicaragua	..	..	..	..	0.0	..	..	..
Norway	0.2	..	..	..	..	..	..	..
Paraguay	..	..	..	2.0	1.5	..	1.1	1.0
Peru	..	..	1.5	1.4	1.0	0.7	0.6	0.6
Poland	1.1	1.1	0.9	1.0	1.2	1.0	2.7	3.5
Portugal	2.8	2.8	3.7	4.1	3.5	3.3	3.9	5.1
Puerto Rico	..	..	..	..	0.5	0.9	0.8	0.5
Russia	7.7	..	4.0	..	..	3.5	2.8	3.0
Singapore	4.5	25.0	25.1	20.6	19.6	19.2	19.7	21.7
Slovak Republic	0.6	0.6	0.9	1.0	0.9	1.4	2.0	..
Slovenia	12.0	12.1	12.0	12.3	11.3	11.3	12.5	12.1
South Africa	..	..	..	..	2.3	2.3	2.2	2.9
Spain	2.0	2.0	6.0	2.6	7.7	7.8	8.2	8.2
Sweden	8.2	7.2	6.0	7.9	6.3	4.1	3.1	3.0
Switzerland	13.9	14.7	12.3	13.5	14.5	13.8	12.7	13.3
Tunisia	..	..	..	..	..	..	..	1.2
Turkey	..	4.0	3.2	2.9	2.7	5.0	3.1	5.9
United Kingdom	5.6	5.7	7.9	8.1	9.7	9.9	11.1	37.3
United States	20.9	20.4	20.5	20.7	21.5	21.8	22.8	22.3

.. Not available

Note: Detailed metadata at: http://metalinks.oecd.org/ins/20180621/57fd.

Disclaimer: http://oe.cd/disclaimer

1. Information on data for Israel: http://oe.cd/israel-disclaimer.

Source: Insurance activity indicators, OECD Insurance Statistics (database)

Table 25. Ratio of reinsurance accepted (Life)

Per cent

	2009	2010	2011	2012	2013	2014	2015	2016
Argentina	..	..	..	1.1	0.6	3.0	2.3	3.0
Australia	5.5	5.8	6.4	7.6	8.1	7.5	8.4	9.7
Austria	..	..	..	..	0.2	0.2	0.2	0.2
Belgium	0.2	0.4	0.5	0.2	0.4	0.4	0.3	0.4
Bolivia	..	..	..	0.4	..	..	..	0.0
Brazil	..	..	..	..	..	0.0	0.0	0.0
Canada	4.1	6.9	8.3	8.8	9.7	16.6	17.5	..
Chile	0.1	0.1	0.1	0.0	0.0	0.1	0.4	1.0
Colombia	..	..	..	0.4	..	..	..	0.0
Costa Rica	..	0.1	0.0	0.1	0.0	0.0	0.0	0.0
Czech Republic	0.0	0.0	0.0	0.0	0.0	0.0	0.0	0.6
Denmark	..	..	0.0	0.6	..	0.5	0.5	0.6
Ecuador	..	..	..	..	..	..	0.6	0.0
El Salvador	..	..	..	..	..	..	..	..
Estonia	..	0.0	0.0	..	..	..	..	..
Finland	0.1	0.1	0.1	0.1	0.1	0.2	0.0	0.0
France	11.2	12.0	5.6	9.1	8.0	8.9	6.3	16.4
Germany	..	..	..	0.7	0.7	0.6	0.6	0.6
Greece	..	0.3	1.1	0.2	0.2	0.2	0.2	0.1
Guatemala	..	..	..	2.1	1.0	1.6	1.7	1.9
Honduras	..	..	..	..	0.0	0.0	0.0	..
Hong Kong, China	1.0	1.1	1.0	1.0	1.1	1.6	1.7	2.8
Hungary	0.0	0.0	0.0	0.0	0.0	0.0	0.0	0.0
India	..	..	0.0	..	..	..	..	0.0
Indonesia	..	..	..	0.0	0.0	..	..	..
Iceland	0.0	0.0	0.0	0.0	0.0	0.0	0.1	..
Ireland	0.8	0.9	0.9	1.2	1.1	1.1	1.2	0.7
Israel[1]	0.0	0.0	0.0	..	..	..	..	0.0
Italy	2.2	2.1	2.4	2.6	1.9	1.3	1.3	1.5
Japan	3.2	1.8	2.0	9.9	7.4	5.5	4.1	3.4
Korea	3.8	2.7	1.4	1.1	1.1	1.1	1.1	1.3
Latvia	..	0.0	0.0	0.0	0.0	0.0	0.0	0.0
Lithuania	..	0.0	0.0	0.0	0.0	0.0	0.0	0.0
Luxembourg	0.1	0.7	1.9	1.3	1.0	1.3	0.8	0.4
Malaysia	1.0	1.1	1.1	1.2	1.3	1.4	1.4	1.4
Mexico	0.8	0.6	0.6	0.5	0.6	0.7	0.4	0.5
Netherlands	11.2	11.2	0.1	0.1	0.0	0.0	0.0	..
New Zealand	..	..	..	..	..	..	..	..
Nicaragua	..	..	..	..	0.0	..	..	..
Norway	..	..	..	..	..	..	..	..
Paraguay	..	..	..	..	0.8	..	0.7	0.0
Peru	..	..	1.8	1.6	1.2	0.6	0.5	0.3
Poland	0.2	0.2	0.1	0.1	0.1	0.1	0.1	0.1
Portugal	0.1	0.2	0.0	0.0	0.0	0.0	0.0	0.0
Puerto Rico	..	..	..	..	0.0	0.0	0.0	0.4
Russia	0.0	..	0.0	..	..	0.0	0.0	0.0
Singapore	2.1	12.3	10.2	11.8	10.9	10.8	10.4	14.7
Slovak Republic	0.0	0.0	0.0	0.0	0.0	0.0	0.0	..
Slovenia	0.0	0.0	0.0	..	..	..	..	..
South Africa	..	..	..	..	0.0	0.0	0.0	0.0
Spain	0.2	0.1	1.1	0.2	1.3	1.6	1.5	1.5
Sweden	0.3	0.3	0.2	2.3	0.2	0.0	0.0	0.0
Switzerland	0.9	1.0	0.5	1.1	1.5	1.4	1.5	1.7
Tunisia	..	..	..	..	..	..	..	1.5
Turkey	..	1.7	2.0	1.6	2.1	1.5	1.6	4.3
United Kingdom	3.2	3.4	6.8	7.1	9.3	9.0	10.0	43.8
United States	8.4	8.4	9.2	9.8	11.3	10.4	15.1	13.8

.. Not available

Note: Detailed metadata at: http://metalinks.oecd.org/ins/20180621/57fd.

Disclaimer: http://oe.cd/disclaimer

1. Information on data for Israel: http://oe.cd/israel-disclaimer.

Source: Insurance activity indicators, OECD Insurance Statistics (database)

Table 26. Ratio of reinsurance accepted (Non-life)

Per cent

	2009	2010	2011	2012	2013	2014	2015	2016
Argentina	..	..	..	0.4	0.3	8.0	7.8	7.5
Australia	14.0	13.6	14.8	15.2	14.2	14.3	14.7	16.0
Austria	..	..	..	..	18.2	14.7	13.6	13.7
Belgium	4.8	7.4	7.5	7.3	7.1	7.6	6.4	5.7
Bolivia	..	..	..	0.6	..	..	..	1.4
Brazil	..	..	..	..	..	0.1	0.0	0.0
Canada	11.3	8.1	8.2	8.3	9.7	18.1	17.7	..
Chile	0.8	0.6	0.7	1.2	1.4	1.5	1.6	1.3
Colombia	..	..	..	0.6	..	..	..	1.4
Costa Rica	..	0.1	0.1	0.2	0.4	0.3	0.4	0.3
Czech Republic	1.5	2.6	3.2	3.5	3.3	2.9	3.4	3.7
Denmark	..	..	0.8	1.1	1.1	1.3	1.4	8.0
Ecuador	..	..	..	..	..	..	2.4	2.2
El Salvador	..	..	..	..	..	..	..	..
Estonia	0.1	0.0	0.1	..	..	..	..	..
Finland	3.7	3.5	3.7	3.7	3.3	3.0	3.0	3.0
France	12.6	13.1	14.0	13.3	13.4	13.3	13.5	17.9
Germany	..	..	..	35.6	34.6	34.7	37.0	36.4
Greece	..	1.8	2.1	3.3	3.7	2.2	1.9	1.8
Guatemala	..	..	..	3.1	3.2	3.0	3.4	3.2
Honduras	..	..	..	..	0.0	0.0	0.0	..
Hong Kong, China	20.4	23.2	26.2	26.2	26.0	26.1	24.2	23.3
Hungary	1.1	1.2	1.5	2.2	2.9	1.9	2.1	2.0
India	..	..	11.6	..	..	..	..	3.0
Indonesia	..	..	..	14.4	15.2	7.3	6.8	7.5
Iceland	1.1	0.9	2.0	2.5	2.5	2.7	2.6	1.9
Ireland	2.0	2.4	4.1	5.3	5.0	5.3	4.6	5.5
Israel[1]	0.0	0.0	0.0	..	..	..	..	0.0
Italy	2.1	2.2	2.6	2.4	3.4	3.4	3.8	3.9
Japan	13.2	13.7	14.3	..	..	..	..	16.0
Korea	12.5	11.0	10.7	10.2	11.1	10.1	10.3	10.2
Latvia	0.5	0.8	1.8	1.7	0.0	0.0	0.0	0.0
Lithuania	..	0.1	0.2	0.2	0.2	0.0	0.0	0.0
Luxembourg	0.3	0.3	2.0	1.3	0.3	0.2	0.2	0.2
Malaysia	12.5	15.0	14.8	16.4	16.5	16.7	17.3	17.8
Mexico	2.4	2.4	3.1	2.9	2.7	2.7	2.7	2.6
Netherlands	2.8	2.8	1.5	2.5	2.9	2.8	2.9	..
New Zealand	2.1	1.6	..	1.3	0.6	0.6	3.8	1.8
Nicaragua	..	..	..	..	0.0	..	..	..
Norway	0.2	..	..	..	..	..	..	..
Paraguay	..	..	..	2.2	1.5	..	1.2	1.0
Peru	..	..	1.4	1.3	1.0	0.8	0.7	0.8
Poland	2.3	2.2	1.9	2.3	2.5	2.1	5.3	6.1
Portugal	9.4	10.3	10.3	11.0	11.7	12.3	12.1	12.6
Puerto Rico	..	..	..	..	0.5	1.0	0.9	0.5
Russia	10.9	..	4.5	..	..	5.0	3.3	3.7
Singapore	20.2	52.5	55.3	37.6	38.1	37.3	40.7	39.2
Slovak Republic	1.2	1.2	1.9	2.1	2.1	3.1	4.0	..
Slovenia	15.4	15.6	15.4	15.8	14.6	14.6	16.3	15.7
South Africa	..	..	..	..	10.8	11.6	11.1	14.2
Spain	3.6	3.8	10.3	4.8	12.9	12.6	13.5	14.1
Sweden	16.4	13.8	11.8	14.6	12.9	13.5	11.4	11.8
Switzerland	25.7	27.0	23.3	24.9	26.6	25.4	23.4	23.6
Tunisia	..	..	..	..	..	..	..	1.1
Turkey	..	4.5	3.5	3.1	2.8	5.4	3.3	6.1
United Kingdom	13.3	12.2	11.0	11.2	10.9	12.6	14.1	24.3
United States	29.1	28.2	28.1	28.2	27.8	28.2	27.4	27.0

.. Not available

Note: Detailed metadata at: http://metalinks.oecd.org/ins/20180621/57fd.

Disclaimer: http://oe.cd/disclaimer

1. Information on data for Israel: http://oe.cd/israel-disclaimer.

Source: Insurance activity indicators, OECD Insurance Statistics (database)

Table 27. Market share of foreign companies in the domestic market (Life)

Per cent

	2009	2010	2011	2012	2013	2014	2015	2016
Argentina	..	..	..	18.3	31.8	31.4	30.8	30.4
Australia	28.7	15.0	10.3	15.8	16.8	15.5	17.7	20.8
Austria	..	..	..	..	37.5	39.2	37.7	39.3
Belgium	..	..	..	..	..	..	..	..
Bolivia	..	..	..	..	..	..	..	29.9
Brazil	..	..	..	..	..	18.6	18.3	17.2
Canada	10.9	10.1	7.9	6.3	5.6	26.0	21.0	..
Chile	53.7	49.0	37.6	43.7	46.7	45.0	41.8	41.6
Colombia	..	..	..	..	..	..	..	29.9
Costa Rica	..	0.2	3.4	5.5	12.4	17.0	23.0	24.8
Czech Republic	97.2	97.4	97.2	97.1	96.8	96.7	96.3	96.8
Denmark	..	..	20.4	19.3	2.5	19.5	18.6	18.8
Ecuador	..	..	..	..	..	..	..	11.7
El Salvador	..	..	9.3	9.7	17.4	9.6	9.4	9.6
Estonia	..	100.0	100.0	100.0	100.0	100.0	100.0	100.0
Finland	36.1	..	..	38.3	42.0	43.0	38.5	..
France	..	..	..	..	..	..	..	..
Germany	26.8	27.0	27.4	30.1	27.4	26.0	26.7	25.3
Greece	59.3	57.2	63.4	63.3	53.8	48.0	55.7	76.9
Guatemala	..	..	..	..	..	..	..	..
Honduras	..	..	..	..	13.8	59.6	62.2	..
Hong Kong, China	..	..	..	..	..	..	..	..
Hungary	95.9	93.4	92.8	93.5	95.6	96.2	95.8	96.9
India	..	..	0.0	..	..	..	..	0.0
Indonesia	..	..	..	..	..	..	..	..
Iceland	2.0	3.0	3.6	3.9	4.3	5.0	5.8	..
Ireland	3.3	8.2	4.7	3.9	4.9	4.5	4.7	..
Israel[1]	30.6	30.6	30.4	0.3	0.4	0.4	0.4	0.4
Italy	30.8	30.2	30.1	27.4	28.9	31.3	30.5	33.1
Japan	17.8	17.6	19.2	22.4	20.7	20.1	20.6	21.8
Korea	20.1	19.7	18.9	16.3	16.1	13.2	12.4	14.7
Latvia	59.0	97.3	90.1	90.0	91.8	91.0	89.8	90.3
Lithuania	..	97.0	96.9	96.8	97.0	97.4	97.4	97.5
Luxembourg	96.6	95.1	95.6	94.6	96.2	96.4	92.5	77.2
Malaysia	71.1	62.0	67.9	68.1	68.6	68.8	69.6	69.7
Mexico	74.0	72.5	69.9	71.1	6.3	74.0	72.3	70.6
Netherlands	22.5	25.2	21.1	21.1	19.2	4.6	18.5	..
New Zealand	..	..	..	..	..	..	..	..
Nicaragua	..	..	..	32.6	29.1	26.6	26.4	18.0
Norway	..	9.7	9.3	10.7	12.3	13.3	15.1	0.7
Paraguay	..	..	..	..	6.2	..	0.0	0.0
Peru	..	..	22.3	20.7	23.5	30.7	56.8	28.1
Poland	49.4	49.8	50.9	51.1	48.8	50.0	50.7	54.3
Portugal	7.1	5.8	9.3	7.9	6.8	54.0	64.2	77.5
Puerto Rico	..	..	..	..	10.4	7.8	0.0	59.9
Russia	3.0	..	..	..	..	8.5	18.1	15.5
Singapore	41.5	44.0	61.0	66.3	67.2	71.3	70.6	70.0
Slovak Republic	91.6	91.0	90.4	90.2	90.4	90.0	89.0	..
Slovenia	16.7	16.6	17.1	16.8	17.6	17.2	17.0	17.1
South Africa	..	..	20.8	33.0	31.9	35.2	33.3	34.6
Spain	10.0	10.3	8.8	19.1	12.4	12.8	12.3	..
Sweden	14.0	16.8	17.3	18.4	19.5	7.9	8.8	11.2
Switzerland	3.3	30.5	29.9	30.6	31.2	27.9	26.9	25.6
Tunisia	..	..	..	..	..	..	..	..
Turkey	50.5	27.5	27.7	27.1	47.1	47.9	59.7	54.2
United Kingdom	20.6	18.8	21.0	26.4	23.3	16.0	16.9	..
United States	25.6	20.6	19.8	19.6	20.0	21.0	17.4	22.5

.. Not available

Note: Detailed metadata at: http://metalinks.oecd.org/ins/20180621/57fd.

Disclaimer: http://oe.cd/disclaimer

1. Information on data for Israel: http://oe.cd/israel-disclaimer.

Source: Insurance activity indicators, OECD Insurance Statistics (database)

Table 28. Market share of foreign undertakings in total domestic business (Life)
Branches or agencies

Per cent

	2009	2010	2011	2012	2013	2014	2015	2016
Argentina	..	..	..	1.5	1.8	3.9	3.2	3.4
Australia	..	..	..	..	..	..	..	..
Austria	..	..	..	..	0.0	0.0	0.0	0.0
Belgium	..	..	..	..	..	..	..	..
Bolivia	..	..	..	..	..	..	..	..
Brazil	..	..	..	..	..	..	0.0	0.0
Canada	2.6	2.8	2.4	2.6	2.2	15.5	15.8	..
Chile	0.0	0.0	..	..	..	..	..	..
Colombia	..	..	..	..	..	..	..	..
Costa Rica	..	0.0	0.0	0.0	0.2	0.6	1.1	1.0
Czech Republic	10.2	8.4	8.3	8.1	7.5	7.2	10.8	10.9
Denmark	..	..	..	..	..	..	..	..
Ecuador	..	..	..	..	..	..	..	..
El Salvador	..	..	9.3	9.7	17.4	9.6	9.4	9.6
Estonia	..	0.0	0.0	2.9	2.5	2.7	2.8	2.2
Finland	..	..	..	..	..	..	..	..
France	..	..	..	..	..	..	..	..
Germany	1.2	0.4	3.1	4.0	4.0	3.9	4.0	3.9
Greece	12.9	13.6	6.2	0.4	0.0	0.0	0.0	0.0
Guatemala	..	..	..	..	..	..	..	..
Honduras	..	..	..	..	13.8	25.6	23.1	..
Hong Kong, China	..	..	..	..	..	..	..	..
Hungary	..	..	..	..	..	..	..	..
India	..	..	0.0	..	..	..	..	0.0
Indonesia	..	..	..	..	..	..	..	..
Iceland	0.0	0.0	0.0	..	..	..	..	..
Ireland	3.3	8.2	4.7	3.9	4.9	4.5	4.7	..
Israel[1]	0.0	0.0	..	..	..	..	..	..
Italy	0.0	0.0	0.0	0.0	0.0	0.0	0.0	0.0
Japan	7.3	7.7	9.2	5.5	4.9	4.2	4.1	4.3
Korea	3.2	2.9	2.7	2.2	2.2	2.4	0.2	2.0
Latvia	32.2	38.0	51.5	55.7	56.3	58.5	59.3	64.8
Lithuania	..	47.7	46.7	41.5	41.6	43.1	41.8	40.8
Luxembourg	0.5	0.2	0.4	0.3	0.5	0.1	0.1	0.1
Malaysia	0.2	0.4	0.4	0.4	0.5	0.5	0.5	0.5
Mexico	..	..	..	..	..	..	..	..
Netherlands	2.7	3.0	2.7	2.7	2.0	0.0	0.0	..
New Zealand	..	..	..	..	..	..	..	..
Nicaragua	..	..	..	..	..	..	..	..
Norway	..	1.2	1.0	0.8	1.3	1.4	0.7	0.7
Paraguay	..	..	..	..	..	..	0.0	0.0
Peru	..	..	..	..	..	..	..	..
Poland	0.0	..	..	..	..	..	..	..
Portugal	0.7	0.5	0.8	0.0	0.0	0.0	0.0	0.0
Puerto Rico	..	..	..	..	..	..	..	35.3
Russia	..	..	..	..	..	..	..	..
Singapore	..	30.0	29.8	15.1	15.0	32.6	30.7	32.3
Slovak Republic	3.8	4.2	4.5	4.3	5.4	4.4	4.8	..
Slovenia	..	..	..	..	..	..	..	..
South Africa	..	..	..	..	0.0	..	..	..
Spain	0.2	0.3	0.3	0.2	0.0	0.0	0.0	..
Sweden	..	..	..	..	..	0.7	..	..
Switzerland	3.3	4.0	1.6	2.1	1.5	0.0	0.0	0.0
Tunisia	..	..	..	..	..	..	..	..
Turkey	..	0.0	..	..	..	..	..	0.0
United Kingdom	0.3	0.9	0.1	0.0	0.0	0.0	0.0	..
United States	0.0	0.0	0.0	..	..	..	..	0.0

.. Not available

Note: Detailed metadata at: http://metalinks.oecd.org/ins/20180621/57fd.

Disclaimer: http://oe.cd/disclaimer

1. Information on data for Israel: http://oe.cd/israel-disclaimer.

Source: Insurance activity indicators, OECD Insurance Statistics (database)

Table 29. Market share of foreign companies in the domestic market (Non-life)

Per cent

	2009	2010	2011	2012	2013	2014	2015	2016
Argentina	..	..	..	17.6	20.1	21.1	22.0	23.4
Australia	28.6	28.7	27.3	27.1	27.7	28.7	28.2	28.7
Austria	..	..	..	..	35.2	37.5	36.9	36.6
Belgium	..	..	..	..	..	..	..	..
Bolivia	..	..	..	..	..	..	..	27.9
Brazil	..	..	..	..	..	51.3	32.4	35.7
Canada	30.1	30.9	29.8	29.0	27.9	44.8	41.6	..
Chile	67.9	66.8	66.5	65.7	63.7	63.5	62.7	79.0
Colombia	..	..	..	..	..	..	..	27.9
Costa Rica	..	0.9	5.8	7.6	10.0	14.2	17.5	20.5
Czech Republic	90.9	89.0	88.6	88.6	88.2	89.4	90.0	89.1
Denmark	..	..	16.0	16.6	16.4	27.5	27.9	28.3
Ecuador	..	..	..	..	..	..	..	0.4
El Salvador	..	..	2.3	2.4	0.0	0.0	0.0	0.0
Estonia	74.0	91.7	90.4	92.7	94.3	95.1	95.2	94.8
Finland	24.3	..	..	25.0	23.8	23.7	100.0	..
France	0.3	0.1	0.1	0.1	0.1	0.1	0.1	..
Germany	17.5	17.1	18.2	13.2	14.0	14.5	14.3	13.3
Greece	35.3	33.8	36.6	41.2	34.5	41.2	43.0	57.3
Guatemala	..	..	..	..	..	..	..	..
Honduras	..	..	..	..	10.5	40.3	42.8	..
Hong Kong, China	..	..	..	..	..	..	..	..
Hungary	95.0	97.3	96.8	95.7	94.9	94.7	92.8	91.7
India	..	..	0.0	..	..	..	..	..
Indonesia	..	..	..	..	..	..	..	..
Iceland	11.8	9.2	9.7	9.9	10.4	10.9	11.3	..
Ireland	8.2	8.9	8.2	17.6	14.3	24.3	22.2	..
Israel[1]	11.4	11.1	11.2	3.3	3.3	3.4	4.0	3.8
Italy	30.0	27.3	27.6	27.5	27.8	28.9	32.2	31.8
Japan	10.2	10.9	12.8	..	..	..	..	9.4
Korea	5.4	4.7	3.9	3.8	4.0	3.7	3.7	3.7
Latvia	60.9	58.6	44.3	48.1	49.4	48.7	57.1	79.0
Lithuania	..	95.9	98.0	98.5	98.8	99.0	99.0	99.3
Luxembourg	62.0	61.6	62.7	58.9	52.1	53.3	52.8	51.7
Malaysia	33.1	32.3	42.7	43.9	45.8	46.6	47.8	48.5
Mexico	50.0	53.5	51.1	52.4	9.7	48.7	52.2	48.5
Netherlands	17.0	17.0	29.4	29.4	22.7	11.6	16.3	..
New Zealand	..	..	..	..	..	..	..	..
Nicaragua	..	..	..	24.6	25.7	24.7	25.7	26.0
Norway	43.3	42.6	42.3	43.9	43.4	41.1	40.2	40.3
Paraguay	..	..	..	0.0	26.4	..	0.0	22.8
Peru	..	..	18.8	19.1	19.9	20.6	45.9	24.8
Poland	56.1	59.3	61.1	62.8	61.3	61.3	61.8	59.1
Portugal	34.6	28.3	26.7	26.5	26.6	84.2	84.3	91.0
Puerto Rico	..	..	..	..	52.6	51.8	41.0	57.0
Russia	33.4	..	..	..	..	2.2	13.7	13.7
Singapore	66.4	67.0	85.6	86.8	86.2	89.0	89.2	90.2
Slovak Republic	95.1	94.7	94.4	94.0	93.8	93.6	93.2	..
Slovenia	4.2	4.9	5.1	4.9	5.1	5.2	5.3	5.7
South Africa	..	..	27.3	63.5	45.2	39.5	34.6	37.4
Spain	22.2	18.6	17.0	32.2	29.1	28.8	23.6	..
Sweden	53.9	53.1	51.9	63.8	57.6	55.4	44.8	46.7
Switzerland	3.1	19.9	19.8	20.4	20.6	19.6	20.3	20.1
Tunisia	..	..	..	..	..	..	..	..
Turkey	52.5	55.2	57.9	53.8	62.2	59.3	66.7	63.7
United Kingdom	54.2	53.1	55.2	55.2	58.0	57.8	57.5	0.5
United States	18.5	13.9	13.9	10.1	10.4	9.4	9.5	10.2

.. Not available

Note: Detailed metadata at: http://metalinks.oecd.org/ins/20180621/57fd.

Disclaimer: http://oe.cd/disclaimer

1. Information on data for Israel: http://oe.cd/israel-disclaimer.

Source: Insurance activity indicators, OECD Insurance Statistics (database)

Table 30. Market share of foreign undertakings in total domestic business (Non-life)

Branches or agencies

Per cent

	2009	2010	2011	2012	2013	2014	2015	2016
Argentina	..	..	..	0.1	0.1	3.2	2.5	2.4
Australia	11.2	11.6	9.7	9.7	9.7	10.1	9.1	9.9
Austria	..	..	..	..	0.1	0.1	0.0	0.0
Belgium	..	..	..	..	..	..	..	..
Bolivia	..	..	..	..	..	..	..	..
Brazil	..	..	..	..	..	..	0.0	0.0
Canada	14.3	15.1	14.3	13.4	13.1	23.2	21.0	..
Chile	0.0	0.0	..	..	..	..	..	..
Colombia	..	..	..	..	..	..	..	..
Costa Rica	..	0.0	0.0	0.1	0.3	0.4	0.8	1.3
Czech Republic	2.8	3.2	3.1	2.7	3.7	4.7	4.9	5.3
Denmark	..	..	..	..	..	..	..	..
Ecuador	..	..	..	..	..	..	..	..
El Salvador	..	..	2.3	2.4	0.0	0.0	0.0	0.0
Estonia	16.7	0.0	0.0	14.5	13.6	14.8	13.5	15.0
Finland	..	..	..	..	..	..	..	..
France	0.3	0.1	0.1	0.1	0.1	0.1	0.1	..
Germany	2.1	1.5	3.0	3.1	2.7	3.2	3.5	3.1
Greece	6.2	4.0	4.6	7.9	0.0	0.0	0.0	0.0
Guatemala	..	..	..	..	..	..	..	..
Honduras	..	..	..	..	10.5	4.4	3.6	..
Hong Kong, China	..	..	..	..	..	..	..	..
Hungary	..	..	..	..	..	..	..	..
India	..	..	0.0	..	..	..	..	..
Indonesia	..	..	..	..	..	..	..	..
Iceland	0.0	0.0	0.0	..	..	..	..	..
Ireland	8.2	8.9	8.2	17.6	14.3	24.3	22.2	..
Israel[1]	0.0	0.0	..	..	..	..	..	..
Italy	4.9	1.0	1.1	1.1	1.1	1.1	1.4	1.6
Japan	5.3	5.6	7.8	..	..	..	..	2.3
Korea	3.7	3.2	2.6	2.0	3.1	2.3	2.3	2.3
Latvia	10.2	11.2	10.9	13.3	18.5	20.4	20.2	22.6
Lithuania	..	19.8	40.4	39.7	52.9	53.1	53.9	46.8
Luxembourg	8.3	7.9	7.2	7.5	6.5	3.6	3.6	3.5
Malaysia	2.2	3.8	4.4	5.8	6.7	7.3	8.4	9.6
Mexico	..	..	..	..	..	..	..	..
Netherlands	1.9	1.9	1.9	1.9	0.3	0.3	0.0	..
New Zealand	..	..	..	..	..	..	..	..
Nicaragua	..	..	..	..	..	..	..	..
Norway	41.7	41.4	41.5	43.2	43.4	41.1	40.2	40.3
Paraguay	..	..	..	..	..	..	0.0	0.0
Peru	..	..	..	..	..	..	..	..
Poland	0.3	..	..	..	..	..	..	..
Portugal	0.6	0.3	0.3	0.0	0.0	0.0	0.0	0.0
Puerto Rico	..	..	..	..	..	..	..	3.1
Russia	..	..	..	..	..	..	..	0.1
Singapore	..	44.1	44.0	42.7	46.8	39.6	38.2	37.4
Slovak Republic	5.1	6.2	6.2	7.1	8.0	8.7	8.5	..
Slovenia	..	..	..	..	..	..	..	..
South Africa	..	..	..	..	0.0	..	..	..
Spain	0.2	0.2	0.2	0.2	0.0	0.0	0.0	..
Sweden	..	..	..	..	..	8.2	..	..
Switzerland	3.1	4.8	4.8	4.9	5.0	5.5	6.0	7.1
Tunisia	..	..	..	..	..	..	..	..
Turkey	0.1	0.2	0.2	0.3	0.3	0.3	0.4	0.4
United Kingdom	5.9	5.3	5.4	4.7	3.7	4.1	4.6	0.5
United States	0.1	0.1	0.1	0.1	0.0	0.0	0.1	0.1

.. Not available

Note: Detailed metadata at: http://metalinks.oecd.org/ins/20180621/57fd.

Disclaimer: http://oe.cd/disclaimer

1. Information on data for Israel: http://oe.cd/israel-disclaimer.

Source: Insurance activity indicators, OECD Insurance Statistics (database)

PART II
Country tables

Australia
Table 1. Selected aggregates

Million AUD

	2009	2010	2011	2012	2013	2014	2015	2016
1.1 Insurance business written in the reporting country								
1.1.1 Insurance business, by ownership								
Gross premiums								
Domestic undertakings	70 384	73 331	78 509	79 230	86 754	103 414	100 992	95 348
Foreign controlled undertakings	17 570	12 274	11 038	13 757	15 722	17 983	19 150	19 836
Foreign companies (branches)	3 639	3 844	3 450	3 713	3 977	4 206	3 893	4 393
All undertakings	74 023	77 176	81 959	82 943	90 731	107 620	104 885	99 741
Premiums ceded								
Domestic undertakings	9 406	9 989	11 246	11 507	12 121	13 268	15 209	17 826
Foreign controlled undertakings	2 797	2 770	3 170	4 111	4 666	5 483	5 986	6 268
Foreign companies (branches)	1 202	1 402	1 442	1 659	1 947	1 842	1 739	1 759
All undertakings	10 607	11 391	12 688	13 166	14 068	15 110	16 948	19 585
Net written premiums								
Domestic undertakings	60 978	63 343	67 263	67 724	74 633	90 147	85 783	77 522
Foreign controlled undertakings	14 773	9 439	7 868	9 646	11 055	12 500	13 164	13 568
Foreign companies (branches)	2 437	2 441	2 008	2 054	2 030	2 365	2 154	2 634
All undertakings	63 415	65 785	69 271	69 778	76 663	92 511	87 937	80 156
1.1.2 Insurance business on foreign risks, gross premiums								
Life	494	495	475	491	574	686	701	711
Non-life	694	..	..	..	..	..	..	..
Composite total	..	..	..	..	..	..	..	..
Total	1 187	495	475	491	574	686	701	711
1.1.3 Life insurance payments, by class, gross premiums								
Annuities	..	..	..	..	..	..	..	..
Unit linked	..	..	..	..	..	..	..	..
Other life insurance	..	..	..	..	..	..	..	..
Total life insurance	..	..	..	41 091	45 794	60 881	56 868	49 890
***of which:** Pension contracts*	..	..	..	..	..	..	..	..
1.1.4 Non-life insurance payments, by class, gross premiums								
Motor vehicle insurance	10 670	..	11 474	12 114	12 924	13 467	13 749	14 512
Marine, aviation and other transport insurance	1 324	..	1 457	1 484	1 523	1 598	1 673	1 648
Freight insurance	..	..	..	..	..	..	..	..
Fire and other property damage insurance	8 106	..	9 537	10 918	12 038	11 836	12 031	12 297
Pecuniary loss insurance	1 384	..	1 161	1 207	1 258	1 454	1 493	1 443
General liability insurance	4 858	..	4 821	5 008	5 283	5 418	5 435	5 348
Accident and health	1 039	..	1 038	1 049	1 134	1 124	1 130	1 064
***of which:** Health*	..	..	..	..	..	..	..	..
Other non-life insurance	654	..	751	835	900	951	1 029	1 071
Treaty reinsurance	4 578	..	5 235	5 836	5 823	5 970	6 271	7 115
Total non-life insurance	32 612	33 223	35 475	38 450	40 884	41 818	42 811	44 498
1.2 Gross claims payments								
Life								
Domestic undertakings	37 546	41 639	44 988	45 777	47 647	64 828	56 547	59 350
Foreign controlled undertakings	9 499	5 355	4 301	4 181	5 212	5 876	6 681	7 133
Foreign companies (branches)	..	..	..	..	..	..	..	..
All undertakings	37 546	41 639	44 988	45 777	47 647	64 828	56 547	59 350
Non-life								
Domestic undertakings	18 193	21 552	31 597	22 048	24 141	26 293	29 311	28 324
Foreign controlled undertakings	3 579	4 120	6 668	4 538	4 542	5 446	6 183	5 534
Foreign companies (branches)	1 951	2 401	7 061	1 749	1 984	3 318	2 585	3 217
All undertakings	20 144	23 953	38 658	23 797	26 126	29 611	31 896	31 541
Composite, all undertakings	..	..	..	..	..	..	..	..
Total								
Domestic undertakings	55 739	63 191	76 585	67 825	71 788	91 121	85 858	87 674
Foreign controlled undertakings	13 078	9 475	10 969	8 719	9 754	11 322	12 864	12 667
Foreign companies (branches)	1 951	2 401	7 061	1 749	1 984	3 318	2 585	3 217
All undertakings	57 690	65 592	83 646	69 574	73 773	94 439	88 443	90 891

Australia
Table 1. Selected aggregates *(cont.)*

Million AUD

	2009	2010	2011	2012	2013	2014	2015	2016
1.3 Commissions								
Life								
Domestic undertakings	2 588	2 738	2 852	3 007	3 015	3 118	3 087	3 129
Foreign controlled undertakings	907	440	455	252	447	451	460	464
Foreign companies (branches)	..	..	..	..	..	..	..	..
All undertakings	2 588	2 738	2 852	3 007	3 015	3 118	3 087	3 129
Non-life								
Domestic undertakings	..	..	..	..	506	566	816	1 038
Foreign controlled undertakings	..	..	..	..	239	270	276	308
Foreign companies (branches)	..	..	..	..	264	287	301	327
All undertakings	..	..	..	..	770	853	1 117	1 364
Composite, all undertakings	..	..	..	..	..	..	..	..
Total								
Domestic undertakings	2 588	2 738	2 852	3 007	3 521	3 684	3 903	4 167
Foreign controlled undertakings	907	440	455	252	686	721	736	772
Foreign companies (branches)	..	..	..	..	264	287	301	327
All undertakings	2 588	2 738	2 852	3 007	3 785	3 971	4 204	4 493
1.4 Gross operating expenses								
Life								
Domestic undertakings	6 355	6 640	6 777	7 274	7 830	8 128	8 041	8 666
Foreign controlled undertakings	2 138	1 608	1 709	1 430	2 392	2 393	2 487	3 038
Foreign companies (branches)	..	..	..	..	..	..	..	..
All undertakings	6 355	6 640	6 777	7 274	7 830	8 128	8 041	8 666
Non-life								
Domestic undertakings	6 043	6 027	6 658	7 197	7 361	7 502	7 497	7 368
Foreign controlled undertakings	1 089	1 172	1 370	1 490	1 618	1 704	1 850	1 829
Foreign companies (branches)	627	559	571	559	597	629	660	618
All undertakings	6 670	6 586	7 229	7 756	7 959	8 131	8 157	7 987
Composite, all undertakings	..	..	..	..	..	..	..	..
Total								
Domestic undertakings	12 399	12 667	13 435	14 471	15 191	15 630	15 538	16 034
Foreign controlled undertakings	3 226	2 780	3 079	2 920	4 010	4 097	4 337	4 867
Foreign companies (branches)	627	559	571	559	597	629	660	618
All undertakings	13 025	13 226	14 006	15 030	15 789	16 259	16 198	16 653
1.5 Insurance business written abroad by branches, gross premiums								
Life								
Branches and agencies	..	..	..	..	..	..	..	..
Subsidaries	..	..	..	..	..	..	..	..
Total	..	..	..	..	..	..	..	..
Non-life								
Branches and agencies	..	..	..	..	..	..	..	..
Subsidaries	..	..	..	..	..	..	..	..
Total	..	..	..	..	..	..	..	..
Composite total	..	..	..	..	..	..	..	..
Total								
Branches and agencies	..	..	..	..	..	..	..	..
Subsidaries	..	..	..	..	..	..	..	..
Total	..	..	..	..	..	..	..	..

.. Not available

Note: Detailed metadata at: http://metalinks.oecd.org/ins/20180621/50dc.

Disclaimer: http://oe.cd/disclaimer

Source: OECD Insurance Statistics (database)

Australia
Table 2. Number of companies and employees

	2009	2010	2011	2012	2013	2014	2015	2016
2.1 Number of companies								
Life								
Domestic undertakings	26	26	31	28	28	28	28	29
Foreign controlled undertakings	8	8	14	14	14	14	13	13
Foreign companies (branches)	..	..	..	..	..	..	..	..
All undertakings	26	26	31	28	28	28	28	29
Non-life								
Domestic undertakings	85	84	81	79	75	74	70	68
Foreign controlled undertakings	22	20	19	17	18	19	19	17
Foreign companies (branches)	35	34	31	30	29	29	29	31
All undertakings	120	118	112	109	104	103	99	99
Composite, all undertakings	..	..	..	..	..	..	0	..
Reinsurance								
Domestic undertakings	8	2	3	3	3	3	2	2
Foreign controlled undertakings	7	1	1	1	1	1	1	1
Foreign companies (branches)	12	10	9	9	9	9	9	8
All undertakings	20	12	12	12	12	12	11	10
Total								
Domestic undertakings	119	112	115	110	106	105	100	99
Foreign controlled undertakings	37	29	34	32	33	34	33	31
Foreign companies (branches)	47	44	40	39	38	38	38	39
All undertakings	166	156	155	149	144	143	138	138
2.2 Number of employees								
Insurance undertakings	..	..	..	..	..	..	..	..
Intermediaries	..	..	..	..	..	..	..	..
Total	..	..	..	..	..	..	..	..

.. Not available

Note: Detailed metadata at: http://metalinks.oecd.org/ins/20180621/50dc.

Disclaimer: http://oe.cd/disclaimer

Source: OECD Insurance Statistics (database)

Austria
Table 1. Selected aggregates

Million EUR

	2009	2010	2011	2012	2013	2014	2015	2016
1.1 Insurance business written in the reporting country								
1.1.1 Insurance business, by ownership								
Gross premiums								
Domestic undertakings	..	..	..	..	18 879	18 889	19 003	18 647
Foreign controlled undertakings	..	..	..	..	6 781	7 196	7 060	6 979
Foreign companies (branches)	..	..	..	..	8	6	6	6
All undertakings	..	..	..	..	18 887	18 895	19 009	18 653
Premiums ceded								
Domestic undertakings	..	..	..	..	3 539	3 102	2 996	3 521
Foreign controlled undertakings	..	..	..	..	1 127	1 171	1 113	1 636
Foreign companies (branches)	..	..	..	..	0	0	0	0
All undertakings	..	..	..	..	3 539	3 102	2 996	3 522
Net written premiums								
Domestic undertakings	..	..	..	..	15 340	15 787	16 007	15 126
Foreign controlled undertakings	..	..	..	..	5 654	6 024	5 948	5 343
Foreign companies (branches)	..	..	..	..	8	6	6	6
All undertakings	..	..	..	..	15 348	15 793	16 013	15 131
1.1.2 Insurance business on foreign risks, gross premiums								
Life	83	991	174	72	157	22	20	14
Non-life	121	4 630	722	662	717	726	702	753
Composite	398	13 176	523	626	595	489	391	371
of which:								
Life	243	6 471	252	188	202	158	111	95
Non-life	155	6 704	270	438	393	331	280	276
Total	602	18 797	1 419	1 360	1 469	1 237	1 114	1 138
1.1.3 Life insurance payments, by class, gross premiums								
Annuities	..	..	..	..	1 441	1 822	1 946	1 531
Unit linked	2 521	2 860	2 255	1 846	1 248	1 011	933	864
Other life insurance	4 797	4 578	4 644	4 588	3 738	3 852	3 812	3 646
Total life insurance	..	7 438	6 899	6 434	6 427	6 685	6 692	6 041
***of which:** Pension contracts*	..	..	..	..	997	1 116	1 031	940
1.1.4 Non-life insurance payments, by class, gross premiums								
Motor vehicle insurance	1 243	1 260	1 316	1 386	1 487	1 447	3 920	4 043
Marine, aviation and other transport insurance	118	124	140	165	174	138	11	9
Freight insurance	0	..	..	..	..	..	155	148
Fire and other property damage insurance	957	973	978	1 008	1 081	1 058	3 153	3 178
Pecuniary loss insurance	211	220	237	167	174	183	178	176
General liability insurance	870	888	922	834	860	886	889	905
Accident and health	2 503	2 572	2 873	3 024	3 150	3 143	3 257	3 391
***of which:** Health*	1 598	1 653	1 704	1 762	1 841	1 905	2 007	2 096
Other non-life insurance	4 798	5 193	5 517	5 672	5 517	5 340	742	749
Treaty reinsurance	..	..	..	..	..	..	..	..
Total non-life insurance	10 701	11 230	11 983	12 255	12 444	12 195	12 303	12 599
1.2 Gross claims payments								
Life								
Domestic undertakings	167	256	314	360	358	1 110	1 254	947
Foreign controlled undertakings	0	0	0	145	140	714	837	920
Foreign companies (branches)	0	0	0	..	0	0	0	0
All undertakings	167	256	314	360	358	1 110	1 254	947
Non-life								
Domestic undertakings	3 229	3 019	2 290	2 675	1 107	1 632	2 072	2 203
Foreign controlled undertakings	1 108	1 531	875	1 490	905	873	1 288	2 620
Foreign companies (branches)	12	5	5	5	4	3	2	3
All undertakings	3 241	3 024	2 296	2 681	1 111	1 636	2 075	2 206
Composite								
Domestic undertakings	10 317	10 023	10 854	11 652	11 676	11 289	12 780	12 440
Foreign controlled undertakings	3 315	3 565	3 751	3 829	3 846	3 026	3 760	10 479
Foreign companies (branches)	0	0	0	..	0	0	0	0
All undertakings	10 317	10 023	10 854	11 652	11 676	11 289	12 780	12 440
of which:								
Life	5 631	5 599	6 338	6 047	6 011	5 955	7 193	6 817
Domestic undertakings	5 631	5 599	6 338	6 047	6 011	5 955	7 193	6 817
Foreign controlled undertakings	1 786	2 117	2 297	2 281	2 274	1 630	2 205	3 500
Foreign companies (branches)	0	0	0	..	0	0	0	0
All undertakings	5 631	5 599	6 338	6 047	6 011	5 955	7 193	6 817
Non-life	4 685	4 425	4 516	5 605	5 665	5 335	5 588	5 623
Domestic undertakings	4 685	4 425	4 516	5 605	5 665	5 335	5 588	5 623
Foreign controlled undertakings	1 529	1 448	1 454	1 549	1 572	1 396	1 525	6 979
Foreign companies (branches)	0	0	0	..	0	0	0	0
All undertakings	4 685	4 425	4 516	5 605	5 665	5 335	5 588	5 623
Total								
Domestic undertakings	13 713	13 298	13 458	14 687	13 141	14 032	16 107	15 590
Foreign controlled undertakings	4 424	5 096	4 626	5 464	4 891	4 613	5 885	14 018
Foreign companies (branches)	12	5	5	5	4	3	2	3
All undertakings	13 725	13 304	13 463	14 692	13 145	14 036	16 109	15 593

Austria
Table 1. Selected aggregates *(cont.)*

Million EUR

	2009	2010	2011	2012	2013	2014	2015	2016
1.3 Commissions								
Life								
Domestic undertakings	118	129	138	75	99	98	98	80
Foreign controlled undertakings	0	0	0	17	5	70	70	79
Foreign companies (branches)	0	0	0	..	0	0	0	0
All undertakings	118	129	138	75	99	98	98	80
Non-life								
Domestic undertakings	518	519	548	338	354	398	386	399
Foreign controlled undertakings	97	295	302	309	319	329	341	348
Foreign companies (branches)	9	1	2	2	2	1	1	1
All undertakings	527	521	549	340	356	399	387	400
Composite								
Domestic undertakings	1 805	1 916	1 962	2 309	2 285	2 279	2 354	2 392
Foreign controlled undertakings	638	712	717	750	752	666	739	734
Foreign companies (branches)	0	0	0	..	0	0	0	0
All undertakings	1 805	1 916	1 962	2 309	2 285	2 279	2 354	2 392
of which:								
Life	616	688	669	692	644	624	623	579
Domestic undertakings	616	688	669	692	644	624	623	579
Foreign controlled undertakings	194	256	255	253	238	163	188	163
Foreign companies (branches)	0	0	0	..	0	0	0	0
All undertakings	616	688	669	692	644	624	623	579
Non-life	1 189	1 228	1 292	1 616	1 641	1 655	1 731	1 812
Domestic undertakings	1 189	1 228	1 292	1 616	1 641	1 655	1 731	1 812
Foreign controlled undertakings	444	456	462	497	514	503	551	571
Foreign companies (branches)	0	0	0	..	0	0	0	0
All undertakings	1 189	1 228	1 292	1 616	1 641	1 655	1 731	1 812
Total								
Domestic undertakings	2 440	2 564	2 647	2 722	2 738	2 775	2 839	2 871
Foreign controlled undertakings	734	1 008	1 019	1 077	1 076	1 065	1 150	1 161
Foreign companies (branches)	9	1	2	2	2	1	1	1
All undertakings	2 450	2 565	2 649	2 724	2 740	2 776	2 840	2 872
1.4 Gross operating expenses								
Life								
Domestic undertakings	136	146	157	95	120	43	40	37
Foreign controlled undertakings	0	0	0	0	14	30	30	36
Foreign companies (branches)	0	0	0	..	0	0	0	0
All undertakings	136	146	157	95	120	43	40	37
Non-life								
Domestic undertakings	801	906	672	860	697	153	143	192
Foreign controlled undertakings	266	443	263	447	414	116	92	111
Foreign companies (branches)	16	3	3	3	3	1	1	1
All undertakings	818	909	675	863	700	154	144	193
Composite								
Domestic undertakings	2 026	2 115	2 054	1 918	2 306	623	678	702
Foreign controlled undertakings	644	723	667	695	699	167	185	177
Foreign companies (branches)	0	0	0	..	0	0	0	0
All undertakings	2 026	2 115	2 054	1 918	2 306	623	678	702
of which:								
Life	845	908	879	513	848	194	202	223
Domestic undertakings	845	908	879	513	848	194	202	223
Foreign controlled undertakings	279	341	344	339	323	61	68	63
Foreign companies (branches)	0	0	0	..	0	0	0	0
All undertakings	845	908	879	513	848	194	202	223
Non-life	1 181	1 208	1 175	1 405	1 458	428	476	479
Domestic undertakings	1 181	1 208	1 175	1 405	1 458	428	476	479
Foreign controlled undertakings	365	382	323	356	376	106	117	114
Foreign companies (branches)	0	0	0	..	0	0	0	0
All undertakings	1 181	1 208	1 175	1 405	1 458	428	476	479
Total								
Domestic undertakings	2 963	3 167	2 883	2 873	3 124	819	861	930
Foreign controlled undertakings	910	1 166	930	1 143	1 128	313	308	324
Foreign companies (branches)	16	3	3	3	3	1	1	1
All undertakings	2 980	3 170	2 885	2 876	3 127	820	862	931

Austria
Table 1. Selected aggregates *(cont.)*

Million EUR

	2009	2010	2011	2012	2013	2014	2015	2016
1.5 Insurance business written abroad by branches, gross premiums								
Life								
Branches and agencies	85 |	139	174	72	157	22	19	13
Subsidaries	..	..	..	..	..	..	..	..
Total	85 |	139	174	72	157	22	19	13
Non-life								
Branches and agencies	111 |	141	219	149	159	198	204	217
Subsidaries	..	..	..	..	..	..	..	..
Total	111 |	141	219	149	159	198	204	217
Composite								
Branches and agencies	331 |	539	480	557	480	368	284	251
Subsidaries	..	..	..	..	..	..	..	..
Total	331 |	539	480	557	480	368	284	251
of which:								
Life	226 |	407	233	168	140	103	78	83
Branches and agencies	226 |	407	233	168	140	103	78	83
Subsidaries	..	..	..	..	..	..	..	..
Total	226 |	407	233	168	140	103	78	83
Non-life	105 |	132	246	389	340	266	206	168
Branches and agencies	105 |	132	246	389	340	266	206	168
Subsidaries	..	..	..	..	..	..	..	..
Total	105 |	132	246	389	340	266	206	168
Total								
Branches and agencies	528	818	873	778	796	587	507	481
Subsidaries	..	..	..	..	..	..	..	..
Total	528	818	873	778	796	587	507	481

.. Not available; | Break in series

Note: Detailed metadata at: http://metalinks.oecd.org/ins/20180621/de0e.

Disclaimer: http://oe.cd/disclaimer

Source: OECD Insurance Statistics (database)

Austria
Table 2. Number of companies and employees

	2009	2010	2011	2012	2013	2014	2015	2016
2.1 Number of companies								
Life								
Domestic undertakings	3	3	3	3	3	7	7	6
Foreign controlled undertakings	0	0	0	1	1	3	3	4
Foreign companies (branches)	0	0	0	0	0	0	0	0
All undertakings	3	3	3	3	3	7	7	6
Non-life								
Domestic undertakings	16	17	17	14	14	12	12	12
Foreign controlled undertakings	8	9	8	7	7	8	8	8
Foreign companies (branches)	2	1	1	1	1	1	1	1
All undertakings	18	18	18	15	15	13	13	13
Composite								
Domestic undertakings	28	28	28	27	26	21	20	17
Foreign controlled undertakings	9	10	10	10	9	6	5	4
Foreign companies (branches)	0	0	0	0	0	0	0	0
All undertakings	28	28	28	27	26	21	20	17
Reinsurance								
Domestic undertakings	3	3	3	3	3	3	2	3
Foreign controlled undertakings	2	2	2	2	1	2	1	1
Foreign companies (branches)	0	0	0	0	0	0	0	0
All undertakings	3	3	3	3	3	3	2	3
Total								
Domestic undertakings	50	51	51	47	46	43	41	38
Foreign controlled undertakings	19	21	20	20	18	19	17	17
Foreign companies (branches)	2	1	1	1	1	1	1	1
All undertakings	52	52	52	48	47	44	42	39
2.2 Number of employees								
Insurance undertakings	27 896	27 755	27 671	27 430	27 738	27 791	27 911	28 336
Intermediaries	9 693	9 872	9 839	9 255	..	..	..	..
Total	27 896	27 755	27 671	27 430	27 738	27 791	27 911	28 336

.. Not available

Note: Detailed metadata at: http://metalinks.oecd.org/ins/20180621/de0e.

Disclaimer: http://oe.cd/disclaimer

Source: OECD Insurance Statistics (database)

Belgium
Table 1. Selected aggregates

Million EUR

	2009	2010	2011	2012	2013	2014	2015	2016
1.1 Insurance business written in the reporting country								
1.1.1 Insurance business, by ownership								
Gross premiums								
Domestic undertakings	28 488	29 575	29 363	32 640	28 251	28 863	27 712	27 497
Foreign controlled undertakings	..	..	..	..	..	..	..	..
Foreign companies (branches)	..	..	..	..	..	..	..	..
All undertakings	28 488	29 575	29 363	32 640	28 251	28 863	27 712	27 497
Premiums ceded								
Domestic undertakings	1 645	1 773	1 441	2 417	2 474	3 251	3 183	3 514
Foreign controlled undertakings	..	..	..	..	..	..	..	..
Foreign companies (branches)	..	..	..	..	..	..	..	..
All undertakings	1 645	1 773	1 441	2 417	2 474	3 251	3 183	3 514
Net written premiums								
Domestic undertakings	26 843	27 802	27 922	30 223	25 777	25 612	24 529	23 983
Foreign controlled undertakings	..	..	..	..	..	..	..	..
Foreign companies (branches)	..	..	..	..	..	..	..	..
All undertakings	26 843	27 802	27 922	30 223	25 777	25 612	24 529	23 983
1.1.2 Insurance business on foreign risks, gross premiums								
Life	..	..	..	31	25	15	24	20
Non-life	..	..	..	242	268	563	436	532
Composite	..	..	..	230	218	223	321	325
of which:								
Life	..	..	..	77	53	39	38	17
Non-life	..	..	..	153	165	184	282	308
Total	..	..	..	502	511	801	781	877
1.1.3 Life insurance payments, by class, gross premiums								
Annuities	..	..	..	..	..	..	..	..
Unit linked	1 664	2 049	2 142	4 844	2 743	2 524	3 008	2 220
Other life insurance	16 740	17 092	16 324	16 235	13 501	13 723	12 302	12 669
Total life insurance	18 404	19 141	18 467	21 078	16 244	16 247	15 310	14 889
of which: *Pension contracts*	..	..	..	..	..	..	..	..
1.1.4 Non-life insurance payments, by class, gross premiums								
Motor vehicle insurance	..	..	..	3 459	3 487	3 542	3 585	..
Marine, aviation and other transport insurance	..	..	..	78	71	69	81	..
Freight insurance	..	..	..	116	104	100	73	..
Fire and other property damage insurance	..	..	..	2 573	2 696	2 755	2 708	..
Pecuniary loss insurance	..	..	..	407	404	725	598	..
General liability insurance	..	..	..	780	770	785	762	..
Accident and health	..	..	..	3 361	3 592	3 695	3 653	..
of which: *Health*	..	..	..	1 517	1 618	1 708	1 849	..
Other non-life insurance	..	..	..	737	825	885	888	..
Treaty reinsurance	..	..	..	7	..	..	..	..
Total non-life insurance	..	..	..	11 516	11 949	12 556	12 349	12 542
1.2 Gross claims payments								
Life								
Domestic undertakings	1 207	514	547	592	528	626	469	623
Foreign controlled undertakings	..	..	..	..	..	..	..	..
Foreign companies (branches)	..	..	..	..	..	..	..	..
All undertakings	..	..	..	592	528	626	469	623
Non-life								
Domestic undertakings	1 120	1 496	1 512	1 898	1 960	2 272	2 363	2 538
Foreign controlled undertakings	..	..	..	..	..	..	..	..
Foreign companies (branches)	..	..	..	..	..	..	..	..
All undertakings	..	..	..	1 898	1 960	2 272	2 363	2 538
Composite								
Domestic undertakings	16 620	17 461	20 798	23 438	23 890	24 323	25 926	25 246
Foreign controlled undertakings	..	..	..	..	..	..	..	..
Foreign companies (branches)	..	..	..	..	..	..	..	..
All undertakings	..	..	..	23 438	23 890	24 323	25 926	25 246
of which:								
Life	..	..	..	17 427	17 746	17 418	19 244	18 345
Domestic undertakings	11 992	12 194	15 232	17 427	17 746	17 418	19 244	18 345
Foreign controlled undertakings	..	..	..	..	..	..	..	..
Foreign companies (branches)	..	..	..	..	..	..	..	..
All undertakings	..	..	..	17 427	17 746	17 418	19 244	18 345
Non-life	..	..	..	6 010	6 144	6 905	6 682	6 901
Domestic undertakings	4 628	5 267	5 566	6 010	6 144	6 905	6 682	6 901
Foreign controlled undertakings	..	..	..	..	..	..	..	..
Foreign companies (branches)	..	..	..	..	..	..	..	..
All undertakings	..	..	..	6 010	6 144	6 905	6 682	6 901
Total								
Domestic undertakings	18 947	19 470	22 857	25 928	26 378	27 222	28 758	28 407
Foreign controlled undertakings	..	..	..	..	..	..	..	..
Foreign companies (branches)	..	..	..	..	..	..	..	..
All undertakings	..	..	..	25 928	26 378	27 222	28 758	28 407

Belgium
Table 1. Selected aggregates *(cont.)*

Million EUR

	2009	2010	2011	2012	2013	2014	2015	2016
1.3 Commissions								
Life								
Domestic undertakings	140	74	54	59	55	45	47	25
Foreign controlled undertakings	..	..	..	..	..	..	..	..
Foreign companies (branches)	..	..	..	..	..	..	..	..
All undertakings	..	..	..	59	55	45	47	25
Non-life								
Domestic undertakings	207	340	318	394	391	450	550	617
Foreign controlled undertakings	..	..	..	..	..	..	..	..
Foreign companies (branches)	..	..	..	..	..	..	..	..
All undertakings	..	..	..	394	391	450	550	617
Composite								
Domestic undertakings	1 926	2 118	2 209	2 397	2 446	2 478	2 493	2 514
Foreign controlled undertakings	..	..	..	..	..	..	..	..
Foreign companies (branches)	..	..	..	..	..	..	..	..
All undertakings	..	..	..	2 397	2 446	2 478	2 493	2 514
of which:								
Life	..	..	..	905	875	852	833	795
Domestic undertakings	695	808	826	905	875	852	833	795
Foreign controlled undertakings	..	..	..	..	..	..	..	..
Foreign companies (branches)	..	..	..	..	..	..	..	..
All undertakings	..	..	..	905	875	852	833	795
Non-life	..	..	..	1 493	1 572	1 626	1 660	1 719
Domestic undertakings	1 231	1 310	1 382	1 493	1 572	1 626	1 660	1 719
Foreign controlled undertakings	..	..	..	..	..	..	..	..
Foreign companies (branches)	..	..	..	..	..	..	..	..
All undertakings	..	..	..	1 493	1 572	1 626	1 660	1 719
Total								
Domestic undertakings	2 273	2 531	2 581	2 851	2 892	2 973	3 090	3 157
Foreign controlled undertakings	..	..	..	..	..	..	..	..
Foreign companies (branches)	..	..	..	..	..	..	..	..
All undertakings	..	..	..	2 851	2 892	2 973	3 090	3 157
1.4 Gross operating expenses								
Life								
Domestic undertakings	219	135	115	118	58	41	45	42
Foreign controlled undertakings	..	..	..	..	..	..	..	..
Foreign companies (branches)	..	..	..	..	..	..	..	..
All undertakings	..	..	..	118	58	41	45	42
Non-life								
Domestic undertakings	451	648	621	806	386	643	618	641
Foreign controlled undertakings	..	..	..	..	..	..	..	..
Foreign companies (branches)	..	..	..	..	..	..	..	..
All undertakings	..	..	..	806	386	643	618	641
Composite								
Domestic undertakings	3 645	4 007	4 176	4 401	2 084	2 197	2 205	2 325
Foreign controlled undertakings	..	..	..	..	..	..	..	..
Foreign companies (branches)	..	..	..	..	..	..	..	..
All undertakings	..	..	..	4 401	2 084	2 197	2 205	2 325
of which:								
Life	..	..	..	1 702	830	833	824	864
Domestic undertakings	1 407	1 560	1 597	1 702	830	833	824	864
Foreign controlled undertakings	..	..	..	..	..	..	..	..
Foreign companies (branches)	..	..	..	..	..	..	..	..
All undertakings	..	..	..	1 702	830	833	824	864
Non-life	..	..	..	2 699	1 254	1 364	1 382	1 461
Domestic undertakings	2 238	2 446	2 579	2 699	1 254	1 364	1 382	1 461
Foreign controlled undertakings	..	..	..	..	..	..	..	..
Foreign companies (branches)	..	..	..	..	..	..	..	..
All undertakings	..	..	..	2 699	1 254	1 364	1 382	1 461
Total								
Domestic undertakings	4 315	4 790	4 912	5 325	2 528	2 881	2 868	3 007
Foreign controlled undertakings	..	..	..	..	..	..	..	..
Foreign companies (branches)	..	..	..	..	..	..	..	..
All undertakings	..	..	..	5 325	2 528	2 881	2 868	3 007

Belgium
Table 1. Selected aggregates *(cont.)*

Million EUR

	2009	2010	2011	2012	2013	2014	2015	2016
1.5 Insurance business written abroad by branches, gross premiums								
Life								
Branches and agencies	..	..	..	2	2	2	0	0
Subsidaries	..	..	..	..	..	..	..	..
Total	..	..	..	2	2	2	..	..
Non-life								
Branches and agencies	..	..	..	698	727	1 572	1 931	1 837
Subsidaries	..	..	..	..	..	..	..	..
Total	..	..	..	698	727	1 572	1 931	1 837
Composite								
Branches and agencies	..	..	..	442	448	1 121	1 156	1 185
Subsidaries	..	..	..	..	..	..	..	..
Total	..	..	..	442	448	1 121	1 156	1 185
of which:								
Life	..	..	..	32	28	16	16	2
Branches and agencies	..	..	..	32	28	16	16	2
Subsidaries	..	..	..	..	..	..	..	..
Total	..	..	..	32	28	16	16	2
Non-life	..	..	..	409	421	1 105	1 141	1 183
Branches and agencies	..	..	..	409	421	1 105	1 141	1 183
Subsidaries	..	..	..	..	..	..	..	..
Total	..	..	..	409	421	1 105	1 141	1 183
Total								
Branches and agencies	..	..	..	1 142	1 178	2 696	3 087	3 022
Subsidaries	..	..	..	..	..	..	..	..
Total	..	..	..	1 142	1 178	2 696	3 087	3 022

.. Not available; | Break in series

Note: Detailed metadata at: http://metalinks.oecd.org/ins/20180621/4c44.

Disclaimer: http://oe.cd/disclaimer

Source: OECD Insurance Statistics (database)

Belgium
Table 2. Number of companies and employees

	2009	2010	2011	2012	2013	2014	2015	2016
2.1 Number of companies								
Life								
Domestic undertakings	21	20	18	17	16	15	15	12
Foreign controlled undertakings	..	..	..	..	..	..	..	..
Foreign companies (branches)	8	8	8	7	7	8	8	10
All undertakings	29	28	26	24	23	23	23	22
Non-life								
Domestic undertakings	54	54	53	49	44	42	41	38
Foreign controlled undertakings	..	..	..	..	..	..	..	..
Foreign companies (branches)	41	40	44	36	36	36	32	32
All undertakings	95	94	97	85	80	78	73	70
Composite								
Domestic undertakings	21	23	24	23	23	23	23	22
Foreign controlled undertakings	..	..	..	..	..	..	..	..
Foreign companies (branches)	2	2	2	2	2	2	2	2
All undertakings	23	25	26	25	25	25	25	24
Reinsurance								
Domestic undertakings	1	2	2	1	1	1	1	1
Foreign controlled undertakings	..	..	..	..	..	..	..	..
Foreign companies (branches)	0	0	0	1	1	1	1	1
All undertakings	1	2	2	2	2	2	2	2
Total								
Domestic undertakings	97	99	97	90	84	81	80	73
Foreign controlled undertakings	..	..	..	..	..	..	..	..
Foreign companies (branches)	51	50	54	46	46	47	43	45
All undertakings	148	149	151	136	130	128	123	118
2.2 Number of employees								
Insurance undertakings	23 588	23 833	25 083	..	..	..	..	..
Intermediaries	20 897	18 075	..	..	..	..	..	..
Total	44 485	41 908	..	..	..	..	..	..

.. Not available

Note: Detailed metadata at: http://metalinks.oecd.org/ins/20180621/4c44.

Disclaimer: http://oe.cd/disclaimer

Source: OECD Insurance Statistics (database)

Canada
Table 1. Selected aggregates

Million CAD

	2009	2010	2011	2012	2013	2014	2015	2016
1.1 Insurance business written in the reporting country								
1.1.1 Insurance business, by ownership								
Gross premiums								
Domestic undertakings	77 487	78 875	83 513	87 337	91 830	81 347	86 082	..
Foreign controlled undertakings	11 354	11 288	11 273	11 465	11 237	18 957	17 321	..
Foreign companies (branches)	8 730	9 464	9 502	9 621	9 651	21 604	20 840	..
All undertakings	86 217	88 339	93 014	96 958	101 481	102 951	106 922	..
Premiums ceded								
Domestic undertakings	16 856	16 638	21 174	23 483	25 176	22 771	25 855	..
Foreign controlled undertakings	2 227	2 465	2 550	2 413	2 504	5 070	4 912	..
Foreign companies (branches)	1 791	2 014	1 923	2 405	2 094	4 469	4 735	..
All undertakings	18 648	18 651	23 097	25 888	27 270	27 240	30 590	..
Net written premiums								
Domestic undertakings	60 631	62 237	62 338	63 854	66 655	58 576	60 227	..
Foreign controlled undertakings	9 127	8 823	8 723	9 052	8 733	13 888	12 410	..
Foreign companies (branches)	6 939	7 450	7 579	7 216	7 557	17 135	16 104	..
All undertakings	67 570	69 687	69 917	71 070	74 212	75 710	76 331	..
1.1.2 Insurance business on foreign risks, gross premiums								
Life	..	..	..	..	..	..	..	..
Non-life	..	..	..	..	..	..	..	..
Composite	..	..	..	..	..	..	..	..
of which:								
Life	..	..	..	..	..	..	..	..
Non-life	..	..	..	..	..	..	..	..
Total	..	..	..	..	..	..	..	..
1.1.3 Life insurance payments, by class, gross premiums								
Annuities	8 943	7 815	6 457	5 276	6 263	5 562	5 539	..
Unit linked	68	70	..	..	..	..	..	..
Other life insurance	18 483	19 212	..	..	..	..	..	..
Total life insurance	38 923	39 093	..	..	..	..	..	..
***of which:** Pension contracts*	1 837	1 598	..	..	..	..	..	..
1.1.4 Non-life insurance payments, by class, gross premiums								
Motor vehicle insurance	17 993	18 191	20 277	21 805	22 857	21 007	21 426	..
Marine, aviation and other transport insurance	628	650	656	672	630	773	716	..
Freight insurance	..	..	..	..	..	..	..	..
Fire and other property damage insurance	13 097	13 483	15 268	16 577	16 687	18 994	19 992	..
Pecuniary loss insurance	1 391	1 643	1 716	1 785	1 748	2 271	2 613	..
General liability insurance	4 766	4 797	5 054	5 197	5 267	5 830	6 289	..
Accident and health	17 371	18 043	25 743	19 672	20 262	25 708	26 370	..
***of which:** Health*	..	..	..	..	..	..	..	..
Other non-life insurance	12	6	8	14	32	138	275	..
Treaty reinsurance	..	..	..	..	..	..	..	..
Total non-life insurance	55 258	56 813	68 723	65 723	67 482	74 721	77 682	..
1.2 Gross claims payments								
Life								
Domestic undertakings	0	0	0	0	0	0	0	..
Foreign controlled undertakings	0	0	0	0	0	0	0	..
Foreign companies (branches)	24	25	27	28	36	41	13	..
All undertakings	24	25	27	28	36	41	13	..
Non-life								
Domestic undertakings	22 318	21 444	23 354	24 435	28 506	25 194	25 500	..
Foreign controlled undertakings	5 102	4 666	5 150	4 939	5 566	8 332	8 552	..
Foreign companies (branches)	4 531	5 971	5 840	4 875	5 242	5 901	4 694	..
All undertakings	26 849	27 415	29 193	29 310	33 748	31 095	30 193	..
Composite								
Domestic undertakings	13 064	13 016	10 525	10 851	11 227	9 477	10 030	..
Foreign controlled undertakings	742	773	666	731	736	881	303	..
Foreign companies (branches)	193	220	160	163	159	7 182	7 161	..
All undertakings	13 257	13 236	10 685	11 014	11 386	16 659	17 190	..
of which:								
Life	5 039	5 224	4 599	4 749	4 969	5 480	5 747	..
Domestic undertakings	4 931	5 096	4 523	4 650	4 869	3 858	4 186	..
Foreign controlled undertakings	311	301	190	189	100	344	100	..
Foreign companies (branches)	108	128	76	99	99	1 622	1 561	..
All undertakings	5 039	5 224	4 599	4 749	4 969	5 480	5 747	..
Non-life	8 218	8 012	6 085	6 264	6 417	11 179	11 444	..
Domestic undertakings	8 133	7 920	6 002	6 201	6 357	5 620	5 844	..
Foreign controlled undertakings	431	472	475	542	546	537	115	..
Foreign companies (branches)	85	92	83	63	60	5 560	5 600	..
All undertakings	8 218	8 012	6 085	6 264	6 417	11 179	11 444	..
Total								
Domestic undertakings	35 381	34 460	33 879	35 286	39 733	34 671	35 529	..
Foreign controlled undertakings	5 844	5 440	5 816	5 670	6 301	9 213	8 854	..
Foreign companies (branches)	4 748	6 216	6 026	5 066	5 437	13 124	11 867	..
All undertakings	40 129	40 676	39 905	40 351	45 170	47 795	47 396	..

Canada
Table 1. Selected aggregates *(cont.)*

Million CAD

	2009	2010	2011	2012	2013	2014	2015	2016
1.3 Commissions								
Life								
Domestic undertakings	0	0	0	0	0	..	0	..
Foreign controlled undertakings	0	0	0	0	0	..	..	..
Foreign companies (branches)	0	11	10	12	10	..	0	..
All undertakings	0	11	10	12	10	..	0	..
Non-life								
Domestic undertakings	3 855	4 055	4 305	4 719	4 781	..	5 441	..
Foreign controlled undertakings	934	932	91	1 115	1 092	..	1 882	..
Foreign companies (branches)	1 003	1 070	1 102	1 077	1 095	..	1 104	..
All undertakings	4 858	5 125	5 407	5 796	5 876	..	6 545	..
Composite								
Domestic undertakings	2 654	5 232	5 539	5 505	5 558	..	4 787	..
Foreign controlled undertakings	0	377	377	258	239	..	97	..
Foreign companies (branches)	171	169	158	147	145	..	193	..
All undertakings	2 825	5 401	5 697	5 652	5 703	..	4 980	..
of which:								
Life	2 382	4 026	4 212	4 239	4 291	..	3 572	..
Domestic undertakings	2 276	3 920	4 115	4 150	4 213	..	3 457	..
Foreign controlled undertakings	0	273	285	172	173	..	65	..
Foreign companies (branches)	107	106	97	89	78	..	115	..
All undertakings	2 382	4 026	4 212	4 239	4 291	..	3 572	..
Non-life	443	1 375	1 485	1 413	1 412	..	1 408	..
Domestic undertakings	379	1 312	1 424	1 355	1 345	..	1 330	..
Foreign controlled undertakings	0	104	91	86	66	..	32	..
Foreign companies (branches)	64	63	61	58	67	..	78	..
All undertakings	443	1 375	1 485	1 413	1 412	..	1 408	..
Total								
Domestic undertakings	6 509	9 287	9 844	10 224	10 339	..	10 228	..
Foreign controlled undertakings	934	1 309	467	1 373	1 331	..	1 979	..
Foreign companies (branches)	1 174	1 250	1 270	1 235	1 249	..	1 298	..
All undertakings	7 683	10 537	11 114	11 460	11 588	..	11 526	..
1.4 Gross operating expenses								
Life								
Domestic undertakings	17	18	20	22	23	24	22	..
Foreign controlled undertakings	0	0	0	0	..	0	0	..
Foreign companies (branches)	30	27	29	32	27	28	15	..
All undertakings	46	45	49	53	50	52	37	..
Non-life								
Domestic undertakings	4 412	4 707	5 235	5 774	6 023	4 032	4 493	..
Foreign controlled undertakings	1 282	1 310	1 385	1 465	1 409	1 385	1 488	..
Foreign companies (branches)	888	929	931	1 001	1 017	855	689	..
All undertakings	5 300	5 636	6 166	6 775	7 040	4 887	5 182	..
Composite								
Domestic undertakings	12 118	13 129	10 675	12 274	13 728	12 612	14 400	..
Foreign controlled undertakings	583	557	558	557	571	736	187	..
Foreign companies (branches)	127	124	119	110	117	206	272	..
All undertakings	12 245	13 253	10 794	12 384	13 845	12 818	14 672	..
of which:								
Life	..	..	..	..	..	..	..	..
Domestic undertakings	..	..	..	..	..	..	..	..
Foreign controlled undertakings	..	..	..	..	..	..	..	..
Foreign companies (branches)	..	..	..	..	..	..	..	..
All undertakings	..	..	..	..	..	..	..	..
Non-life	..	..	..	..	..	..	..	..
Domestic undertakings	..	..	..	..	..	..	..	..
Foreign controlled undertakings	..	..	..	..	..	..	..	..
Foreign companies (branches)	..	..	..	..	..	..	..	..
All undertakings	..	..	..	..	..	..	..	..
Total								
Domestic undertakings	16 546	17 854	15 930	18 069	19 774	16 668	18 915	..
Foreign controlled undertakings	1 864	1 868	1 943	2 021	1 981	2 121	1 675	..
Foreign companies (branches)	1 045	1 079	1 079	1 143	1 161	1 089	976	..
All undertakings	17 591	18 933	17 009	19 212	20 934	17 757	19 891	..

Canada
Table 1. Selected aggregates *(cont.)*

Million CAD

	2009	2010	2011	2012	2013	2014	2015	2016
1.5 Insurance business written abroad by branches, gross premiums								
Life								
Branches and agencies	..	..	..	..	..	..	..	..
Subsidaries	..	..	..	..	..	..	..	..
Total	0 |	..	..	..	..	0	0	..
Non-life								
Branches and agencies	..	..	..	..	..	..	..	..
Subsidaries	..	..	..	..	..	..	..	..
Total	325 |	250	545	548	1 018	1 320	1 500	..
Composite								
Branches and agencies	..	..	..	..	..	..	..	..
Subsidaries	..	..	..	..	..	..	..	..
Total	41 003 |	36 677	34 423	37 741	7 942	31 162	40 235	..
of which:								
Life	..	..	..	..	..	27 224	..	..
Branches and agencies	..	..	..	..	..	..	..	..
Subsidaries	..	..	..	..	..	..	..	..
Total	..	..	..	..	..	27 224	..	..
Non-life	..	..	..	..	..	3 939	..	..
Branches and agencies	..	..	..	..	..	..	..	..
Subsidaries	..	..	..	..	..	..	..	..
Total	..	..	..	..	..	3 939	..	..
Total								
Branches and agencies	..	..	..	..	..	..	..	..
Subsidaries	..	..	..	..	..	..	..	..
Total	41 328	36 927	34 968	38 289	8 959	32 482	41 736	..

.. Not available; | Break in series

Note: Detailed metadata at: http://metalinks.oecd.org/ins/20180621/10bf.

Disclaimer: http://oe.cd/disclaimer

Source: OECD Insurance Statistics (database)

Canada
Table 2. Number of companies and employees

	2009	2010	2011	2012	2013	2014	2015	2016
2.1 Number of companies								
Life								
Domestic undertakings	1	1	1	1	1	1	1	..
Foreign controlled undertakings	0	0	0	0	0	0	0	..
Foreign companies (branches)	9	7	5	5	5	5	5	..
All undertakings	10	8	6	6	6	6	6	..
Non-life								
Domestic undertakings	89	87	86	84	60	66	66	..
Foreign controlled undertakings	24	23	23	23	22	28	28	..
Foreign companies (branches)	67	66	61	60	60	60	58	..
All undertakings	156	153	147	144	120	126	124	..
Composite								
Domestic undertakings	46	44	43	43	34	34	33	..
Foreign controlled undertakings	11	11	10	10	10	9	7	..
Foreign companies (branches)	27	26	26	21	26	23	22	..
All undertakings	73	70	69	64	60	57	55	..
Reinsurance								
Domestic undertakings	6	6	6	6	6	5	5	..
Foreign controlled undertakings	5	5	6	6	6	5	5	..
Foreign companies (branches)	27	24	28	27	28	25	26	..
All undertakings	33	30	34	33	34	30	31	..
Total								
Domestic undertakings	142	138	136	134	101	106	105	..
Foreign controlled undertakings	40	39	39	39	38	42	40	..
Foreign companies (branches)	130	123	120	113	119	113	111	..
All undertakings	272	261	256	247	220	219	216	..
2.2 Number of employees								
Insurance undertakings	..	..	..	..	..	..	..	..
Intermediaries	..	..	..	..	..	..	..	..
Total	..	..	..	..	..	..	..	..

.. Not available

Note: Detailed metadata at: http://metalinks.oecd.org/ins/20180621/10bf.

Disclaimer: http://oe.cd/disclaimer

Source: OECD Insurance Statistics (database)

Chile
Table 1. Selected aggregates

Million CLP

	2009	2010	2011	2012	2013	2014	2015	2016
1.1 Insurance business written in the reporting country								
1.1.1 Insurance business, by ownership								
Gross premiums								
Domestic undertakings	3 504 520	4 239 694	4 691 200	5 496 223	5 832 221	6 260 019	7 465 743	8 394 971
Foreign controlled undertakings	2 056 579	2 335 007	2 270 671	2 821 041	3 056 166	3 211 682	3 614 011	4 422 880
Foreign companies (branches)	0	0	..	..	..	..	..	..
All undertakings	3 504 520	4 239 694	4 691 200	5 496 223	5 832 221	6 260 019	7 465 743	8 394 971
Premiums ceded								
Domestic undertakings	644 272	..	911 543	930 906	906 942	998 507	1 135 872	1 310 392
Foreign controlled undertakings	486 353	..	648 512	671 333	647 814	676 439	749 522	953 240
Foreign companies (branches)	0	..	..	..	..	..	..	..
All undertakings	644 272	..	911 543	930 906	906 942	998 507	1 135 872	1 310 392
Net written premiums								
Domestic undertakings	2 860 248	..	3 779 657	4 565 317	4 925 279	5 261 513	6 329 871	7 084 578
Foreign controlled undertakings	1 570 226	..	1 622 159	2 149 709	2 408 352	2 535 243	2 864 489	3 469 640
Foreign companies (branches)	0	..	..	..	..	..	..	..
All undertakings	2 860 248	..	3 779 657	4 565 317	4 925 279	5 261 513	6 329 871	7 084 578
1.1.2 Insurance business on foreign risks, gross premiums								
Life	..	..	0	..	..	..	..	..
Non-life	..	..	0	..	..	..	..	..
Composite total	..	..	..	..	..	..	..	..
Total	..	..	0	..	..	..	..	..
1.1.3 Life insurance payments, by class, gross premiums								
Annuities	808 248	1 067 841	1 105 236	1 623 894	1 729 819	1 692 693	2 343 736	2 759 473
Unit linked	201 107	196 316	201 183	213 028	318 975	475 508	613 110	712 539
Other life insurance	1 268 495	1 531 021	1 625 966	1 761 476	1 827 419	1 948 628	2 123 123	2 373 130
Total life insurance	2 277 850	2 795 177	2 932 385	3 598 399	3 876 213	4 116 829	5 079 969	5 845 142
***of which:** Pension contracts*	0	0	1 340 726	..	..	..	..	..
1.1.4 Non-life insurance payments, by class, gross premiums								
Motor vehicle insurance	293 508	348 409	420 964	480 767	467 370	509 632	554 020	607 928
Marine, aviation and other transport insurance	69 483	75 737	92 530	93 208	117 884	129 698	148 074	132 318
Freight insurance	0	0	0	0	0	0	0	0
Fire and other property damage insurance	439 527	539 516	663 739	726 707	711 066	788 536	901 636	926 988
Pecuniary loss insurance	44 298	49 420	58 737	62 661	55 877	62 708	73 291	81 763
General liability insurance	50 340	52 327	69 048	80 035	52 154	56 828	41 342	34 468
Accident and health	121 524	123 267	115 563	117 127	25 789	30 296	46 180	53 105
***of which:** Health*	195	571	943	1 362	1 349	6 186	2 268	8 145
Other non-life insurance	204 829	252 717	336 427	335 850	524 059	561 863	602 569	651 596
Treaty reinsurance	0	0	0	0	0	0	0	0
Total non-life insurance	1 223 509	1 441 393	1 757 008	1 896 354	1 954 198	2 139 562	2 367 113	2 488 165
1.2 Gross claims payments								
Life								
Domestic undertakings	2 771 258	2 989 991	2 914 714	3 393 850	3 714 398	4 027 828	2 853 170	3 342 724
Foreign controlled undertakings	1 177 463	1 103 085	989 305	1 353 122	1 551 286	1 580 430	1 020 903	1 219 666
Foreign companies (branches)	0	0	0	..	..	..	..	..
All undertakings	2 771 258	2 989 991	2 914 714	3 393 850	3 714 398	4 027 828	2 853 170	3 342 724
Non-life								
Domestic undertakings	501 155	4 196 890	658 815	874 913	896 672	260 092	1 421 296	1 491 740
Foreign controlled undertakings	300 774	3 421 645	420 283	524 939	541 982	157 970	889 183	1 193 951
Foreign companies (branches)	0	0	0	..	..	..	..	..
All undertakings	501 155	4 196 890	658 815	874 913	896 672	260 092	1 421 296	1 491 740
Composite, all undertakings	..	..	..	..	..	..	..	..
Total								
Domestic undertakings	3 272 413	7 186 881	3 573 529	4 268 763	4 611 070	4 287 920	4 274 466	4 834 464
Foreign controlled undertakings	1 478 237	4 524 730	1 409 588	1 878 061	2 093 268	1 738 400	1 910 087	2 413 617
Foreign companies (branches)	0	0	0	..	..	..	..	..
All undertakings	3 272 413	7 186 881	3 573 529	4 268 763	4 611 070	4 287 920	4 274 466	4 834 464
1.3 Commissions								
Life								
Domestic undertakings	153 504	183 002	182 335	228 573	248 645	263 060	301 418	318 445
Foreign controlled undertakings	80 584	97 836	86 321	118 560	131 550	139 650	164 172	159 299
Foreign companies (branches)	0	0	0	..	..	..	..	..
All undertakings	153 504	183 002	182 335	228 573	248 645	263 060	301 418	318 445
Non-life								
Domestic undertakings	145 287	171 903	205 222	224 665	230 945	260 092	287 918	312 001
Foreign controlled undertakings	98 178	114 424	134 674	142 291	140 238	157 970	171 469	242 835
Foreign companies (branches)	0	0	0	..	..	..	..	..
All undertakings	145 287	171 903	205 222	224 665	230 945	260 092	287 918	312 001
Composite, all undertakings	..	..	..	..	..	..	..	..
Total								
Domestic undertakings	298 791	354 905	387 557	453 238	479 590	523 153	589 336	630 445
Foreign controlled undertakings	178 762	212 260	220 996	260 851	271 787	297 621	335 641	402 134
Foreign companies (branches)	0	0	0	..	..	..	..	..
All undertakings	298 791	354 905	387 557	453 238	479 590	523 153	589 336	630 445

Chile
Table 1. Selected aggregates *(cont.)*

Million CLP

	2009	2010	2011	2012	2013	2014	2015	2016
1.4 Gross operating expenses								
Life								
Domestic undertakings	445 121	497 317	502 620	519 184	549 344	583 313	612 178	664 997
Foreign controlled undertakings	238 613	271 689	242 660	250 271	268 515	284 692	308 320	316 103
Foreign companies (branches)	0	0	0	..	..	..	..	..
All undertakings	445 121	497 317	502 620	519 184	549 344	583 313	612 178	664 997
Non-life								
Domestic undertakings	263 732	290 845	331 560	339 044	359 066	382 886	412 676	457 861
Foreign controlled undertakings	200 942	214 753	241 486	239 100	251 791	266 721	288 658	367 114
Foreign companies (branches)	0	0	0	..	..	..	..	..
All undertakings	263 732	290 845	331 560	339 044	359 066	382 886	412 676	457 861
Composite, all undertakings	..	..	..	..	..	..	..	..
Total								
Domestic undertakings	708 853	788 162	834 180	858 228	908 410	966 199	1 024 854	1 122 857
Foreign controlled undertakings	439 555	486 443	484 145	489 370	520 306	551 413	596 978	683 216
Foreign companies (branches)	0	0	0	..	..	..	..	..
All undertakings	708 853	788 162	834 180	858 228	908 410	966 199	1 024 854	1 122 857
1.5 Insurance business written abroad by branches, gross premiums								
Life								
Branches and agencies	..	..	0	..	..	..	..	..
Subsidaries	..	..	0	..	..	..	..	..
Total	..	..	0	..	..	..	..	..
Non-life								
Branches and agencies	..	..	0	..	..	..	..	..
Subsidaries	..	..	0	..	..	..	..	..
Total	..	..	0	..	..	..	..	..
Composite total	..	..	..	..	..	..	..	..
Total								
Branches and agencies	..	..	0	..	..	..	..	..
Subsidaries	..	..	0	..	..	..	..	..
Total	..	..	0	..	..	..	..	..

.. Not available

Note: Detailed metadata at: http://metalinks.oecd.org/ins/20180621/b3e9.

Disclaimer: http://oe.cd/disclaimer

Source: OECD Insurance Statistics (database)

Chile
Table 2. Number of companies and employees

	2009	2010	2011	2012	2013	2014	2015	2016
2.1 Number of companies								
Life								
Domestic undertakings	30	31	30	32	33	34	36	36
Foreign controlled undertakings	12	12	12	11	12	12	13	13
Foreign companies (branches)	0	0	0	..	..	..	..	0
All undertakings	30	31	30	32	33	34	36	36
Non-life								
Domestic undertakings	25	26	27	28	29	29	30	30
Foreign controlled undertakings	14	15	16	16	18	17	18	11
Foreign companies (branches)	0	0	0	..	..	..	..	0
All undertakings	25	26	27	28	29	29	30	30
Composite, all undertakings	**0**	**0**	**0**	**0**	**0**	**0**	**0**	**0**
Reinsurance								
Domestic undertakings	1	1	1	1	1	1	1	1
Foreign controlled undertakings	1	1	1	1	1	1	..	1
Foreign companies (branches)	0	0	0	..	..	..	..	0
All undertakings	1	1	1	1	1	1	1	1
Total								
Domestic undertakings	56	58	58	61	63	64	67	67
Foreign controlled undertakings	27	28	29	28	31	30	31	25
Foreign companies (branches)	0	0	0	..	..	..	..	0
All undertakings	56	58	58	61	63	64	67	67
2.2 Number of employees								
Insurance undertakings	13 236	13 554	14 366	16 304	16 686	17 039	15 368	16 414
Intermediaries	6 492	6 828	7 211	6 828	7 046	6 959	7 499	7 599
Total	19 728	20 382	21 577	23 132	23 732	23 998	22 867	24 013

.. Not available

Note: Detailed metadata at: http://metalinks.oecd.org/ins/20180621/b3e9.

Disclaimer: http://oe.cd/disclaimer

Source: OECD Insurance Statistics (database)

Czech Republic
Table 1. Selected aggregates

Million CZK

	2009	2010	2011	2012	2013	2014	2015	2016
1.1 Insurance business written in the reporting country								
1.1.1 Insurance business, by ownership								
Gross premiums								
Domestic undertakings	135 645	147 259	146 494	145 572	147 955	148 755	140 688	135 581
Foreign controlled undertakings	126 354	136 170	134 999	134 114	135 671	137 200	129 432	124 165
Foreign companies (branches)	8 512	8 723	8 598	8 026	8 567	9 164	11 159	11 102
All undertakings	144 157	155 981	155 092	153 597	156 522	157 919	151 846	146 683
Premiums ceded								
Domestic undertakings	23 094	26 327	27 642	27 730	29 333	29 915	29 857	28 913
Foreign controlled undertakings	21 993	23 843	24 903	24 826	26 054	26 601	26 578	25 450
Foreign companies (branches)	1 121	1 174	1 120	984	1 016	1 250	1 561	1 993
All undertakings	24 215	27 502	28 762	28 714	30 349	31 165	31 418	30 905
Net written premiums								
Domestic undertakings	112 551	120 931	118 852	117 842	118 623	118 839	110 831	106 669
Foreign controlled undertakings	104 361	112 327	110 096	109 288	109 617	110 598	102 854	98 714
Foreign companies (branches)	7 391	7 548	7 478	7 041	7 550	7 914	9 598	9 109
All undertakings	119 942	128 480	126 330	124 884	126 173	126 754	120 429	115 778
1.1.2 Insurance business on foreign risks, gross premiums								
Life	3 626	..	2	3	0	0	0	0
Non-life	86 665	..	814	931	741	993	524	274
Composite	..	..	1 553	1 681	1 780	2 121	1 867	1 843
of which:								
Life	..	..	1	0	37	360	4	0
Non-life	..	..	1 553	1 681	1 742	1 761	1 863	1 843
Total	90 291	..	2 370	2 614	2 521	3 113	2 390	2 117
1.1.3 Life insurance payments, by class, gross premiums								
Annuities	2 314	2 082	1 881	1 810	1 775	1 505	1 413	..
Unit linked	24 126	33 956	36 584	37 799	34 764	37 632	35 125	26 131
Other life insurance	33 791	35 710	33 543	32 437	35 030	32 042	25 876	33 110
Total life insurance	60 232	71 748	72 008	72 046	71 569	71 179	62 414	59 240
of which: *Pension contracts*	..	..	..	..	..	..	..	..
1.1.4 Non-life insurance payments, by class, gross premiums								
Motor vehicle insurance	41 099	38 467	35 827	34 350	35 804	37 855	39 633	38 212
Marine, aviation and other transport insurance	255	289	274	243	214	294	331	912
Freight insurance	376	378	385	336	393	461	466	0
Fire and other property damage insurance	19 847	20 151	20 586	20 832	21 442	21 687	22 655	23 042
Pecuniary loss insurance	3 873	5 047	5 413	5 190	5 920	4 933	3 770	3 959
General liability insurance	11 642	12 128	12 416	12 420	12 869	13 164	13 810	13 609
Accident and health	4 628	5 491	5 708	5 523	5 482	5 342	5 393	5 136
of which: *Health*	0	0	0	0	0	0	0	0
Other non-life insurance	2 204	2 284	2 477	2 656	2 825	3 002	3 374	2 223
Treaty reinsurance	0	0	0	0	0	0	0	0
Total non-life insurance	83 925	84 234	83 084	81 550	84 950	86 738	89 431	87 092

Czech Republic
Table 1. Selected aggregates *(cont.)*

Million CZK

	2009	2010	2011	2012	2013	2014	2015	2016
1.2 Gross claims payments								
Life								
Domestic undertakings	29 536	247 |	934	968	765	1 307	702	.. c
Foreign controlled undertakings	28 702	247 |	934	968	765	1 307	702	.. c
Foreign companies (branches)	3 864	4 041	4 193	4 402	7 219	6 044	6 376	6 094
All undertakings	33 400	4 287 |	5 127	5 370	7 984	7 352	7 077	6 456
Non-life								
Domestic undertakings	41 439	3 939 |	2 981	3 594	5 208	6 045	2 285	2 103
Foreign controlled undertakings	37 426	1 983 |	1 463	1 648	2 171	1 734	1 288	1 072
Foreign companies (branches)	903	1 001	922	746	1 184	1 353	1 216	1 674
All undertakings	42 343	4 940 |	3 903	4 340	6 392	7 398	3 501	3 777
Composite								
Domestic undertakings	..	72 968 |	76 178	78 484	86 244	90 284	84 909	81 024
Foreign controlled undertakings	..	69 071 |	72 105	74 012	81 355	84 712	79 681	75 835
Foreign companies (branches)	..	0	0	0	0	0	0	0
All undertakings	..	72 968 |	76 178	78 484	86 244	90 284	84 909	81 024
of which:								
Life	..	31 760 |	36 944	41 040	43 395	50 972	44 105	37 676
Domestic undertakings	..	31 760 |	36 944	41 040	43 395	50 972	44 105	37 676
Foreign controlled undertakings	..	30 834 |	35 822	39 685	42 174	49 092	42 631	36 570
Foreign companies (branches)	..	0	0	0	0	0	0	0
All undertakings	..	31 760 |	36 944	41 040	43 395	50 972	44 105	37 676
Non-life	..	41 208 |	39 235	37 444	42 849	39 312	40 805	43 348
Domestic undertakings	..	41 208 |	39 235	37 444	42 849	39 312	40 805	43 348
Foreign controlled undertakings	..	38 237 |	36 283	34 327	39 180	35 620	37 050	39 265
Foreign companies (branches)	..	0	0	0	0	0	0	0
All undertakings	..	41 208 |	39 235	37 444	42 849	39 312	40 805	43 348
Total								
Domestic undertakings	70 975	77 154	80 094	83 046	92 217	97 636	87 896	83 490
Foreign controlled undertakings	66 128	71 301	74 502	76 628	84 291	87 754	81 671	77 269
Foreign companies (branches)	4 768	5 041	5 116	5 148	8 403	7 397	7 592	7 767
All undertakings	75 743	82 196	85 209	88 194	100 620	105 033	95 488	91 257
1.3 Commissions								
Life								
Domestic undertakings	..	9 |	628	..	..	..	..	..
Foreign controlled undertakings	..	9 |	628	..	..	..	..	..
Foreign companies (branches)	..	0	486	..	..	..	..	..
All undertakings	..	9 |	1 114	..	..	..	..	..
Non-life								
Domestic undertakings	..	313 |	466	..	..	..	..	..
Foreign controlled undertakings	..	257 |	273	..	..	..	..	..
Foreign companies (branches)	..	214	418	..	..	..	..	..
All undertakings	..	528 |	884	..	..	..	..	..
Composite								
Domestic undertakings	..	5 035 |	12 386	..	..	..	..	..
Foreign controlled undertakings	..	4 607 |	11 419	..	..	..	..	..
Foreign companies (branches)	..	0	0	..	..	..	..	..
All undertakings	..	5 035 |	12 386	..	..	..	..	..
of which:								
Life	..	414 |	7 407	..	..	..	..	..
Domestic undertakings	..	414 |	7 407	..	..	..	..	..
Foreign controlled undertakings	..	414 |	7 243	..	..	..	..	..
Foreign companies (branches)	..	0	0	..	..	..	..	..
All undertakings	..	414 |	7 407	..	..	..	..	..
Non-life	..	4 620 |	4 980	..	..	..	..	..
Domestic undertakings	..	4 620 |	4 980	..	..	..	..	..
Foreign controlled undertakings	..	4 193 |	4 176	..	..	..	..	..
Foreign companies (branches)	..	0	0	..	..	..	..	..
All undertakings	..	4 620 |	4 980	..	..	..	..	..
Total								
Domestic undertakings	..	5 357	13 481	..	..	..	..	..
Foreign controlled undertakings	..	4 873	12 320	..	..	..	..	..
Foreign companies (branches)	..	214	904	..	..	..	..	..
All undertakings	..	5 572	14 384	..	..	..	..	..

Czech Republic
Table 1. Selected aggregates *(cont.)*

Million CZK

	2009	2010	2011	2012	2013	2014	2015	2016
1.4 Gross operating expenses								
Life								
Domestic undertakings	12 964	1 060 |	1 085	1 132	748	759	739	.. c
Foreign controlled undertakings	12 557	1 060 |	1 085	1 132	748	759	739	.. c
Foreign companies (branches)	1 387	1 440	1 617	1 659	1 587	1 459	2 036	2 015
All undertakings	14 351	2 499 |	2 702	2 791	2 335	2 219	2 775	2 520
Non-life								
Domestic undertakings	22 391	2 303 |	2 559	1 970	1 795	1 805	1 571	1 203
Foreign controlled undertakings	19 946	1 446 |	1 509	1 152	987	937	883	622
Foreign companies (branches)	735	874	933	277	715	841	1 203	1 224
All undertakings	23 126	3 177 |	3 491	2 247	2 510	2 646	2 773	2 427
Composite								
Domestic undertakings	..	31 688 |	33 219	21 405	21 863	22 207	20 341	21 319
Foreign controlled undertakings	..	25 999 |	31 001	20 417	20 499	21 233	19 120	19 893
Foreign companies (branches)	..	0	0	0	0	0	0	0
All undertakings	..	31 688 |	33 219	21 405	21 863	22 207	20 341	21 319
of which:								
Life	..	12 087 |	13 363	12 009	11 670	11 475	9 613	9 217
Domestic undertakings	..	12 087 |	13 363	12 009	11 670	11 475	9 613	9 217
Foreign controlled undertakings	..	11 605 |	12 861	11 604	11 231	11 050	9 059	8 637
Foreign companies (branches)	..	0	0	0	0	0	0	0
All undertakings	..	12 087 |	13 363	12 009	11 670	11 475	9 613	9 217
Non-life	..	19 601 |	19 856	9 396	10 193	10 733	10 728	12 102
Domestic undertakings	..	19 601 |	19 856	9 396	10 193	10 733	10 728	12 102
Foreign controlled undertakings	..	17 994 |	18 140	8 814	9 268	10 184	10 061	11 256
Foreign companies (branches)	..	0	0	0	0	0	0	0
All undertakings	..	19 601 |	19 856	9 396	10 193	10 733	10 728	12 102
Total								
Domestic undertakings	35 356	35 050	36 863	24 507	24 407	24 772	22 650	23 027
Foreign controlled undertakings	32 503	28 505	33 595	22 701	22 234	22 929	20 742	21 020
Foreign companies (branches)	2 122	2 314	2 550	1 936	2 302	2 301	3 239	3 239
All undertakings	37 477	37 364	39 413	26 443	26 708	27 072	25 889	26 266
1.5 Insurance business written abroad by branches, gross premiums								
Life								
Branches and agencies	1 077	0 |	0	0	0	0	0	0
Subsidaries	..	..	..	..	..	..	..	..
Total	1 077	0 |	0	0	0	0	0	..
Non-life								
Branches and agencies	421	437 |	318	307	323	313	351	377
Subsidaries	..	..	..	..	..	..	..	..
Total	421	437 |	318	307	323	313	351	377
Composite								
Branches and agencies	..	1 264 |	1 294	1 359	3 714	4 528	5 164	1 697
Subsidaries	..	..	..	..	..	..	..	..
Total	..	1 264 |	1 294	1 359	3 714	4 528	5 164	1 697
of which:								
Life	..	1 254 |	1 244	1 317	1 737	1 434	1 460	1 697
Branches and agencies	..	1 254 |	1 244	1 317	1 737	1 434	1 460	1 697
Subsidaries	..	..	..	..	..	..	..	..
Total	..	1 254 |	1 244	1 317	1 737	1 434	1 460	1 697
Non-life	..	10 |	49	42	1 977	3 095	3 704	..
Branches and agencies	..	10 |	49	42	1 977	3 095	3 704	0
Subsidaries	..	..	..	..	..	..	..	..
Total	..	10 |	49	42	1 977	3 095	3 704	..
Total								
Branches and agencies	1 498	1 701	1 612	1 666	4 037	4 841	5 516	2 074
Subsidaries	..	..	..	..	..	..	..	..
Total	1 498	1 701	1 612	1 666	4 037	4 841	5 516	2 074

.. Not available; | Break in series; c Confidential data

Note: Detailed metadata at: http://metalinks.oecd.org/ins/20180621/3162.

Disclaimer: http://oe.cd/disclaimer

Source: OECD Insurance Statistics (database)

Czech Republic
Table 2. Number of companies and employees

	2009	2010	2011	2012	2013	2014	2015	2016
2.1 Number of companies								
Life								
Domestic undertakings	3	3	3	3	2	2	2	1
Foreign controlled undertakings	3	3	3	3	2	2	2	1
Foreign companies (branches)	4	4	4	3	3	4	5	5
All undertakings	7	7	7	6	5	6	7	6
Non-life								
Domestic undertakings	17	17	17	16	16	15	15	13
Foreign controlled undertakings	9	9	9	8	8	7	5	4
Foreign companies (branches)	12	13	14	15	15	16	18	19
All undertakings	29	30	31	31	31	31	33	32
Composite								
Domestic undertakings	15	15	15	15	15	15	14	14
Foreign controlled undertakings	12	12	12	12	12	12	11	11
Foreign companies (branches)	1	0	0	0	0	0	0	0
All undertakings	16	15	15	15	15	15	14	14
Reinsurance								
Domestic undertakings	1	1	1	1	1	1	1	1
Foreign controlled undertakings	1	1	1	1	1	1	1	1
Foreign companies (branches)	0	0	..	..	..	..	..	..
All undertakings	1	1	1	1	1	1	1	1
Total								
Domestic undertakings	36	36	36	35	34	33	32	29
Foreign controlled undertakings	25	25	25	24	23	22	19	17
Foreign companies (branches)	17	17	18	18	18	20	23	24
All undertakings	53	53	54	53	52	53	55	53
2.2 Number of employees								
Insurance undertakings	14 594	..	..	..	..	..	..	..
Intermediaries	96 957	..	..	..	..	..	..	..
Total	111 551	..	..	..	..	..	..	..

.. Not available

Note: Detailed metadata at: http://metalinks.oecd.org/ins/20180621/3162.

Disclaimer: http://oe.cd/disclaimer

Source: OECD Insurance Statistics (database)

Denmark
Table 1. Selected aggregates

Million DKK

	2009	2010	2011	2012	2013	2014	2015	2016
1.1 Insurance business written in the reporting country								
1.1.1 Insurance business, by ownership								
Gross premiums								
Domestic undertakings	161 090	171 554	181 700	189 673	1 268 025	208 213	215 276	225 500
Foreign controlled undertakings	25 454	27 763	34 560	34 996	39 736	46 022	46 192	49 042
Foreign companies (branches)	..	..	..	..	..	..	..	..
All undertakings	..	..	181 700	189 673	1 268 025	208 213	215 276	225 500
Premiums ceded								
Domestic undertakings	4 213	6 015	7 676	7 009	7 417	5 875	6 309	6 943
Foreign controlled undertakings	706	1 456	3 427	3 293	3 199	2 080	2 462	2 355
Foreign companies (branches)	..	..	..	..	..	..	..	..
All undertakings	..	..	7 676	7 009	7 417	5 875	6 309	6 943
Net written premiums								
Domestic undertakings	156 877	165 540	174 024	182 664	1 260 608	202 338	208 966	218 557
Foreign controlled undertakings	24 748	26 307	31 132	31 703	36 537	43 942	43 730	46 687
Foreign companies (branches)	..	..	..	..	..	..	..	..
All undertakings	..	..	174 024	182 664	1 260 608	202 338	208 966	218 557
1.1.2 Insurance business on foreign risks, gross premiums								
Life	..	..	3 099	3 530	1 125	631	631	..
Non-life	..	..	13 950	14 359	14 611	23 099	22 611	..
Composite total	..	..	..	..	..	..	..	..
Total	..	..	17 050	17 889	15 737	23 730	23 242	..
1.1.3 Life insurance payments, by class, gross premiums								
Annuities	..	..	..	..	..	..	..	..
Unit linked	..	..	..	..	..	..	..	..
Other life insurance	..	..	..	..	..	..	..	..
Total life insurance	..	..	..	129 477	133 294	140 314	147 662	153 907
***of which:** Pension contracts*	..	..	..	..	..	..	..	..
1.1.4 Non-life insurance payments, by class, gross premiums								
Motor vehicle insurance	..	..	16 520	16 511	16 304	19 310	19 146	21 247
Marine, aviation and other transport insurance	..	..	1 328	1 397	1 263	1 174	1 105	1 857
Freight insurance	..	..	..	..	..	..	0	..
Fire and other property damage insurance	..	..	15 003	20 461	20 737	22 855	22 642	25 107
Pecuniary loss insurance	..	..	336	359	372	402	417	1 113
General liability insurance	..	..	1 857	2 023	2 061	2 377	2 314	3 203
Accident and health	..	..	13 403	13 553	12 611	15 063	15 282	15 965
***of which:** Health*	..	..	900	1 013	1 051	1 265	1 337	4 498
Other non-life insurance	..	..	3 983	4 465	4 659	5 156	5 052	1 635
Treaty reinsurance	..	..	451	638	653	867	937	538
Total non-life insurance	..	..	52 882	59 407	58 661	67 204	66 895	70 665
1.2 Gross claims payments								
Life								
Domestic undertakings	69 241	77 577	86 498	92 230	111 119	124 323	98 376	115 270
Foreign controlled undertakings	13 699	16 488	20 780	22 286	24 154	24 385	20 765	23 573
Foreign companies (branches)	..	..	..	..	..	..	..	..
All undertakings	82 940	77 577	86 498	92 230	111 119	124 323	98 376	115 270
Non-life								
Domestic undertakings	39 988	42 282	45 935	40 906	43 547	46 601	47 833	44 773
Foreign controlled undertakings	6 018	6 002	7 484	6 308	6 731	13 007	13 316	11 816
Foreign companies (branches)	..	..	..	..	..	..	..	..
All undertakings	46 006	42 282	45 935	40 906	43 547	46 601	47 833	44 773
Composite, all undertakings	..	..	..	..	..	..	..	..
Total								
Domestic undertakings	109 229	119 859	132 433	133 136	154 666	170 924	146 209	160 043
Foreign controlled undertakings	19 716	22 490	28 264	28 594	30 885	37 392	34 081	35 389
Foreign companies (branches)	..	..	..	..	..	..	..	..
All undertakings	128 945	119 859	132 433	133 136	154 666	170 924	146 209	160 043

Denmark
Table 1. Selected aggregates *(cont.)*

Million DKK

	2009	2010	2011	2012	2013	2014	2015	2016
1.3 Commissions								
Life								
Domestic undertakings	493	226	235	194	182	195	199	175
Foreign controlled undertakings	98	97	77	59	43	60	36	34
Foreign companies (branches)	..	..	..	..	..	..	..	..
All undertakings	..	..	235	194	182	195	199	175
Non-life								
Domestic undertakings	1 194	1 309	1 257	1 434	1 380	1 613	1 879	1 361
Foreign controlled undertakings	230	292	257	367	361	579	891	494
Foreign companies (branches)	..	..	..	..	..	..	..	..
All undertakings	..	..	1 257	1 434	1 380	1 613	1 879	1 361
Composite, all undertakings	..	..	..	..	..	..	..	..
Total								
Domestic undertakings	1 687	1 535	1 492	1 629	1 562	1 808	2 079	1 536
Foreign controlled undertakings	328	389	334	426	405	639	927	528
Foreign companies (branches)	..	..	..	..	..	..	..	..
All undertakings	..	..	1 492	1 629	1 562	1 808	2 079	1 536
1.4 Gross operating expenses								
Life								
Domestic undertakings	4 930	4 685	5 136	5 088	4 954	4 887	4 570	4 788
Foreign controlled undertakings	1 385	1 340	1 325	1 316	1 326	1 377	1 284	1 268
Foreign companies (branches)	..	..	..	..	..	..	..	..
All undertakings	6 315	4 685	5 136	5 088	4 954	4 887	4 570	4 788
Non-life								
Domestic undertakings	9 179	9 713	10 241	10 292	10 391	11 564	11 856	12 050
Foreign controlled undertakings	1 688	1 577	1 940	2 124	2 200	3 867	4 065	3 780
Foreign companies (branches)	..	..	..	..	..	..	..	..
All undertakings	10 867	9 713	10 241	10 292	10 391	11 564	11 856	12 050
Composite, all undertakings	..	..	..	..	..	..	..	..
Total								
Domestic undertakings	14 109	14 398	15 377	15 380	15 345	16 451	16 426	16 838
Foreign controlled undertakings	3 073	2 917	3 265	3 440	3 526	5 244	5 349	5 048
Foreign companies (branches)	..	..	..	..	..	..	..	..
All undertakings	17 182	14 398	15 377	15 380	15 345	16 451	16 426	16 838
1.5 Insurance business written abroad by branches, gross premiums								
Life								
Branches and agencies	478	423	353	..	..	..	..	..
Subsidaries	..	..	..	..	..	..	..	..
Total	..	..	353	..	..	..	..	..
Non-life								
Branches and agencies	647	8 805	9 995	10 646	10 031	9 286	8 607	19 043
Subsidaries	..	..	..	..	..	..	..	..
Total	..	..	9 995	10 646	10 031	9 286	8 607	19 043
Composite total	..	..	..	..	..	..	..	..
Total								
Branches and agencies	1 126	9 227	10 348	10 646	10 031	9 286	8 607	19 043
Subsidaries	..	..	..	..	..	..	..	..
Total	..	..	10 348	10 646	10 031	9 286	8 607	19 043

.. Not available

Note: Detailed metadata at: http://metalinks.oecd.org/ins/20180621/899a.

Disclaimer: http://oe.cd/disclaimer

Source: OECD Insurance Statistics (database)

Denmark
Table 2. Number of companies and employees

	2009	2010	2011	2012	2013	2014	2015	2016
2.1 Number of companies								
Life								
Domestic undertakings	59	55	55	47	39	37	33	33
Foreign controlled undertakings	8	8	8	7	5	4	4	4
Foreign companies (branches)	4	4	6	6	1	1	1	1
All undertakings	71	59	61	53	40	38	34	34
Non-life								
Domestic undertakings	100	87	85	76	77	63	63	63
Foreign controlled undertakings	10	8	8	6	6	6	6	6
Foreign companies (branches)	10	45	41	38	48	49	49	53
All undertakings	120	132	126	114	125	112	112	116
Composite, all undertakings	**0**	**0**	**0**	**0**	**0**	**0**	**0**	**0**
Reinsurance								
Domestic undertakings	10	9	9	9	7	7	7	5
Foreign controlled undertakings	1	0	0	..	..	..	..	0
Foreign companies (branches)	..	..	..	..	..	..	..	..
All undertakings	11	..	9	9	7	7	7	5
Total								
Domestic undertakings	169	..	149	132	123	107	103	101
Foreign controlled undertakings	19	..	16	13	11	10	10	10
Foreign companies (branches)	14	..	47	44	49	50	50	54
All undertakings	202	..	196	176	172	157	153	155
2.2 Number of employees								
Insurance undertakings	16 455	16 051	16 130	15 835	15 377	17 057	16 472	16 112
Intermediaries	..	..	..	..	..	..	..	..
Total	..	..	16 130	15 835	15 377	17 057	16 472	16 112

.. Not available

Note: Detailed metadata at: http://metalinks.oecd.org/ins/20180621/899a.

Disclaimer: http://oe.cd/disclaimer

Source: OECD Insurance Statistics (database)

Estonia
Table 1. Selected aggregates

Million EUR

	2009	2010	2011	2012	2013	2014	2015	2016
1.1 Insurance business written in the reporting country								
1.1.1 Insurance business, by ownership								
Gross premiums								
Domestic undertakings	281	427	403	430	523	561	619	654
Foreign controlled undertakings	188	406	380	407	499	539	596	627
Foreign companies (branches)	41	0	0	51	60	70	70	82
All undertakings	247	427	403	480	583	631	689	736
Premiums ceded								
Domestic undertakings	25	20	20	..	27	28	29	31
Foreign controlled undertakings	10	13	11	..	18	2	20	22
Foreign companies (branches)	..	0	0	..	..	..	..	..
All undertakings	..	20	20	..	..	..	..	..
Net written premiums								
Domestic undertakings	256	406	383	..	496	534	590	624
Foreign controlled undertakings	178	393	368	..	481	217	576	605
Foreign companies (branches)	..	0	0	..	..	..	..	..
All undertakings	..	406	383	..	..	..	..	..
1.1.2 Insurance business on foreign risks, gross premiums								
Life	..	96	90	..	..	..	..	..
Non-life	..	62	68	..	..	..	..	..
Composite total	..	..	..	..	..	..	..	..
Total	..	158	158	..	..	..	..	..
1.1.3 Life insurance payments, by class, gross premiums								
Annuities	6	8	9	10	17	19	24	27
Unit linked	33	104	84	27	87	109	118	116
Other life insurance	37	61	67	30	66	63	72	80
Total life insurance	76	173	160	68	171	191	215	221
***of which:** Pension contracts*	0	1	26	30	33	37	36	40
1.1.4 Non-life insurance payments, by class, gross premiums								
Motor vehicle insurance	161	148	142	143	229	244	259	292
Marine, aviation and other transport insurance	1	1	1	3	2	2	2	6
Freight insurance	1	2	2	..	3	4	4	..
Fire and other property damage insurance	56	63	63	59	99	107	115	127
Pecuniary loss insurance	12	4	5	5	8	9	9	12
General liability insurance	5	8	9	6	15	16	19	21
Accident and health	7	28	30	15	40	42	42	54
***of which:** Health*	..	..	..	..	9	..	..	..
Other non-life insurance	0	1	1	1	9	16	23	4
Treaty reinsurance	..	0	0	..	8	..	..	..
Total non-life insurance	242	254	253	231	412	440	474	515
1.2 Gross claims payments								
Life								
Domestic undertakings	44	82	115	112	101	..	97	87
Foreign controlled undertakings	16	82	115	112	101	..	97	87
Foreign companies (branches)	..	0	0	..	..	..	..	0
All undertakings	44	82	115	112	101	..	97	87
Non-life								
Domestic undertakings	121	153	154	147	197	..	230	243
Foreign controlled undertakings	86	139	141	134	184	..	217	228
Foreign companies (branches)	28	0	0	..	33	..	40	43
All undertakings	149	153	154	147	230	246	271	287
Composite, all undertakings	..	..	..	..	..	..	..	..
Total								
Domestic undertakings	165	235	270	259	298	..	328	369
Foreign controlled undertakings	102	221	256	246	285	..	314	354
Foreign companies (branches)	28	0	0	..	33	..	40	47
All undertakings	193	235	270	259	331	246	368	416
1.3 Commissions								
Life								
Domestic undertakings	..	3	8	9	19	21	23	..
Foreign controlled undertakings	..	3	8	9	19	21	23	..
Foreign companies (branches)	..	0	0	..	..	..	..	..
All undertakings	..	3	8	9	10	..	23	..
Non-life								
Domestic undertakings	..	17	17	4	72	73	78	..
Foreign controlled undertakings	..	16	15	2	67	69	73	..
Foreign companies (branches)	..	0	0	..	..	..	..	..
All undertakings	..	17	17	4	72	..	78	..
Composite, all undertakings	..	..	..	..	..	..	..	..
Total								
Domestic undertakings	..	20	25	13	90	94	101	..
Foreign controlled undertakings	..	18	23	11	86	89	95	..
Foreign companies (branches)	..	0	0	..	..	..	..	..
All undertakings	..	20	25	13	90	..	101	..

Estonia
Table 1. Selected aggregates *(cont.)*

Million EUR

	2009	2010	2011	2012	2013	2014	2015	2016
1.4 Gross operating expenses								
Life								
Domestic undertakings	..	21	24	23	9	9	11	..
Foreign controlled undertakings	..	21	24	23	9	9	11	..
Foreign companies (branches)	..	0	0	..	..	..	..	..
All undertakings	..	21	24	23	9	..	11	..
Non-life								
Domestic undertakings	..	71	74	73	27	30	27	115
Foreign controlled undertakings	..	64	67	67	25	29	26	..
Foreign companies (branches)	..	0	0	..	..	..	..	..
All undertakings	..	71	74	73	27	..	27	..
Composite, all undertakings	..	..	..	..	..	..	..	..
Total								
Domestic undertakings	..	92	98	96	37	40	38	115
Foreign controlled undertakings	..	85	91	90	35	38	36	..
Foreign companies (branches)	..	0	0	..	..	..	..	..
All undertakings	..	92	98	96	37	..	38	..
1.5 Insurance business written abroad by branches, gross premiums								
Life								
Branches and agencies	47	96	90	85	94	114	130	96
Subsidaries	..	0	0	..	..	..	..	..
Total	47	96	90	85	94	114	130	96
Non-life								
Branches and agencies	28	62	68	96	170	174	190	201
Subsidaries	..	0	0	..	..	..	..	..
Total	28	62	68	96	170	174	190	201
Composite total	..	..	..	..	..	..	..	..
Total								
Branches and agencies	75	158	158	181	264	288	320	349
Subsidaries	..	0	0	..	..	..	..	..
Total	75	158	158	181	264	288	320	349

.. Not available

Note: Detailed metadata at: http://metalinks.oecd.org/ins/20180621/5ba4.

Disclaimer: http://oe.cd/disclaimer

Source: OECD Insurance Statistics (database)

Estonia
Table 2. Number of companies and employees

	2009	2010	2011	2012	2013	2014	2015	2016
2.1 Number of companies								
Life								
Domestic undertakings	5	5	4	4	4	4	4	2
Foreign controlled undertakings	4	5	4	4	4	4	4	2
Foreign companies (branches)	0	0	0	1	1	1	1	0
All undertakings	5	5	4	5	5	5	5	2
Non-life								
Domestic undertakings	7	8	8	8	8	8	8	8
Foreign controlled undertakings	4	5	5	5	5	5	5	5
Foreign companies (branches)	5	0	0	4	4	4	3	4
All undertakings	12	8	8	12	12	12	11	12
Composite, all undertakings	**0**	**0**	**0**	**0**	**0**	**0**	**0**	**0**
Reinsurance								
Domestic undertakings	..	0	0	..	0	0	0	0
Foreign controlled undertakings	..	0	0	..	0	0	0	0
Foreign companies (branches)	..	0	0	..	..	..	0	0
All undertakings	..	0	0	..	..	..	0	0
Total								
Domestic undertakings	..	13	12	12	12	12	12	12
Foreign controlled undertakings	..	10	9	9	9	9	9	9
Foreign companies (branches)	..	0	0	5	5	5	4	5
All undertakings	..	13	12	17	17	17	16	17
2.2 Number of employees								
Insurance undertakings	1 737	2 702	1 867	1 903	2 596	2 561	2 581	..
Intermediaries	..	..	814	849	1 271	1 217	1 232	..
Total	1 737	..	2 681	2 752	3 867	3 778	3 813	..

.. Not available

Note: Detailed metadata at: http://metalinks.oecd.org/ins/20180621/5ba4.

Disclaimer: http://oe.cd/disclaimer

Source: OECD Insurance Statistics (database)

Finland
Table 1. Selected aggregates

Million EUR

	2009	2010	2011	2012	2013	2014	2015	2016
1.1 Insurance business written in the reporting country								
1.1.1 Insurance business, by ownership								
Gross premiums								
Domestic undertakings	6 817	8 770	7 279	7 279	9 834	10 632	10 741	9 045
Foreign controlled undertakings	2 053	..	..	2 317	3 357	3 698	6 892	..
Foreign companies (branches)	..	..	..	..	..	..	..	..
All undertakings	6 817	8 770	7 279	7 279	9 834	10 632	10 741	9 045
Premiums ceded								
Domestic undertakings	245	242	240	240	257	259	246	241
Foreign controlled undertakings	28	..	..	20	19	15	217	..
Foreign companies (branches)	..	..	..	..	..	..	..	..
All undertakings	245	242	240	240	257	259	246	241
Net written premiums								
Domestic undertakings	6 781	8 528	7 039	7 039	9 577	10 373	10 495	8 804
Foreign controlled undertakings	2 053	..	..	2 297	3 338	3 683	6 675	..
Foreign companies (branches)	..	..	..	..	..	..	..	..
All undertakings	6 781	8 528	7 039	7 039	9 577	10 373	10 495	8 804
1.1.2 Insurance business on foreign risks, gross premiums								
Life	..	..	..	..	..	..	..	..
Non-life	..	..	..	..	..	..	..	..
Composite total	..	..	..	..	..	..	..	..
Total	..	..	..	..	..	..	..	..
1.1.3 Life insurance payments, by class, gross premiums								
Annuities	1 127	2 798	1 988	1 988	2 458	2 544	2 287	694
Unit linked	2 114	1 297	1 255	1 255	2 509	2 929	3 224	2 446
Other life insurance	104	1 120	505	505	614	619	745	1 433
Total life insurance	3 345	5 215	3 749	3 749	5 581	6 092	6 256	4 573
***of which:** Pension contracts*	949	1 491	828	828	819	756	597	675
1.1.4 Non-life insurance payments, by class, gross premiums								
Motor vehicle insurance	1 292	1 282	1 389	1 474	1 520	1 591	1 639	1 639
Marine, aviation and other transport insurance	57	60	64	68	70	70	68	73
Freight insurance	54	49	50	53	55	56	52	57
Fire and other property damage insurance	765	750	828	864	929	985	1 030	1 028
Pecuniary loss insurance	36	41	38	33	33	30	28	22
General liability insurance	167	169	191	191	239	392	385	234
Accident and health	852	846	938	1 024	1 048	1 060	1 058	1 119
***of which:** Health*	176	191	218	245	264	299	290	368
Other non-life insurance	115	117	129	131	144	152	88	163
Treaty reinsurance	..	122	132	149	149	135	135	136
Total non-life insurance	3 467	3 435	3 759	3 986	4 187	4 471	4 483	4 471
1.2 Gross claims payments								
Life								
Domestic undertakings	2 855	3 919	3 592	3 917	3 927	3 871	3 957	4 324
Foreign controlled undertakings	..	..	1 013	1 479	1 399	1 160	1 124	.. c
Foreign companies (branches)	..	..	..	..	..	..	..	..
All undertakings	2 855	3 919	3 592	3 917	3 927	3 871	3 957	4 324
Non-life								
Domestic undertakings	2 345	2 568	2 706	2 873	2 858	2 939	2 872	3 103
Foreign controlled undertakings	..	..	676	696	741	724	2 872	.. c
Foreign companies (branches)	..	..	..	..	..	..	..	..
All undertakings	2 345	2 568	2 706	2 873	2 858	2 939	2 872	3 103
Composite, all undertakings	..	..	..	..	..	..	..	..
Total								
Domestic undertakings	5 201	6 487	6 298	6 790	6 785	6 810	6 829	7 427
Foreign controlled undertakings	..	..	1 689	2 175	2 140	1 884	3 996	..
Foreign companies (branches)	..	..	..	..	..	..	..	..
All undertakings	5 201	6 487	6 298	6 790	6 785	6 810	6 829	7 427

Finland
Table 1. Selected aggregates *(cont.)*

Million EUR

	2009	2010	2011	2012	2013	2014	2015	2016
1.3 Commissions								
Life								
Domestic undertakings	54	64	81	68	90	-83	101	126
Foreign controlled undertakings	..	..	7	6	9	-10	15	.. c
Foreign companies (branches)	..	..	..	..	..	..	..	..
All undertakings	54	64	81	68	90	-83	101	126
Non-life								
Domestic undertakings	68	99	90	102	58	-142	113	166
Foreign controlled undertakings	..	..	13	16	21	-18	23	.. c
Foreign companies (branches)	..	..	..	..	..	..	..	..
All undertakings	68	99	90	102	58	-142	113	166
Composite, all undertakings	..	..	..	..	..	..	..	..
Total								
Domestic undertakings	122	163	171	170	148	-225	214	292
Foreign controlled undertakings	..	..	21	22	30	-28	38	..
Foreign companies (branches)	..	..	..	..	..	..	..	..
All undertakings	122	163	171	170	148	-225	214	292
1.4 Gross operating expenses								
Life								
Domestic undertakings	230	255	275	283	302	317	316	341
Foreign controlled undertakings	..	..	39	36	34	36	34	.. c
Foreign companies (branches)	..	..	..	..	..	..	..	..
All undertakings	230	255	275	283	302	317	316	341
Non-life								
Domestic undertakings	690	699	738	778	827	844	847	876
Foreign controlled undertakings	..	..	138	143	161	158	847	.. c
Foreign companies (branches)	..	..	..	..	..	..	..	..
All undertakings	690	699	738	778	827	844	847	876
Composite, all undertakings	..	..	..	..	..	..	..	..
Total								
Domestic undertakings	921	954	1 013	1 061	1 129	1 161	1 163	1 217
Foreign controlled undertakings	..	..	177	179	195	194	881	..
Foreign companies (branches)	..	..	..	..	..	..	..	..
All undertakings	921	954	1 013	1 061	1 129	1 161	1 163	1 217
1.5 Insurance business written abroad by branches, gross premiums								
Life								
Branches and agencies	480	598	614	203	162	107	17	..
Subsidaries	..	..	..	..	..	..	..	..
Total	480	598	614	203	162	107	17	..
Non-life								
Branches and agencies	9	..	..	..	..	..	..	..
Subsidaries	..	..	..	..	..	..	..	..
Total	9	..	..	..	..	..	..	..
Composite total	..	..	..	..	..	..	..	..
Total								
Branches and agencies	490	598	614	203	162	107	17	..
Subsidaries	..	..	..	..	..	..	..	..
Total	490	598	614	203	162	107	17	..

.. Not available; c Confidential data

Note: Detailed metadata at: http://metalinks.oecd.org/ins/20180621/cd90.

Disclaimer: http://oe.cd/disclaimer

Source: OECD Insurance Statistics (database)

Finland
Table 2. Number of companies and employees

	2009	2010	2011	2012	2013	2014	2015	2016
2.1 Number of companies								
Life								
Domestic undertakings	12	11	11	13	13	13	13	11
Foreign controlled undertakings	..	..	1	1	1	1	1	1
Foreign companies (branches)	..	..	..	..	..	..	..	..
All undertakings	12	11	11	13	13	13	13	11
Non-life								
Domestic undertakings	103	79	78	42	42	38	38	37
Foreign controlled undertakings	..	..	1	1	1	1	1	2
Foreign companies (branches)	..	..	..	..	..	..	..	..
All undertakings	103	79	78	42	42	38	38	37
Composite, all undertakings	..	..	..	..	..	..	..	..
Reinsurance								
Domestic undertakings	2	2	2	..	..	..	..	..
Foreign controlled undertakings	..	..	..	..	..	..	..	..
Foreign companies (branches)	..	..	..	..	..	..	..	..
All undertakings	2	2	2	..	..	..	..	..
Total								
Domestic undertakings	117	92	91	55	55	51	51	48
Foreign controlled undertakings	..	..	2	2	2	2	2	3
Foreign companies (branches)	..	..	..	..	..	..	..	..
All undertakings	117	92	91	55	55	51	51	48
2.2 Number of employees								
Insurance undertakings	9 316	9 221	9 321	9 321	9 231	8 980	8 750	8 815
Intermediaries	331	331	338	342	203	216	221	244
Total	9 647	9 552	9 659	9 663	9 434	9 196	8 971	9 059

.. Not available

Note: Detailed metadata at: http://metalinks.oecd.org/ins/20180621/cd90.

Disclaimer: http://oe.cd/disclaimer

Source: OECD Insurance Statistics (database)

France
Table 1. Selected aggregates

Million EUR

	2009	2010	2011	2012	2013	2014	2015	2016
1.1 Insurance business written in the reporting country								
1.1.1 Insurance business, by ownership								
Gross premiums								
Domestic undertakings	216 463	224 190	207 586	201 207	207 521	221 223	226 000	295 909
Foreign controlled undertakings	..	..	..	..	..	..	..	..
Foreign companies (branches)	190	84	95	104	103	103	111	..
All undertakings	216 654	224 274	207 680	201 310	207 624	221 327	226 111	295 909
Premiums ceded								
Domestic undertakings	18 050	19 192	20 994	21 638	22 115	19 932	25 840	45 137
Foreign controlled undertakings	..	..	..	..	..	..	..	..
Foreign companies (branches)	17	18	19	18	19	22	21	..
All undertakings	18 067	19 210	21 013	21 657	22 135	19 954	25 861	45 137
Net written premiums								
Domestic undertakings	198 413	204 998	186 592	179 568	185 406	201 291	200 160	250 772
Foreign controlled undertakings	..	..	..	..	..	..	..	..
Foreign companies (branches)	178	66	76	85	84	82	90	..
All undertakings	198 591	205 064	186 668	179 654	185 490	201 373	200 250	250 772
1.1.2 Insurance business on foreign risks, gross premiums								
Life	430	429	107	83	259	73	60	..
Non-life	367	391	1 592	1 589	1 735	1 876	2 188	..
Composite	..	..	227	206	636	468	485	..
of which:								
Life	..	..	226	206	167	456	482	..
Non-life	..	..	1	1	469	12	3	..
Total	797	821	1 926	1 879	2 631	2 416	2 734	..
1.1.3 Life insurance payments, by class, gross premiums								
Annuities	..	..	..	..	..	..	..	1 080
Unit linked	46 699	220 612	..	..	..	..	..	30 066
Other life insurance	..	..	..	..	..	..	..	119 133
Total life insurance	..	..	..	..	..	..	..	150 279
***of which:** Pension contracts*	..	..	..	..	..	..	..	..
1.1.4 Non-life insurance payments, by class, gross premiums								
Motor vehicle insurance	..	..	..	..	..	..	..	22 712
Marine, aviation and other transport insurance	..	..	..	..	..	..	..	1 721
Freight insurance	..	..	..	..	..	..	..	..
Fire and other property damage insurance	..	..	..	..	..	..	..	21 498
Pecuniary loss insurance	..	..	..	..	..	..	..	2 887
General liability insurance	..	..	..	..	..	..	..	6 884
Accident and health	..	..	..	..	..	..	..	49 416
***of which:** Health*	..	..	..	..	..	..	..	..
Other non-life insurance	..	..	..	..	..	..	..	10 953
Treaty reinsurance	..	..	..	..	..	..	..	..
Total non-life insurance	68 945	71 329	71 324	76 295	..	..	..	116 071
1.2 Gross claims payments								
Life								
Domestic undertakings	21 613 |	22 766	30 961	31 131	25 663	26 144	26 794	26 184
Foreign controlled undertakings	..	..	..	..	..	..	..	..
Foreign companies (branches)	..	..	..	..	..	..	..	..
All undertakings	21 613 |	22 766	30 961	31 131	25 663	26 144	26 794	26 184
Non-life								
Domestic undertakings	43 467 |	49 368	48 584	50 472	45 317	61 895	63 029	46 084
Foreign controlled undertakings	..	..	..	..	..	..	..	..
Foreign companies (branches)	95	44	51	59	59	52	51	..
All undertakings	43 562 |	49 412	48 635	50 531	45 376	61 947	63 080	46 084
Composite								
Domestic undertakings	75 111 |	73 529	93 502	98 016	97 287	86 518	91 862	137 406
Foreign controlled undertakings	..	..	..	..	..	..	..	..
Foreign companies (branches)	..	..	..	..	..	..	..	..
All undertakings	75 111 |	73 529	93 502	98 016	97 287	86 518	91 862	137 406
of which:								
Life	..	..	..	..	88 620	..	..	105 772
Domestic undertakings	..	..	..	..	88 620	..	..	105 772
Foreign controlled undertakings	..	..	..	..	..	..	..	..
Foreign companies (branches)	..	..	..	..	..	..	..	..
All undertakings	..	..	..	..	88 620	..	..	105 772
Non-life	..	..	..	..	8 667	..	..	31 634
Domestic undertakings	..	..	..	..	8 667	..	..	31 634
Foreign controlled undertakings	..	..	..	..	..	..	..	..
Foreign companies (branches)	..	..	..	..	..	..	..	..
All undertakings	..	..	..	..	8 667	..	..	31 634
Total								
Domestic undertakings	140 191	145 663	173 047	179 619	168 267	174 557	181 685	209 674
Foreign controlled undertakings	..	..	..	..	..	..	..	..
Foreign companies (branches)	95	44	51	59	59	52	51	..
All undertakings	140 286	145 707	173 098	179 678	168 326	174 608	181 736	209 674

France
Table 1. Selected aggregates *(cont.)*

Million EUR

	2009	2010	2011	2012	2013	2014	2015	2016
1.3 Commissions								
Life								
Domestic undertakings	6 323	1 323	1 682	1 705	..	..	..	..
Foreign controlled undertakings	..	..	..	..	..	..	..	..
Foreign companies (branches)	..	..	..	..	..	..	..	..
All undertakings	6 323	1 323	1 682	1 705	..	..	..	..
Non-life								
Domestic undertakings	9 983	10 198	10 449	10 610	..	..	..	..
Foreign controlled undertakings	..	..	..	..	..	..	..	..
Foreign companies (branches)	66	18	19	22	..	..	..	..
All undertakings	10 048	10 215	10 468	10 633	..	..	..	..
Composite								
Domestic undertakings	..	5 201	5 915	5 717	..	..	..	..
Foreign controlled undertakings	..	..	..	..	..	..	..	..
Foreign companies (branches)	..	..	..	..	..	..	..	..
All undertakings	..	5 201	5 915	5 717	..	..	..	..
of which:								
Life	..	..	4 985	4 677	..	..	..	..
Domestic undertakings	..	..	4 985	4 677	..	..	..	..
Foreign controlled undertakings	..	..	..	..	..	..	..	..
Foreign companies (branches)	..	..	..	..	..	..	..	..
All undertakings	..	..	4 985	4 677	..	..	..	..
Non-life	..	..	930	1 041	..	..	..	..
Domestic undertakings	..	..	930	1 041	..	..	..	..
Foreign controlled undertakings	..	..	..	..	..	..	..	..
Foreign companies (branches)	..	..	..	..	..	..	..	..
All undertakings	..	..	930	1 041	..	..	..	..
Total								
Domestic undertakings	16 306	16 722	18 046	18 033	..	..	..	..
Foreign controlled undertakings	..	..	..	..	..	..	..	..
Foreign companies (branches)	66	18	19	22	..	..	..	..
All undertakings	16 371	16 739	18 065	18 055	..	..	..	..
1.4 Gross operating expenses								
Life								
Domestic undertakings	2 481	719	842	2 982	2 828	2 893	2 914	3 436
Foreign controlled undertakings	..	..	..	..	..	..	..	..
Foreign companies (branches)	..	..	..	..	..	..	..	..
All undertakings	2 481	719	842	2 982	2 828	2 893	2 914	3 436
Non-life								
Domestic undertakings	14 448	5 842	5 487	15 726	15 969	16 156	15 936	20 162
Foreign controlled undertakings	..	..	..	..	..	..	..	..
Foreign companies (branches)	17	8	10	9	..	8	..	..
All undertakings	14 465	5 849	5 497	15 726	15 969	16 164	15 936	20 162
Composite								
Domestic undertakings	11 460	4 505	4 937	12 392	12 957	13 439	14 727	23 144
Foreign controlled undertakings	..	..	..	..	..	..	..	..
Foreign companies (branches)	..	..	..	..	..	..	..	..
All undertakings	11 460	4 505	4 937	12 392	12 957	13 439	14 727	23 144
of which:								
Life	..	..	..	..	10 533	10 808	11 414	17 608
Domestic undertakings	..	..	..	..	10 533	..	..	17 608
Foreign controlled undertakings	..	..	..	..	..	..	..	..
Foreign companies (branches)	..	..	..	..	..	..	..	..
All undertakings	..	..	..	..	10 533	10 808	11 414	17 608
Non-life	..	..	..	..	2 424	2 631	3 313	5 536
Domestic undertakings	..	..	..	..	2 424	..	..	5 536
Foreign controlled undertakings	..	..	..	..	..	..	..	..
Foreign companies (branches)	..	..	..	..	..	..	..	..
All undertakings	..	..	..	..	2 424	2 631	3 313	5 536
Total								
Domestic undertakings	28 389	11 066	11 266	31 100	31 754	32 488	33 578	46 742
Foreign controlled undertakings	..	..	..	..	..	..	..	..
Foreign companies (branches)	17	8	10	9	..	8	..	..
All undertakings	28 406	11 074	11 276	31 100	31 754	32 497	33 578	46 742

France
Table 1. Selected aggregates *(cont.)*

Million EUR

	2009	2010	2011	2012	2013	2014	2015	2016
1.5 Insurance business written abroad by branches, gross premiums								
Life								
Branches and agencies	1 205	1 761	1 929	1 895	2 691	2 860	3 373	107
Subsidaries	..	..	..	..	..	..	..	..
Total	1 205	1 761	1 929	1 895	2 691	2 860	3 373	..
Non-life								
Branches and agencies	4 191	5 111	5 592	4 107	4 176	4 960	5 460	3 024
Subsidaries	..	..	..	..	..	..	..	..
Total	4 191	5 111	5 592	4 107	4 176	4 960	5 460	..
Composite								
Branches and agencies	..	..	..	..	..	..	..	9 037
Subsidaries	..	..	..	..	..	..	..	..
Total	..	..	..	..	..	..	..	..
of which:								
Life	..	..	..	..	..	..	..	..
Branches and agencies	..	..	..	..	..	..	..	..
Subsidaries	..	..	..	..	..	..	..	..
Total	..	..	..	..	..	..	..	..
Non-life	..	..	..	..	..	..	..	..
Branches and agencies	..	..	..	..	..	..	..	..
Subsidaries	..	..	..	..	..	..	..	..
Total	..	..	..	..	..	..	..	..
Total								
Branches and agencies	5 396	6 872	7 521	6 001	6 867	7 820	8 834	12 168
Subsidaries	..	..	..	..	..	..	..	..
Total	5 396	6 872	7 521	6 001	6 867	7 820	8 834	..

.. Not available; | Break in series

Note: Detailed metadata at: http://metalinks.oecd.org/ins/20180621/624b.

Disclaimer: http://oe.cd/disclaimer

Source: OECD Insurance Statistics (database)

France
Table 2. Number of companies and employees

	2009	2010	2011	2012	2013	2014	2015	2016
2.1 Number of companies								
Life								
Domestic undertakings	63	61	61	62	59	55	51	..
Foreign controlled undertakings	..	..	..	..	..	..	..	..
Foreign companies (branches)	..	..	..	..	..	..	..	..
All undertakings	63	61	61	62	59	55	51	59
Non-life								
Domestic undertakings	259	257	250	221	212	206	191	..
Foreign controlled undertakings	9	8	7	5	..	..	..	..
Foreign companies (branches)	..	..	..	..	4	4	4	..
All undertakings	259	257	250	221	216	210	195	241
Composite								
Domestic undertakings	38	39	40	40	38	38	39	..
Foreign controlled undertakings	..	..	..	..	..	..	..	..
Foreign companies (branches)	..	..	..	..	..	..	..	..
All undertakings	38	39	40	40	38	38	39	173
Reinsurance								
Domestic undertakings	26	24	20	16	16	15	16	..
Foreign controlled undertakings	..	..	..	..	..	..	..	..
Foreign companies (branches)	..	..	..	..	..	..	..	..
All undertakings	26	24	20	16	16	15	16	..
Total								
Domestic undertakings	386	381	371	339	325	314	297	..
Foreign controlled undertakings	..	..	7	5	..	..	..	..
Foreign companies (branches)	..	..	..	..	4	4	4	..
All undertakings	386	381	371	339	329	318	301	473
2.2 Number of employees								
Insurance undertakings	..	..	..	..	..	..	..	..
Intermediaries	..	..	..	..	..	..	..	..
Total	..	..	..	..	..	..	..	..

.. Not available

Note: Detailed metadata at: http://metalinks.oecd.org/ins/20180621/624b.

Disclaimer: http://oe.cd/disclaimer

Source: OECD Insurance Statistics (database)

Germany
Table 1. Selected aggregates

Million EUR

	2009	2010	2011	2012	2013	2014	2015	2016
1.1 Insurance business written in the reporting country								
1.1.1 Insurance business, by ownership								
Gross premiums								
Domestic undertakings	174 647	180 083	178 145	233 661	243 304	246 201	254 407	257 208
Foreign controlled undertakings	35 702	37 912	35 602	37 194	39 396	38 694	39 170	36 978
Foreign companies (branches)	3 000	1 744	5 560	8 062	7 963	8 796	9 751	8 994
All undertakings	177 647	181 828	183 705	235 634	251 267	254 997	264 158	266 203
Premiums ceded								
Domestic undertakings	15 976	14 656	15 996	23 045	25 709	27 853	32 499	31 990
Foreign controlled undertakings	3 899	3 414	3 905	3 947	4 645	4 615	4 593	4 041
Foreign companies (branches)	..	..	..	100	108	103	114	112
All undertakings	..	..	..	23 145	25 817	27 956	32 613	32 102
Net written premiums								
Domestic undertakings	158 671	165 427	162 149	210 616	217 596	218 348	221 907	225 218
Foreign controlled undertakings	31 804	34 499	31 696	33 247	34 751	34 078	34 577	32 937
Foreign companies (branches)	..	..	..	1 873	7 854	8 693	9 637	8 882
All undertakings	..	..	..	212 489	225 450	227 041	231 545	234 100
1.1.2 Insurance business on foreign risks, gross premiums								
Life	..	..	..	..	..	..	..	..
Non-life	..	..	..	..	..	..	..	..
Composite total	..	..	..	..	..	..	..	..
Total	..	..	..	..	..	..	..	..
1.1.3 Life insurance payments, by class, gross premiums								
Annuities	23 949	27 898	27 237	29 443	32 863	34 019	31 782	31 215
Unit linked	12 113	13 466	12 808	12 721	12 919	13 863	13 863	15 351
Other life insurance	44 304	44 734	40 660	40 822	41 934	40 891	41 214	38 845
Total life insurance	80 365	86 098	80 705	82 986	87 716	88 774	86 859	85 411
***of which:** Pension contracts*	..	..	..	..	..	..	..	..
1.1.4 Non-life insurance payments, by class, gross premiums								
Motor vehicle insurance	25 745	24 680	26 350	27 577	28 592	31 425	32 589	36 521
Marine, aviation and other transport insurance	4 689	4 535	4 156	4 537	4 476	4 379	5 116	4 749
Freight insurance	..	..	..	..	..	..	..	..
Fire and other property damage insurance	32 555	33 154	36 611	34 420	36 832	35 422	38 830	42 499
Pecuniary loss insurance	1 245	2 910	2 979	2 754	2 815	2 088	2 197	2 376
General liability insurance	11 887	11 648	12 321	12 623	13 265	14 213	15 425	16 126
Accident and health	50 621	45 055	47 235	48 823	49 395	48 811	49 176	49 721
***of which:** Health*	33 350	37 290	39 555	41 036	41 747	40 924	41 627	37 178
Other non-life insurance	3 819	4 195	4 316	4 794	4 841	4 865	31 030	25 991
Treaty reinsurance	..	..	..	..	..	..	..	..
Total non-life insurance	130 561	126 177	133 968	135 526	140 215	141 203	174 363	177 983
1.2 Gross claims payments								
Life								
Domestic undertakings	62 837	71 181	85 244	66 288	69 267	74 625	73 307	78 596
Foreign controlled undertakings	..	..	..	15 284	17 017	17 510	17 929	17 942
Foreign companies (branches)	..	..	..	..	..	..	..	..
All undertakings	62 837	71 181	85 244	66 288	69 267	74 625	73 307	78 596
Non-life								
Domestic undertakings	91 083	84 864	93 574	101 839	113 293	72 709	77 667	78 086
Foreign controlled undertakings	..	..	..	12 192	12 402	8 955	3 653	9 227
Foreign companies (branches)	..	..	..	..	..	..	..	..
All undertakings	91 083	84 864	93 574	101 839	113 293	72 709	77 667	78 086
Composite, all undertakings	..	..	..	..	..	..	..	..
Total								
Domestic undertakings	153 920	156 045	178 818	168 127	182 560	147 334	150 974	156 682
Foreign controlled undertakings	..	..	..	27 475	29 419	26 465	21 581	27 169
Foreign companies (branches)	..	..	..	..	..	..	..	..
All undertakings	153 920	156 045	178 818	168 127	182 560	147 334	150 974	156 682
1.3 Commissions								
Life								
Domestic undertakings	5 514	5 875	6 312	6 005	5 367	5 583	5 069	4 987
Foreign controlled undertakings	..	..	..	1 771	1 604	1 533	1 488	1 238
Foreign companies (branches)	..	..	..	..	..	..	..	..
All undertakings	5 514	5 875	6 312	6 005	5 367	5 583	5 069	4 987
Non-life								
Domestic undertakings	9 904	9 627	9 908	10 069	10 048	10 221	10 740	11 105
Foreign controlled undertakings	..	..	..	1 985	1 720	1 626	257	1 594
Foreign companies (branches)	..	..	..	..	..	..	..	..
All undertakings	9 904	9 627	9 908	10 069	10 048	10 221	10 740	11 105
Composite, all undertakings	..	..	..	..	..	..	..	..
Total								
Domestic undertakings	15 419	15 502	16 220	16 074	15 416	15 805	15 810	16 092
Foreign controlled undertakings	..	..	..	3 756	3 323	3 159	1 745	2 832
Foreign companies (branches)	..	..	..	..	..	..	..	..
All undertakings	15 419	15 502	16 220	16 074	15 416	15 805	15 810	16 092

Germany
Table 1. Selected aggregates *(cont.)*

Million EUR

	2009	2010	2011	2012	2013	2014	2015	2016
1.4 Gross operating expenses								
Life								
Domestic undertakings	9 827	14 203	14 545	4 051	3 954	3 963	4 008	3 902
Foreign controlled undertakings	..	..	..	925	921	894	1 036	938
Foreign companies (branches)	..	..	..	..	..	..	..	..
All undertakings	9 827	14 203	14 545	4 051	3 954	3 963	4 008	3 902
Non-life								
Domestic undertakings	30 298	27 565	28 382	11 593	11 599	10 296	10 627	10 807
Foreign controlled undertakings	..	..	..	1 528	1 400	1 187	324	1 183
Foreign companies (branches)	..	..	..	..	..	..	..	..
All undertakings	30 298	27 565	28 382	11 593	11 599	10 296	10 627	10 807
Composite, all undertakings	..	..	..	..	..	..	..	..
Total								
Domestic undertakings	40 125	41 768	42 927	15 644	15 553	14 259	14 635	14 709
Foreign controlled undertakings	..	..	..	2 453	2 321	2 081	1 361	2 121
Foreign companies (branches)	..	..	..	..	..	..	..	..
All undertakings	40 125	41 768	42 927	15 644	15 553	14 259	14 635	14 709
1.5 Insurance business written abroad by branches, gross premiums								
Life								
Branches and agencies	142	..	..	..	..	..	..	..
Subsidaries	..	..	..	..	..	..	..	..
Total	142	..	..	..	..	..	..	..
Non-life								
Branches and agencies	988	..	..	..	..	..	..	..
Subsidaries	..	..	..	..	..	..	..	..
Total	988	..	..	..	..	..	..	..
Composite total	..	..	..	..	..	..	..	..
Total								
Branches and agencies	1 129	..	..	..	..	..	..	..
Subsidaries	..	..	..	..	..	..	..	..
Total	1 129	..	..	..	..	..	..	..

.. Not available

Note: Detailed metadata at: http://metalinks.oecd.org/ins/20180621/c2f6.

Disclaimer: http://oe.cd/disclaimer

Source: OECD Insurance Statistics (database)

Germany
Table 2. Number of companies and employees

	2009	2010	2011	2012	2013	2014	2015	2016
2.1 Number of companies								
Life								
Domestic undertakings	96	96	95	90	91	91	85	85
Foreign controlled undertakings	22	19	20	19	17	17	14	14
Foreign companies (branches)	21	21	20	19	2	2	2	2
All undertakings	117	117	115	109	93	93	87	87
Non-life								
Domestic undertakings	266	261	265	256	259	255	257	252
Foreign controlled undertakings	27	25	25	25	23	21	22	18
Foreign companies (branches)	64	72	69	62	3	3	3	2
All undertakings	330	333	334	318	262	258	260	254
Composite, all undertakings	**0**	**0**	**0**	**0**	**0**	**0**	**0**	**0**
Reinsurance								
Domestic undertakings	38	35	33	30	29	27	27	27
Foreign controlled undertakings	5	5	5	6	4	3	3	3
Foreign companies (branches)	0	7	7	7	1	1	1	1
All undertakings	38	42	40	37	30	28	28	28
Total								
Domestic undertakings	400	392	393	376	379	373	369	364
Foreign controlled undertakings	54	49	50	50	44	41	39	35
Foreign companies (branches)	85	100	96	88	6	6	6	5
All undertakings	485	492	489	464	385	379	375	369
2.2 Number of employees								
Insurance undertakings	140 609	123 595	125 783	126 625	128 755	126 755	128 784	..
Intermediaries	8 120	27 927	27 952	27 407	27 331	26 982	25 917	..
Total	148 729	151 522	153 735	154 032	156 086	153 737	154 701	156 675

.. Not available

Note: Detailed metadata at: http://metalinks.oecd.org/ins/20180621/c2f6.

Disclaimer: http://oe.cd/disclaimer

Source: OECD Insurance Statistics (database)

Greece
Table 1. Selected aggregates

Million EUR

	2009	2010	2011	2012	2013	2014	2015	2016
1.1 Insurance business written in the reporting country								
1.1.1 Insurance business, by ownership								
Gross premiums								
Domestic undertakings	2 354	4 818	4 691	4 289	4 071	3 806	3 573	3 531
Foreign controlled undertakings	1 208	1 877	2 130	2 071	1 730	1 696	1 766	2 350
Foreign companies (branches)	481	427	261	211	0	0	0	0
All undertakings	5 194	5 246	4 952	4 499	4 071	3 806	3 573	3 531
Premiums ceded								
Domestic undertakings	193	523	737	534	824	471	459	396
Foreign controlled undertakings	96	226	439	235	214	206	201	244
Foreign companies (branches)	116	96	90	0	0	0	0	0
All undertakings	310	619	827	534	824	471	459	396
Net written premiums								
Domestic undertakings	2 161	4 295	3 954	3 754	3 247	3 334	3 114	3 135
Foreign controlled undertakings	1 111	1 651	1 691	1 836	1 516	1 490	1 565	2 106
Foreign companies (branches)	365	332	171	211	0	0	0	0
All undertakings	2 526	4 627	4 125	3 965	3 247	3 335	3 114	3 135
1.1.2 Insurance business on foreign risks, gross premiums								
Life	..	..	..	..	..	..	..	..
Non-life	..	..	..	..	..	..	..	..
Composite	..	..	..	..	..	..	..	..
of which:								
Life	..	..	..	..	..	..	..	..
Non-life	..	..	..	..	..	..	..	..
Total	..	..	..	..	..	..	..	..
1.1.3 Life insurance payments, by class, gross premiums								
Annuities	..	..	..	165	142	129	125	0
Unit linked	..	..	..	368	240	396	326	250
Other life insurance	..	..	..	1 406	1 299	1 353	1 348	1 416
Total life insurance	..	..	..	1 939	1 681	1 879	1 799	1 666
of which: *Pension contracts*	..	..	..	205	143	151	156	..
1.1.4 Non-life insurance payments, by class, gross premiums								
Motor vehicle insurance	1 713	1 965	1 840	1 569	1 417	1 154	1 006	911
Marine, aviation and other transport insurance	33	28	25	21	19	19	20	32
Freight insurance	37	33	27	24	24	21	21	..
Fire and other property damage insurance	604	576	529	538	529	448	440	410
Pecuniary loss insurance	81	65	69	78	69	30	30	40
General liability insurance	86	81	73	78	76	67	68	65
Accident and health	79	76	76	68	64	57	57	300
of which: *Health*	20	18	19	20	0	0	..	..
Other non-life insurance	181	153	146	179	188	128	129	137
Treaty reinsurance	..	0	0	0	0	0	..	..
Total non-life insurance	2 814	2 995	2 786	2 556	2 386	1 924	1 770	1 896

Greece
Table 1. Selected aggregates *(cont.)*

Million EUR

	2009	2010	2011	2012	2013	2014	2015	2016
1.2 Gross claims payments								
Life								
Domestic undertakings	655	692	822	1 300	1 072	900	744	..
Foreign controlled undertakings	524	506	591	1 017	707	1	502	..
Foreign companies (branches)	240	269	263	0	0	0	0	..
All undertakings	894	961	1 085	1 300	1 072	900	744	..
Non-life								
Domestic undertakings	540	550	501	431	373	355	314	..
Foreign controlled undertakings	139	144	146	142	121	224	109	..
Foreign companies (branches)	70	35	47	0	1	1	0	..
All undertakings	610	586	549	431	375	356	314	..
Composite								
Domestic undertakings	1 270	1 317	1 408	1 291	1 096	1 018	931	..
Foreign controlled undertakings	399	422	430	441	364	412	347	..
Foreign companies (branches)	..	0	0	0	0	0	0	..
All undertakings	1 270	1 317	1 408	1 291	1 096	1 018	931	..
of which:								
Life	648	703	866	791	669	613	573	..
Domestic undertakings	648	703	866	791	669	613	573	..
Foreign controlled undertakings	194	255	285	282	226	7	220	..
Foreign companies (branches)	..	0	0	0	0	0	0	..
All undertakings	648	703	866	791	669	613	573	..
Non-life	622	614	541	501	426	405	358	..
Domestic undertakings	622	614	541	501	426	405	358	..
Foreign controlled undertakings	205	166	145	159	138	405	126	..
Foreign companies (branches)	..	0	0	0	0	0	0	..
All undertakings	622	614	541	501	426	405	358	..
Total								
Domestic undertakings	2 464	2 559	2 731	3 022	2 541	2 273	1 989	..
Foreign controlled undertakings	1 061	1 072	1 167	1 600	1 192	637	957	..
Foreign companies (branches)	310	304	310	0	1	1	0	..
All undertakings	2 774	2 864	3 042	3 022	2 542	2 274	1 989	..
1.3 Commissions								
Life								
Domestic undertakings	..	..	..	..	..	95	91	..
Foreign controlled undertakings	..	..	..	..	..	70	70	..
Foreign companies (branches)	..	..	..	..	..	0	0	..
All undertakings	..	..	..	..	..	95	91	..
Non-life								
Domestic undertakings	..	..	..	..	..	161	158	..
Foreign controlled undertakings	..	..	..	..	..	63	66	..
Foreign companies (branches)	..	..	..	..	..	0	0	..
All undertakings	..	..	..	..	..	162	158	..
Composite								
Domestic undertakings	..	..	..	..	..	276	709	..
Foreign controlled undertakings	..	..	..	..	..	115	115	..
Foreign companies (branches)	..	..	..	..	..	0	0	..
All undertakings	..	..	..	..	..	276	709	..
of which:								
Life	..	..	..	..	..	102	544	..
Domestic undertakings	..	..	..	..	..	102	544	..
Foreign controlled undertakings	..	..	..	..	..	39	40	..
Foreign companies (branches)	..	..	..	..	..	0	0	..
All undertakings	..	..	..	..	..	102	544	..
Non-life	..	..	..	..	..	174	164	..
Domestic undertakings	..	..	..	..	..	174	164	..
Foreign controlled undertakings	..	..	..	..	..	76	75	..
Foreign companies (branches)	..	..	..	..	..	0	0	..
All undertakings	..	..	..	..	..	174	164	..
Total								
Domestic undertakings	..	..	..	..	..	532	957	..
Foreign controlled undertakings	..	..	..	..	..	248	251	..
Foreign companies (branches)	..	..	..	..	..	0	0	..
All undertakings	..	..	..	..	..	532	957	..

Greece
Table 1. Selected aggregates *(cont.)*

Million EUR

	2009	2010	2011	2012	2013	2014	2015	2016
1.4 Gross operating expenses								
Life								
Domestic undertakings	192 |	177	182	82	79	176	163	35
Foreign controlled undertakings	163 |	137	139	75	66	141	132	32
Foreign companies (branches)	62	59	57	0	0	0	..	0
All undertakings	254 |	236	239	82	79	176	163	35
Non-life								
Domestic undertakings	342 |	395	373	104	124	264	247	248
Foreign controlled undertakings	113 |	135	137	59	61	115	116	145
Foreign companies (branches)	64	53	60	1	0	0	0	0
All undertakings	406 |	448	432	106	124	264	247	248
Composite								
Domestic undertakings	509 |	608	543	67	169	404	371	700
Foreign controlled undertakings	158 |	189	191	16	57	154	150	448
Foreign companies (branches)	..	0	0	0	0	0	..	0
All undertakings	509 |	608	543	67	169	404	371	700
of which:								
Life	157 |	195	176	36	53	144	145	315
Domestic undertakings	157 |	195	176	36	53	144	145	315
Foreign controlled undertakings	51 |	70	69	11	21	53	52	231
Foreign companies (branches)	..	0	0	0	0	0	..	0
All undertakings	157 |	195	176	36	53	144	145	315
Non-life	352 |	413	368	31	116	260	226	385
Domestic undertakings	352 |	413	368	31	116	260	226	385
Foreign controlled undertakings	106 |	119	122	4	36	101	98	217
Foreign companies (branches)	..	0	0	0	0	0	..	0
All undertakings	352 |	413	368	31	116	260	226	385
Total								
Domestic undertakings	1 043	1 179	1 098	253	372	844	781	983
Foreign controlled undertakings	434	461	467	150	184	410	398	625
Foreign companies (branches)	125	112	117	1	0	0	0	0
All undertakings	1 169	1 291	1 215	254	372	844	781	983
1.5 Insurance business written abroad by branches, gross premiums								
Life								
Branches and agencies	3	16	0	..	..	..	..	..
Subsidaries	..	..	..	..	..	..	..	..
Total	..	16	0	..	..	..	..	..
Non-life								
Branches and agencies	2	14	0	..	..	..	..	..
Subsidaries	..	..	..	..	..	..	..	..
Total	..	14	0	..	..	..	..	..
Composite								
Branches and agencies	..	..	..	..	..	..	..	..
Subsidaries	..	..	..	..	..	..	..	..
Total	..	..	..	..	..	..	..	..
of which:								
Life	..	..	..	..	..	..	..	..
Branches and agencies	..	..	..	..	..	..	..	..
Subsidaries	..	..	..	..	..	..	..	..
Total	..	..	..	..	..	..	..	..
Non-life	..	..	..	..	..	..	..	..
Branches and agencies	..	..	..	..	..	..	..	..
Subsidaries	..	..	..	..	..	..	..	..
Total	..	..	..	..	..	..	..	..
Total								
Branches and agencies	6	30	0	..	..	..	..	..
Subsidaries	..	..	..	..	..	..	..	..
Total	..	30	0	..	..	..	..	..

.. Not available; | Break in series

Note: Detailed metadata at: http://metalinks.oecd.org/ins/20180621/cc46.

Disclaimer: http://oe.cd/disclaimer

Source: OECD Insurance Statistics (database)

Greece
Table 2. Number of companies and employees

	2009	2010	2011	2012	2013	2014	2015	2016
2.1 Number of companies								
Life								
Domestic undertakings	14	11	10	11	11	11	11	4
Foreign controlled undertakings	9	6	6	7	7	7	7	2
Foreign companies (branches)	3	1	1	0	0	0	0	0
All undertakings	17	12	11	11	11	11	11	4
Non-life								
Domestic undertakings	30	32	31	31	28	24	24	24
Foreign controlled undertakings	10	7	7	7	7	6	5	7
Foreign companies (branches)	17	2	2	2	2	2	2	0
All undertakings	47	34	33	33	30	26	26	24
Composite								
Domestic undertakings	11	12	11	11	11	11	11	17
Foreign controlled undertakings	4	4	4	4	4	4	4	10
Foreign companies (branches)	..	0	0	0	0	0	0	0
All undertakings	11	12	11	11	11	11	11	17
Reinsurance								
Domestic undertakings	..	0	0	0	0	0	0	0
Foreign controlled undertakings	..	0	0	0	0	0	0	0
Foreign companies (branches)	..	0	0	0	0	0	0	0
All undertakings	..	0	0	0	0	0	0	0
Total								
Domestic undertakings	55	55	52	53	50	46	46	45
Foreign controlled undertakings	..	17	17	18	18	17	16	19
Foreign companies (branches)	20	3	3	2	2	2	2	0
All undertakings	75	58	55	55	52	48	48	45
2.2 Number of employees								
Insurance undertakings	..	..	..	..	..	..	..	..
Intermediaries	..	..	..	..	..	..	..	..
Total	..	..	..	..	..	..	..	..

.. Not available

Note: Detailed metadata at: http://metalinks.oecd.org/ins/20180621/cc46.

Disclaimer: http://oe.cd/disclaimer

Source: OECD Insurance Statistics (database)

Hungary
Table 1. Selected aggregates

Million HUF

	2009	2010	2011	2012	2013	2014	2015	2016
1.1 Insurance business written in the reporting country								
1.1.1 Insurance business, by ownership								
Gross premiums								
Domestic undertakings	825 793	842 781	815 038	760 249	801 210	833 664	835 428	885 781
Foreign controlled undertakings	788 388	802 202	770 794	718 932	763 286	796 332	788 248	835 272
Foreign companies (branches)	..	..	..	..	..	..	..	..
All undertakings	825 793	842 781	815 038	760 249	801 210	833 664	835 428	885 781
Premiums ceded								
Domestic undertakings	131 366	134 572	131 231	127 261	111 755	116 117	115 801	118 081
Foreign controlled undertakings	121 701	123 702	120 088	118 373	104 254	108 557	104 464	107 021
Foreign companies (branches)	..	..	..	..	..	..	..	..
All undertakings	131 366	134 572	131 231	127 261	111 755	116 117	115 801	118 081
Net written premiums								
Domestic undertakings	694 427	708 209	683 807	632 989	689 455	717 547	719 627	767 700
Foreign controlled undertakings	666 687	678 500	650 706	600 559	659 032	687 774	683 784	728 251
Foreign companies (branches)	..	..	..	..	..	..	..	..
All undertakings	694 427	708 209	683 807	632 989	689 455	717 547	719 627	767 700
1.1.2 Insurance business on foreign risks, gross premiums								
Life	1 831 |	2 501	30 145	3 284	3 358	3 533	4 234	4 317
Non-life	1 243 |	1 568	2 165	1 257	1 840	1 923	1 052	2 308
Composite	3 701 |	5 030	5 326	7 943	4 500	2 829	4 368	8 142
of which:								
Life	39 |	64	80	279	781	228	216	177
Non-life	3 662 |	4 965	5 246	7 665	3 719	2 602	4 152	7 965
Total	6 775	9 099	37 636	12 484	9 698	8 285	9 654	14 767
1.1.3 Life insurance payments, by class, gross premiums								
Annuities	6 234	4 459	4 247	3 529	2 975	3 147	3 479	..
Unit linked	253 623	295 752	298 106	261 098	286 919	282 059	266 857	..
Other life insurance	155 725	147 947	142 599	138 251	146 439	171 738	156 617	..
Total life insurance	415 582	448 159	444 952	402 878	436 333	456 944	426 953	438 718
***of which:** Pension contracts*	68	51	37	..	19	..	10	..
1.1.4 Non-life insurance payments, by class, gross premiums								
Motor vehicle insurance	219 468	200 559	164 432	147 428	144 515	152 283	175 045	203 396
Marine, aviation and other transport insurance	1 080	1 098	933	663	661	793	879	142
Freight insurance	2 615	2 798	3 082	2 405	2 552	2 856	3 165	5 733
Fire and other property damage insurance	138 136	140 943	147 551	152 904	159 562	158 219	161 160	168 736
Pecuniary loss insurance	4 387	3 829	4 922	2 930	3 739	3 672	4 822	5 430
General liability insurance	18 556	17 560	17 956	18 856	20 074	21 904	23 585	21 274
Accident and health	19 161	20 323	22 596	23 361	25 922	28 358	29 859	22 389
***of which:** Health*	7 593	7 599	5 929	7 128	8 559	9 558	8 668	4 250
Other non-life insurance	6 780	7 479	8 811	8 758	7 781	8 557	9 909	19 916
Treaty reinsurance	..	..	..	..	..	..	..	..
Total non-life insurance	410 183	394 588	370 284	357 305	364 806	376 641	408 424	447 017

Hungary
Table 1. Selected aggregates *(cont.)*

Million HUF

	2009	2010	2011	2012	2013	2014	2015	2016
1.2 Gross claims payments								
Life								
Domestic undertakings	132 391 |	142 272	170 016	153 649	139 994	130 633	150 198	155 047
Foreign controlled undertakings	124 751 |	131 643	158 484	150 320	129 594	121 318	139 595	147 047
Foreign companies (branches)	..	..	..	..	..	..	..	..
All undertakings	132 391 |	142 272	170 016	153 649	139 994	130 633	150 198	155 047
Non-life								
Domestic undertakings	18 943 |	19 173	18 824	22 516	25 692	27 416	30 571	34 112
Foreign controlled undertakings	9 618 |	12 193	11 865	11 387	12 611	13 973	14 605	16 056
Foreign companies (branches)	..	..	..	..	..	..	..	..
All undertakings	18 943 |	19 173	18 824	22 516	25 692	27 416	30 571	34 112
Composite								
Domestic undertakings	359 394 |	441 811	411 093	413 298	422 789	379 879	356 926	361 448
Foreign controlled undertakings	359 394 |	441 811	411 093	413 298	422 789	379 879	356 926	361 448
Foreign companies (branches)	..	..	..	..	..	..	..	..
All undertakings	359 394 |	441 811	411 093	413 298	422 789	379 879	356 926	361 448
of which:								
Life	176 947 |	228 884	236 953	240 059	242 802	212 244	180 098	176 820
Domestic undertakings	176 947 |	228 884	236 953	240 059	242 802	212 244	180 098	176 820
Foreign controlled undertakings	176 947 |	228 884	236 953	240 059	242 802	212 244	180 098	176 820
Foreign companies (branches)	..	..	..	..	..	..	..	..
All undertakings	176 947 |	228 884	236 953	240 059	242 802	212 244	180 098	176 820
Non-life	182 447 |	212 928	174 139	173 240	179 988	167 635	176 829	184 628
Domestic undertakings	182 447 |	212 928	174 139	173 240	179 988	167 635	176 829	184 628
Foreign controlled undertakings	182 447 |	212 928	174 139	173 240	179 988	167 635	176 829	184 628
Foreign companies (branches)	..	..	..	..	..	..	..	..
All undertakings	182 447 |	212 928	174 139	173 240	179 988	167 635	176 829	184 628
Total								
Domestic undertakings	510 729	603 256	599 932	589 464	588 475	537 928	537 695	550 607
Foreign controlled undertakings	493 763	585 648	581 441	575 006	564 995	515 171	511 127	524 551
Foreign companies (branches)	..	..	..	..	..	..	..	..
All undertakings	510 729	603 256	599 932	589 464	588 475	537 928	537 695	550 607
1.3 Commissions								
Life								
Domestic undertakings	21 500 |	23 836	23 907	20 760	14 900	14 024	13 526	16 531
Foreign controlled undertakings	16 617 |	13 107	13 391	14 215	11 559	11 559	11 089	14 360
Foreign companies (branches)	..	..	..	..	..	..	..	..
All undertakings	21 500 |	23 836	23 907	20 760	14 900	14 024	13 526	16 531
Non-life								
Domestic undertakings	5 302 |	5 722	6 479	6 319	7 349	7 243	9 161	10 325
Foreign controlled undertakings	2 933 |	5 088	5 335	4 457	4 813	4 948	5 986	5 650
Foreign companies (branches)	..	..	..	..	..	..	..	..
All undertakings	5 302 |	5 722	6 479	6 319	7 349	7 243	9 161	10 325
Composite								
Domestic undertakings	72 427 |	74 369	74 891	69 058	75 007	72 592	79 086	108 207
Foreign controlled undertakings	72 427 |	74 369	74 891	69 058	75 007	72 592	79 086	108 207
Foreign companies (branches)	..	..	..	..	..	..	..	..
All undertakings	72 427 |	74 369	74 891	69 058	75 007	72 592	79 086	108 207
of which:								
Life	27 160 |	28 121	30 426	26 909	29 847	30 235	29 116	39 083
Domestic undertakings	27 160 |	28 121	30 426	26 909	29 847	30 235	29 116	39 083
Foreign controlled undertakings	27 160 |	28 121	30 426	26 909	29 847	30 235	29 116	39 083
Foreign companies (branches)	..	..	..	..	..	..	..	..
All undertakings	27 160 |	28 121	30 426	26 909	29 847	30 235	29 116	39 083
Non-life	45 267 |	46 248	44 465	42 148	45 160	42 357	49 970	69 124
Domestic undertakings	45 267 |	46 248	44 465	42 148	45 160	42 357	49 970	69 124
Foreign controlled undertakings	45 267 |	46 248	44 465	42 148	45 160	42 357	49 970	69 124
Foreign companies (branches)	..	..	..	..	..	..	..	..
All undertakings	45 267 |	46 248	44 465	42 148	45 160	42 357	49 970	69 124
Total								
Domestic undertakings	99 230	103 927	105 277	96 136	97 256	93 859	101 773	135 063
Foreign controlled undertakings	91 977	92 564	93 617	87 729	91 380	89 099	96 162	128 218
Foreign companies (branches)	..	..	..	..	..	..	..	..
All undertakings	99 230	103 927	105 277	96 136	97 256	93 859	101 773	135 063

Hungary
Table 1. Selected aggregates *(cont.)*

Million HUF

	2009	2010	2011	2012	2013	2014	2015	2016
1.4 Gross operating expenses								
Life								
Domestic undertakings	42 768 |	56 566	52 633	37 846	32 595	35 399	32 897	34 946
Foreign controlled undertakings	15 559 |	37 256	36 587	32 963	27 473	30 053	29 279	31 818
Foreign companies (branches)	..	..	..	..	..	..	..	..
All undertakings	42 768 |	56 566	52 633	37 846	32 595	35 399	32 897	34 946
Non-life								
Domestic undertakings	14 175 |	15 324	17 229	16 277	17 413	17 638	20 337	21 977
Foreign controlled undertakings	7 192 |	11 678	12 859	10 465	11 126	11 890	14 690	13 298
Foreign companies (branches)	..	..	..	..	..	..	..	..
All undertakings	14 175 |	15 324	17 229	16 277	17 413	17 638	20 337	21 977
Composite								
Domestic undertakings	160 403 |	175 554	170 062	155 577	172 680	181 142	167 842	176 431
Foreign controlled undertakings	160 403 |	175 554	170 062	155 577	172 680	181 142	167 842	176 431
Foreign companies (branches)	..	..	..	..	..	..	..	..
All undertakings	160 403 |	175 554	170 062	155 577	172 680	181 142	167 842	176 431
of which:								
Life	47 882 |	65 371	68 791	55 125	56 633	70 675	55 349	56 859
Domestic undertakings	47 882 |	65 371	68 791	55 125	56 633	70 675	55 349	56 859
Foreign controlled undertakings	47 882 |	65 371	68 791	55 125	56 633	70 675	55 349	56 859
Foreign companies (branches)	..	..	..	..	..	..	..	..
All undertakings	47 882 |	65 371	68 791	55 125	56 633	70 675	55 349	56 859
Non-life	112 521 |	110 183	101 271	100 451	116 047	110 467	112 493	119 571
Domestic undertakings	112 521 |	110 183	101 271	100 451	116 047	110 467	112 493	119 571
Foreign controlled undertakings	112 521 |	110 183	101 271	100 451	116 047	110 467	112 493	119 571
Foreign companies (branches)	..	..	..	..	..	..	..	..
All undertakings	112 521 |	110 183	101 271	100 451	116 047	110 467	112 493	119 571
Total								
Domestic undertakings	217 346	247 444	239 924	209 699	222 687	234 179	221 076	233 354
Foreign controlled undertakings	183 154	224 487	219 509	199 004	211 279	223 085	211 811	221 547
Foreign companies (branches)	..	..	..	..	..	..	..	..
All undertakings	217 346	247 444	239 924	209 699	222 687	234 179	221 076	233 354
1.5 Insurance business written abroad by branches, gross premiums								
Life								
Branches and agencies	..	..	..	..	..	..	..	..
Subsidaries	..	..	..	..	..	..	..	..
Total	..	..	..	..	..	..	..	..
Non-life								
Branches and agencies	..	..	..	..	..	..	..	..
Subsidaries	..	..	..	..	..	..	..	..
Total	..	..	..	..	..	..	..	..
Composite								
Branches and agencies	..	..	..	..	..	..	..	..
Subsidaries	..	..	..	..	..	..	..	..
Total	..	..	..	..	..	..	..	..
of which:								
Life	..	..	..	..	..	..	..	..
Branches and agencies	..	..	..	..	..	..	..	..
Subsidaries	..	..	..	..	..	..	..	..
Total	..	..	..	..	..	..	..	..
Non-life	..	..	..	..	..	..	..	..
Branches and agencies	..	..	..	..	..	..	..	..
Subsidaries	..	..	..	..	..	..	..	..
Total	..	..	..	..	..	..	..	..
Total								
Branches and agencies	..	..	..	..	..	..	..	..
Subsidaries	..	..	..	..	..	..	..	..
Total	..	..	..	..	..	..	..	..

.. Not available; | Break in series

Note: Detailed metadata at: http://metalinks.oecd.org/ins/20180621/7518.

Disclaimer: http://oe.cd/disclaimer

Source: OECD Insurance Statistics (database)

Hungary
Table 2. Number of companies and employees

	2009	2010	2011	2012	2013	2014	2015	2016
2.1 Number of companies								
Life								
Domestic undertakings	12	12	12	12	10	10	10	8
Foreign controlled undertakings	9	9	9	9	7	7	7	7
Foreign companies (branches)	0	0	..	..	..	..	0	0
All undertakings	12	12	12	12	10	10	10	8
Non-life								
Domestic undertakings	15	15	15	13	12	12	11	10
Foreign controlled undertakings	7	9	9	7	6	6	6	6
Foreign companies (branches)	11	14	12	14	14	14	13	14
All undertakings	26	29	27	27	26	26	24	24
Composite								
Domestic undertakings	10	10	10	10	10	10	9	9
Foreign controlled undertakings	10	10	10	10	10	10	9	9
Foreign companies (branches)	1	0	1	1	1	1	2	2
All undertakings	11	10	11	11	11	11	11	11
Reinsurance								
Domestic undertakings	..	..	..	..	..	..	..	..
Foreign controlled undertakings	..	..	..	..	..	..	..	..
Foreign companies (branches)	..	..	..	..	..	..	..	..
All undertakings	..	..	..	..	..	..	..	..
Total								
Domestic undertakings	37	37	37	35	32	32	30	27
Foreign controlled undertakings	26	28	28	26	23	23	22	22
Foreign companies (branches)	12	14	13	15	15	15	15	16
All undertakings	49	51	50	50	47	47	45	43
2.2 Number of employees								
Insurance undertakings	..	10 547	9 580	9 701	9 363	9 229	8 728	8 542
Intermediaries	..	17 067	16 950	13 572	13 083	12 768	11 392	9 822
Total	..	27 615	26 530	23 273	22 445	21 997	20 121	18 364

.. Not available

Note: Detailed metadata at: http://metalinks.oecd.org/ins/20180621/7518.

Disclaimer: http://oe.cd/disclaimer

Source: OECD Insurance Statistics (database)

Iceland
Table 1. Selected aggregates

Million ISK

	2009	2010	2011	2012	2013	2014	2015	2016
1.1 Insurance business written in the reporting country								
1.1.1 Insurance business, by ownership								
Gross premiums								
Domestic undertakings	34 293	46 636	48 117	50 490	51 142	51 849	55 346	58 777
Foreign controlled undertakings	3 732	4 082	4 464	4 788	5 088	5 401	6 010	..
Foreign companies (branches)	0	0	0	..	..	..	..	..
All undertakings	34 293	46 636	48 117	50 490	51 142	51 849	55 346	58 777
Premiums ceded								
Domestic undertakings	2 546	3 621	3 425	3 371	3 136	2 918	2 882	2 725
Foreign controlled undertakings	260	476	328	318	310	310	272	..
Foreign companies (branches)	0	0	0	..	..	..	..	..
All undertakings	2 546	3 621	3 425	3 371	3 136	2 918	2 882	2 725
Net written premiums								
Domestic undertakings	31 747	43 015	44 692	47 118	48 005	48 931	52 465	56 052
Foreign controlled undertakings	3 472	3 606	4 136	4 470	4 779	5 091	5 737	..
Foreign companies (branches)	0	0	0	..	..	..	..	..
All undertakings	31 747	43 015	44 692	47 118	48 005	48 931	52 465	56 052
1.1.2 Insurance business on foreign risks, gross premiums								
Life	6 786	3 510	0	0	0	0	0	0
Non-life	41 886	43 506	2 528	2 632	2 156	2 563	3 018	1 010
Composite total	..	..	..	..	..	..	..	..
Total	48 673	47 016	2 528	2 632	2 156	2 563	3 018	1 010
1.1.3 Life insurance payments, by class, gross premiums								
Annuities	47	65	57	61	61	111	473	..
Unit linked	108	104	110	87	86	87	91	20
Other life insurance	3 118	3 216	3 227	3 532	3 913	4 042	4 087	5 141
Total life insurance	3 273	3 385	3 395	3 680	4 061	4 240	4 651	5 161
***of which:** Pension contracts*	0	0	0	0	0	0	0	0
1.1.4 Non-life insurance payments, by class, gross premiums								
Motor vehicle insurance	20 424	20 479	20 205	21 226	21 522	22 084	23 952	28 398
Marine, aviation and other transport insurance	2 204	2 483	2 629	2 746	3 372	3 419	3 690	3 631
Freight insurance	577	602	632	667	638	646	751	0
Fire and other property damage insurance	11 557	12 193	12 838	14 028	13 816	13 903	13 911	12 484
Pecuniary loss insurance	58	77	100	77	45	23	27	33
General liability insurance	2 452	2 372	2 782	2 932	2 556	2 565	2 672	3 078
Accident and health	4 707	5 012	5 318	5 108	5 102	4 947	5 646	5 960
***of which:** Health*	717	..	..	..	..	..	..	..
Other non-life insurance	0	12	27	27	30	22	42	32
Treaty reinsurance	0	0	0	0	0	0	0	0
Total non-life insurance	41 980	43 230	44 530	46 809	47 081	47 608	50 690	53 616
1.2 Gross claims payments								
Life								
Domestic undertakings	1 101	882	1 139	1 434	1 381	1 529	1 325	1 690
Foreign controlled undertakings	26	15	21	56	47	30	58	..
Foreign companies (branches)	..	0	..	..	..	..	..	..
All undertakings	1 101	882	1 139	1 434	1 381	1 529	1 325	1 690
Non-life								
Domestic undertakings	33 871	27 092	28 721	30 190	31 417	32 554	36 082	41 655
Foreign controlled undertakings	2 858	2 859	3 132	2 931	3 412	3 520	4 169	..
Foreign companies (branches)	0	0	..	..	..	..	..	..
All undertakings	33 871	27 092	28 721	30 190	31 417	32 554	36 082	41 655
Composite, all undertakings	..	..	..	..	..	..	..	..
Total								
Domestic undertakings	34 972	27 974	29 861	31 624	32 798	34 083	37 407	43 345
Foreign controlled undertakings	2 884	2 874	3 152	2 987	3 459	3 550	4 227	..
Foreign companies (branches)	0	0	..	..	..	..	..	..
All undertakings	34 972	27 974	29 861	31 624	32 798	34 083	37 407	43 345

Iceland
Table 1. Selected aggregates *(cont.)*

Million ISK

	2009	2010	2011	2012	2013	2014	2015	2016
1.3 Commissions								
Life								
Domestic undertakings	57	41	74	71	66	118	90	..
Foreign controlled undertakings	4	6	4	12	20	42	3	..
Foreign companies (branches)	..	0	..	..	..	..	..	..
All undertakings	57	41	74	71	66	118	90	..
Non-life								
Domestic undertakings	168	121	101	122	102	39	36	..
Foreign controlled undertakings	20	0	0	0	0	0	0	..
Foreign companies (branches)	0	0	..	..	..	..	..	..
All undertakings	168	121	101	122	102	39	36	..
Composite, all undertakings	..	..	..	..	..	..	..	..
Total								
Domestic undertakings	224	162	175	193	168	157	126	..
Foreign controlled undertakings	24	6	4	12	20	42	3	..
Foreign companies (branches)	0	0	..	..	..	..	..	..
All undertakings	224	162	175	193	168	157	126	..
1.4 Gross operating expenses								
Life								
Domestic undertakings	782	851	945	1 119	1 384	1 098	1 498	1 231
Foreign controlled undertakings	43	52	57	77	90	18	161	..
Foreign companies (branches)	..	0	..	..	..	..	..	..
All undertakings	782	851	945	1 119	1 384	1 098	1 498	1 231
Non-life								
Domestic undertakings	7 646	8 563	9 081	9 987	9 860	9 680	4 314	6 931
Foreign controlled undertakings	785	859	965	996	1 084	1 086	1 225	..
Foreign companies (branches)	0	0	..	..	..	..	..	..
All undertakings	7 646	8 563	9 081	9 987	9 860	9 680	4 314	6 931
Composite, all undertakings	..	..	..	..	..	..	..	..
Total								
Domestic undertakings	8 428	9 414	10 027	11 106	11 244	10 778	5 812	8 162
Foreign controlled undertakings	828	911	1 022	1 072	1 173	1 104	1 387	..
Foreign companies (branches)	0	0	..	..	..	..	..	..
All undertakings	8 428	9 414	10 027	11 106	11 244	10 778	5 812	8 162
1.5 Insurance business written abroad by branches, gross premiums								
Life								
Branches and agencies	0	0	0	0	..	..	..	..
Subsidaries	0	0	0	0	..	..	..	..
Total	0	0	0	0	..	..	..	..
Non-life								
Branches and agencies	0	277	551	914	..	..	..	..
Subsidaries	0	0	0	0	..	..	..	..
Total	0	277	551	914	..	..	..	..
Composite total	..	..	..	..	..	..	..	..
Total								
Branches and agencies	0	277	551	914	..	..	..	..
Subsidaries	0	0	0	0	..	..	..	..
Total	0	277	551	914	..	..	..	..

.. Not available

Note: Detailed metadata at: http://metalinks.oecd.org/ins/20180621/00f0.

Disclaimer: http://oe.cd/disclaimer

Source: OECD Insurance Statistics (database)

Iceland
Table 2. Number of companies and employees

	2009	2010	2011	2012	2013	2014	2015	2016
2.1 Number of companies								
Life								
Domestic undertakings	5	5	5	5	5	5	5	4
Foreign controlled undertakings	1	1	1	1	1	1	1	..
Foreign companies (branches)	0	0	0	1	1	1	1	..
All undertakings	5	5	5	6	6	6	6	4
Non-life								
Domestic undertakings	6	6	6	6	5	5	5	4
Foreign controlled undertakings	1	1	1	1	1	1	1	..
Foreign companies (branches)	0	0	0	1	1	1	1	..
All undertakings	6	6	6	7	6	6	6	4
Composite, all undertakings	**0**	**0**	**0**	**0**	**0**	**0**	**0**	**0**
Reinsurance								
Domestic undertakings	2	2	2	2	2	2	2	0
Foreign controlled undertakings	0	0	0	0	..	..	..	..
Foreign companies (branches)	0	0	0	0	..	..	..	..
All undertakings	2	2	2	2	2	2	2	0
Total								
Domestic undertakings	13	13	13	13	12	12	12	8
Foreign controlled undertakings	2	2	2	2	2	2	2	0
Foreign companies (branches)	0	0	0	2	2	2	2	0
All undertakings	13	13	13	15	14	14	14	8
2.2 Number of employees								
Insurance undertakings	615	617	652	641	614	..	582	..
Intermediaries	..	..	0	..	..	592	..	..
Total	617	617	652	..	614	592	582	..

.. Not available

Note: Detailed metadata at: http://metalinks.oecd.org/ins/20180621/00f0.

Disclaimer: http://oe.cd/disclaimer

Source: OECD Insurance Statistics (database)

Ireland
Table 1. Selected aggregates

Million EUR

	2009	2010	2011	2012	2013	2014	2015	2016
1.1 Insurance business written in the reporting country								
1.1.1 Insurance business, by ownership								
Gross premiums								
Domestic undertakings	32 162	31 340	30 304	33 133	31 818	36 377	40 340	48 949
Foreign controlled undertakings	..	0	..	..	..	..	..	..
Foreign companies (branches)	1 425	2 840	1 731	2 348	2 301	3 184	3 645	..
All undertakings	33 587	34 180	32 035	35 481	34 119	39 561	43 985	48 949
Premiums ceded								
Domestic undertakings	3 068	2 950	3 478	3 755	3 908	3 891	4 933	9 985
Foreign controlled undertakings	..	0	..	..	..	..	..	..
Foreign companies (branches)	283	800	772	356	268	371	359	..
All undertakings	3 351	3 750	4 250	4 111	4 176	4 262	5 292	9 985
Net written premiums								
Domestic undertakings	29 094	28 390	26 826	29 379	27 910	32 486	35 407	38 964
Foreign controlled undertakings	..	0	..	..	..	..	..	..
Foreign companies (branches)	1 142	2 040	960	1 992	2 033	2 813	3 286	..
All undertakings	30 236	30 430	27 786	31 371	29 943	35 299	38 693	38 964
1.1.2 Insurance business on foreign risks, gross premiums								
Life	14 534	15 779	15 627	15 038	16 125	21 410	23 192	..
Non-life	2 868	3 016	3 195	3 676	3 826	3 960	4 263	..
Composite total	..	..	..	..	..	..	..	..
Total	17 402	18 796	18 821	18 714	19 951	25 370	27 455	..
1.1.3 Life insurance payments, by class, gross premiums								
Annuities	..	..	..	..	..	..	..	0
Unit linked	..	..	..	..	..	..	..	28 838
Other life insurance	..	..	..	..	..	..	..	4 477
Total life insurance	..	..	..	28 140	27 207	32 171	34 587	33 315
***of which:** Pension contracts*	..	..	..	..	..	..	..	..
1.1.4 Non-life insurance payments, by class, gross premiums								
Motor vehicle insurance	1 687	1 649	1 423	1 486	1 435	1 599	1 795	3 905
Marine, aviation and other transport insurance	175	204	237	243	183	143	163	421
Freight insurance	..	..	0	..	..	..	..	0
Fire and other property damage insurance	1 667	1 785	1 728	1 906	1 763	1 758	1 768	4 023
Pecuniary loss insurance	91	47	67	..	105	124	92	332
General liability insurance	1 133	1 108	1 072	1 147	1 127	1 301	1 400	2 887
Accident and health	1 278	1 267	1 432	1 288	1 171	1 235	2 750	1 935
***of which:** Health*	..	..	..	..	..	..	..	..
Other non-life insurance	474	518	485	563	504	494	585	1 159
Treaty reinsurance	137	168	284	374	330	373	414	746
Total non-life insurance	6 642	6 745	6 729	7 007	6 618	7 027	8 967	15 408
1.2 Gross claims payments								
Life								
Domestic undertakings	16 760	21 393	..	27 921	28 263	27 434	28 474	32 280
Foreign controlled undertakings	..	0	..	..	..	..	..	..
Foreign companies (branches)	1 095	626	..	..	1 235	1 114	1 356	..
All undertakings	17 855	22 019	..	27 921	29 498	28 548	29 830	32 280
Non-life								
Domestic undertakings	4 196	4 438	4 938	4 842	4 369	3 853	5 343	15 941
Foreign controlled undertakings	..	0	..	..	..	..	..	..
Foreign companies (branches)	38	474	1 023	983	677	1 177	1 179	..
All undertakings	4 234	4 912	5 961	5 825	5 046	5 030	6 522	15 941
Composite, all undertakings	..	..	..	..	..	..	..	..
Total								
Domestic undertakings	20 956	25 831	4 938	32 763	32 632	31 287	33 817	48 221
Foreign controlled undertakings	..	0	..	..	..	..	..	..
Foreign companies (branches)	1 133	1 099	1 023	983	1 912	2 291	2 535	..
All undertakings	22 089	26 931	5 961	33 746	34 544	33 578	36 352	48 221
1.3 Commissions								
Life								
Domestic undertakings	1 371	1 310	..	1 593	1 844	2 051	2 281	2 198
Foreign controlled undertakings	..	0	..	..	..	..	..	..
Foreign companies (branches)	37	25	..	..	43	64	59	..
All undertakings	1 408	1 335	..	1 593	1 887	2 115	2 340	2 108
Non-life								
Domestic undertakings	857	767	764	657	737	764	896	2 292
Foreign controlled undertakings	..	0	..	..	..	..	..	..
Foreign companies (branches)	120	130	104	171	130	248	299	..
All undertakings	977	897	868	828	867	1 012	1 195	2 292
Composite, all undertakings	..	..	..	..	..	..	..	..
Total								
Domestic undertakings	2 228	2 077	764	2 250	2 581	2 815	3 177	4 490
Foreign controlled undertakings	..	0	..	..	..	..	..	..
Foreign companies (branches)	157	155	104	171	173	312	358	..
All undertakings	2 385	2 232	868	2 420	2 754	3 127	3 535	4 490

Ireland
Table 1. Selected aggregates *(cont.)*

Million EUR

	2009	2010	2011	2012	2013	2014	2015	2016
1.4 Gross operating expenses								
Life								
Domestic undertakings	1 152	1 127	..	1 268	1 346	1 429	1 437	1 319
Foreign controlled undertakings	..	0	..	..	..	..	..	..
Foreign companies (branches)	99	68	..	..	154	657	158	..
All undertakings	1 251	1 195	..	1 268	1 500	2 086	1 595	1 319
Non-life								
Domestic undertakings	668	726	688	622	650	589	484	1 873
Foreign controlled undertakings	..	0	..	..	..	..	..	..
Foreign companies (branches)	72	79	186	295	159	223	224	..
All undertakings	740	805	874	917	809	812	708	1 873
Composite, all undertakings	..	..	..	..	..	..	..	..
Total								
Domestic undertakings	1 820	1 853	688	1 891	1 996	2 018	1 921	3 192
Foreign controlled undertakings	..	0	..	..	..	..	..	..
Foreign companies (branches)	171	147	186	295	313	880	382	..
All undertakings	1 991	2 000	874	2 185	2 309	2 898	2 303	3 192
1.5 Insurance business written abroad by branches, gross premiums								
Life								
Branches and agencies	3 026	3 701	2 434	3 422	5 563	5 970	6 234	..
Subsidaries	..	0	..	..	..	..	..	..
Total	3 026	3 701	2 434	3 422	5 563	5 970	6 234	..
Non-life								
Branches and agencies	5 322	8 628	9 626	9 599	9 228	9 640	9 835	..
Subsidaries	..	0	..	..	..	..	..	..
Total	5 322	8 628	9 626	9 599	9 228	9 640	9 835	..
Composite total	..	..	..	..	..	..	..	..
Total								
Branches and agencies	8 348	12 329	12 060	13 021	14 791	15 610	16 069	..
Subsidaries	..	0	..	..	..	..	..	..
Total	8 348	12 329	12 060	13 021	14 791	15 610	16 069	..

.. Not available

Note: Detailed metadata at: http://metalinks.oecd.org/ins/20180621/c8db.

Disclaimer: http://oe.cd/disclaimer

Source: OECD Insurance Statistics (database)

Ireland
Table 2. Number of companies and employees

	2009	2010	2011	2012	2013	2014	2015	2016
2.1 Number of companies								
Life								
Domestic undertakings	59	61	62	55	53	51	48	44
Foreign controlled undertakings	..	0	0	0	..	..	..	0
Foreign companies (branches)	10	10	9	8	8	8	11	11
All undertakings	69	71	71	63	61	59	59	55
Non-life								
Domestic undertakings	129	123	121	111	104	102	101	90
Foreign controlled undertakings	..	0	0	0	..	..	..	0
Foreign companies (branches)	29	30	28	28	27	30	32	31
All undertakings	158	153	149	139	131	132	133	121
Composite, all undertakings	**0**	**0**	**0**	**0**	**0**	**0**	**0**	**0**
Reinsurance								
Domestic undertakings	120	115	102	87	77	75	67	61
Foreign controlled undertakings	..	0	0	0	..	..	..	0
Foreign companies (branches)	0	3	0	0	0	0	0	0
All undertakings	120	118	102	87	77	75	67	61
Total								
Domestic undertakings	..	299	285	253	234	228	216	196
Foreign controlled undertakings	..	0	..	..	..	..	..	0
Foreign companies (branches)	..	43	37	36	35	38	43	42
All undertakings	..	342	322	289	269	266	259	238
2.2 Number of employees								
Insurance undertakings	11 476	10 626	9 696	8 682	8 887	8 095	9 404	..
Intermediaries	..	..	..	..	..	..	..	..
Total	..	..	9 696	8 682	8 887	..	..	..

.. Not available

Note: Detailed metadata at: http://metalinks.oecd.org/ins/20180621/c8db.

Disclaimer: http://oe.cd/disclaimer

Source: OECD Insurance Statistics (database)

Israel
Table 1. Selected aggregates

Million ILS

	2009	2010	2011	2012	2013	2014	2015	2016
1.1 Insurance business written in the reporting country								
1.1.1 Insurance business, by ownership								
Gross premiums								
Domestic undertakings	40 320	42 003	45 317	48 086	50 339	51 400	54 869	58 153
Foreign controlled undertakings	8 397	8 903	9 663	840	889	953	1 135	1 165
Foreign companies (branches)	0	0	..	..	..	..	..	..
All undertakings	40 320	42 003	45 317	48 086	50 339	51 400	54 869	58 153
Premiums ceded								
Domestic undertakings	6 367	5 868	6 529	6 877	6 418	5 934	6 356	8 756
Foreign controlled undertakings	..	816	894	185	164	162	232	225
Foreign companies (branches)	..	..	..	..	..	..	..	..
All undertakings	6 367	5 868	6 529	6 877	6 418	5 934	6 356	8 756
Net written premiums								
Domestic undertakings	33 953	36 135	38 788	41 209	43 921	45 466	48 512	49 398
Foreign controlled undertakings	8 397	8 087	8 769	656	726	791	903	940
Foreign companies (branches)	0	..	..	..	..	..	..	..
All undertakings	33 953	36 135	38 788	41 209	43 921	45 466	48 512	49 398
1.1.2 Insurance business on foreign risks, gross premiums								
Life	0	..	..	..	..	..	..	..
Non-life	2 234	..	..	..	..	..	..	..
Composite	38 085	..	3	..	..	..	..	..
of which:								
Life	19 785	..	..	..	..	..	..	..
Non-life	18 300	..	3	..	..	..	..	..
Total	40 320	..	3	..	..	..	..	..
1.1.3 Life insurance payments, by class, gross premiums								
Annuities	1 445	1 772	1 593	1 542	1 361	1 194	1 084	1 273
Unit linked	13 950	14 974	16 662	17 673	18 557	18 236	20 266	20 897
Other life insurance	4 373	4 911	5 654	6 242	6 709	7 141	8 066	8 492
Total life insurance	19 768	21 656	23 909	25 458	26 627	26 571	29 416	30 662
***of which:** Pension contracts*	13 512	14 762	..	..	..	..	..	..
1.1.4 Non-life insurance payments, by class, gross premiums								
Motor vehicle insurance	10 201	9 867	10 358	10 673	11 040	11 439	11 775	13 053
Marine, aviation and other transport insurance	44	43	41	41	38	38	39	38
Freight insurance	156	160	173	180	169	170	174	176
Fire and other property damage insurance	3 256	3 326	3 475	4 082	4 283	4 292	4 238	4 375
Pecuniary loss insurance	209	226	0	277	284	278	307	335
General liability insurance	2 343	2 353	2 354	2 487	2 575	2 697	2 814	2 917
Accident and health	3 402	3 607	3 950	4 396	4 869	5 425	5 678	6 086
***of which:** Health*	2 930	3 066	..	3 580	3 859	4 189	4 203	4 448
Other non-life insurance	927	766	1 056	492	452	492	426	502
Treaty reinsurance	0	0	..	..	..	0	0	0
Total non-life insurance	20 538	20 347	21 408	22 628	23 712	24 830	25 452	27 483

Israel
Table 1. Selected aggregates (*cont.*)

Million ILS

	2009	2010	2011	2012	2013	2014	2015	2016
1.2 Gross claims payments								
Life								
Domestic undertakings	..	..	..	..	0	3	6	8
Foreign controlled undertakings	..	0	..	..	..	..	..	0
Foreign companies (branches)	..	..	..	..	..	..	..	..
All undertakings	..	0	..	..	0	3	6	8
Non-life								
Domestic undertakings	1 082	1 138	1 303	1 395	2 013	2 470	2 589	2 180
Foreign controlled undertakings	12	0	..	..	..	..	39	72
Foreign companies (branches)	..	..	..	..	..	..	..	..
All undertakings	1 082	1 138	1 303	1 395	2 013	2 470	2 589	2 180
Composite								
Domestic undertakings	21 015	22 199	24 636	25 830	24 594	27 644	30 828	31 879
Foreign controlled undertakings	4 256	4 398	5 004	393	280	462	640	538
Foreign companies (branches)	..	..	..	..	..	..	..	..
All undertakings	21 015	22 199	24 636	25 830	24 594	27 644	30 828	31 879
of which:								
Life	9 208	10 349	11 651	12 472	12 644	13 825	15 363	16 243
Domestic undertakings	9 208	10 349	11 651	12 472	12 644	13 825	15 363	16 243
Foreign controlled undertakings	2 716	3 054	3 564	27	18	26	39	36
Foreign companies (branches)	..	..	..	..	..	..	..	..
All undertakings	9 208	10 349	11 651	12 472	12 644	13 825	15 363	16 243
Non-life	11 807	11 849	12 985	13 358	11 949	13 819	15 465	15 636
Domestic undertakings	11 807	11 849	12 985	13 358	11 949	13 819	15 465	15 636
Foreign controlled undertakings	1 540	1 344	1 440	366	262	436	600	502
Foreign companies (branches)	..	..	..	..	..	..	..	..
All undertakings	11 807	11 849	12 985	13 358	11 949	13 819	15 465	15 636
Total								
Domestic undertakings	22 096	23 337	25 939	27 225	26 607	30 117	33 422	34 067
Foreign controlled undertakings	4 268	4 398	5 004	393	280	462	679	609
Foreign companies (branches)	..	..	..	..	..	..	..	..
All undertakings	22 096	23 337	25 939	27 225	26 607	30 117	33 422	34 067
1.3 Commissions								
Life								
Domestic undertakings	..	0	..	..	0	6	15	19
Foreign controlled undertakings	..	0	..	..	..	..	..	0
Foreign companies (branches)	..	..	..	..	..	..	..	..
All undertakings	..	0	..	..	0	6	15	19
Non-life								
Domestic undertakings	143	1 138	159	175	248	281	317	291
Foreign controlled undertakings	0	0	..	..	..	..	0	0
Foreign companies (branches)	..	..	..	..	..	..	..	..
All undertakings	143	1 138	159	175	248	281	317	291
Composite								
Domestic undertakings	4 497	4 783	5 070	5 512	5 688	5 940	6 296	6 709
Foreign controlled undertakings	844	897	947	41	39	..	42	40
Foreign companies (branches)	..	..	..	..	..	..	..	..
All undertakings	4 497	4 783	5 070	5 512	5 688	5 940	6 296	6 709
of which:								
Life	2 011	2 201	2 328	2 577	2 571	2 639	2 912	3 097
Domestic undertakings	2 011	2 201	2 328	2 577	2 571	2 639	2 912	3 097
Foreign controlled undertakings	571	614	635	1	1	1	1	1
Foreign companies (branches)	..	..	..	..	..	..	..	..
All undertakings	2 011	2 201	2 328	2 577	2 571	2 639	2 912	3 097
Non-life	2 486	2 583	2 742	2 936	3 118	3 300	3 384	3 612
Domestic undertakings	2 486	2 583	2 742	2 936	3 118	3 300	3 384	3 612
Foreign controlled undertakings	273	283	312	40	38	38	41	39
Foreign companies (branches)	..	..	..	..	..	..	..	..
All undertakings	2 486	2 583	2 742	2 936	3 118	3 300	3 384	3 612
Total								
Domestic undertakings	4 640	5 921	5 229	5 688	5 936	6 226	6 628	7 019
Foreign controlled undertakings	844	897	947	41	39	..	42	40
Foreign companies (branches)	..	..	..	..	..	..	..	..
All undertakings	4 640	5 921	5 229	5 688	5 936	6 226	6 628	7 019

Israel
Table 1. Selected aggregates *(cont.)*

Million ILS

	2009	2010	2011	2012	2013	2014	2015	2016
1.4 Gross operating expenses								
Life								
Domestic undertakings	..	0	..	..	1	10	32	32
Foreign controlled undertakings	..	0	..	..	..	..	..	0
Foreign companies (branches)	..	..	..	..	..	..	..	..
All undertakings	..	0	..	..	1	10	32	32
Non-life								
Domestic undertakings	250 |	184	306	305	449	322	402	380
Foreign controlled undertakings	24 |	0	..	..	..	..	30	29
Foreign companies (branches)	..	..	..	..	..	..	..	..
All undertakings	250 |	184	306	305	449	322	402	380
Composite								
Domestic undertakings	3 798 |	4 136	5 198	5 270	5 285	5 169	5 719	6 033
Foreign controlled undertakings	812 |	881	1 158	260	272	276	282	275
Foreign companies (branches)	..	..	..	..	..	..	..	..
All undertakings	3 798 |	4 136	5 198	5 270	5 285	5 169	5 719	6 033
of which:								
Life	1 784 |	1 965	2 104	2 323	2 542	2 608	2 790	2 707
Domestic undertakings	1 784 |	1 965	2 104	2 323	2 542	2 608	2 790	2 707
Foreign controlled undertakings	465 |	521	565	53	61	56	54	55
Foreign companies (branches)	..	..	..	..	..	..	..	..
All undertakings	1 784 |	1 965	2 104	2 323	2 542	2 608	2 790	2 707
Non-life	2 014 |	2 172	2 445	2 373	2 502	2 561	2 721	2 785
Domestic undertakings	2 014 |	2 172	2 445	2 373	2 502	2 561	2 721	2 785
Foreign controlled undertakings	347 |	360	368	208	212	220	228	220
Foreign companies (branches)	..	..	..	..	..	..	..	..
All undertakings	2 014 |	2 172	2 445	2 373	2 502	2 561	2 721	2 785
Total								
Domestic undertakings	4 048	4 321	5 504	5 574	5 736	5 501	6 153	6 445
Foreign controlled undertakings	836	881	1 158	260	272	276	312	304
Foreign companies (branches)	..	..	..	..	..	..	..	..
All undertakings	4 048	4 321	5 504	5 574	5 736	5 501	6 153	6 445
1.5 Insurance business written abroad by branches, gross premiums								
Life								
Branches and agencies	..	..	..	..	..	..	..	..
Subsidaries	..	..	..	..	..	..	..	..
Total	..	..	..	..	..	..	..	..
Non-life								
Branches and agencies	..	..	..	..	..	..	..	..
Subsidaries	..	..	..	..	..	..	..	..
Total	..	..	..	..	..	..	..	..
Composite								
Branches and agencies	..	..	..	..	..	..	..	..
Subsidaries	..	..	..	..	..	..	..	..
Total	..	..	..	..	..	..	..	..
of which:								
Life	..	..	..	..	..	..	..	..
Branches and agencies	..	..	..	..	..	..	..	..
Subsidaries	..	..	..	..	..	..	..	..
Total	..	..	..	..	..	..	..	..
Non-life	..	..	..	..	..	..	..	..
Branches and agencies	..	..	..	..	..	..	..	..
Subsidaries	..	..	..	..	..	..	..	..
Total	..	..	..	..	..	..	..	..
Total								
Branches and agencies	..	..	..	..	..	..	..	..
Subsidaries	..	..	..	..	..	..	..	..
Total	..	..	..	..	..	..	..	..

.. Not available; | Break in series

Note: Detailed metadata at: http://metalinks.oecd.org/ins/20180621/22a5.

The statistical data for Israel are supplied by and under the responsibility of the relevant Israeli authorities. The use of such data by the OECD is without prejudice to the status of the Golan Heights, East Jerusalem and Israeli settlements in the West Bank under the terms of international law.

Disclaimer: http://oe.cd/disclaimer

Source: OECD Insurance Statistics (database)

Israel
Table 2. Number of companies and employees

	2009	2010	2011	2012	2013	2014	2015	2016
2.1 Number of companies								
Life								
Domestic undertakings	0	..	..	..	1	1	2	2
Foreign controlled undertakings	..	..	..	..	..	..	0	..
Foreign companies (branches)	..	..	..	..	..	..	0	..
All undertakings	..	0	..	..	1	1	2	2
Non-life								
Domestic undertakings	11	11	10	10	12	12	10	10
Foreign controlled undertakings	1	..	..	..	..	..	1	1
Foreign companies (branches)	2	2	..	2	2	3	3	3
All undertakings	13	13	10	12	14	15	13	13
Composite								
Domestic undertakings	13	13	13	13	10	10	11	10
Foreign controlled undertakings	2	3	2	1	1	1	1	1
Foreign companies (branches)	..	..	2	..	..	..	0	..
All undertakings	..	13	15	13	10	10	11	10
Reinsurance								
Domestic undertakings	0	0	..	..	..	..	0	..
Foreign controlled undertakings	..	..	..	..	..	..	0	..
Foreign companies (branches)	..	..	..	..	..	..	0	..
All undertakings	..	0	..	..	..	0	0	0
Total								
Domestic undertakings	24	24	23	23	23	23	23	22
Foreign controlled undertakings	3	3	2	1	1	1	2	..
Foreign companies (branches)	2	2	2	2	2	3	3	3
All undertakings	13	26	25	25	25	26	26	25
2.2 Number of employees								
Insurance undertakings	..	..	..	..	..	..	..	..
Intermediaries	..	..	..	..	..	..	..	..
Total	..	..	..	..	..	..	..	..

.. Not available

Note: Detailed metadata at: http://metalinks.oecd.org/ins/20180621/22a5.

The statistical data for Israel are supplied by and under the responsibility of the relevant Israeli authorities. The use of such data by the OECD is without prejudice to the status of the Golan Heights, East Jerusalem and Israeli settlements in the West Bank under the terms of international law

Disclaimer: http://oe.cd/disclaimer

Source: OECD Insurance Statistics (database)

Italy
Table 1. Selected aggregates

Million EUR

	2009	2010	2011	2012	2013	2014	2015	2016
1.1 Insurance business written in the reporting country								
1.1.1 Insurance business, by ownership								
Gross premiums								
Domestic undertakings	118 279	127 810	112 362	107 192	120 973	145 244	149 011	136 278
Foreign controlled undertakings	34 921	37 340	32 577	29 138	34 302	44 419	45 694	44 287
Foreign companies (branches)	1 818	355	416	399	373	375	473	521
All undertakings	120 097	128 165	112 778	107 591	121 345	145 619	149 484	136 799
Premiums ceded								
Domestic undertakings	5 436	5 257	5 043	5 178	4 513	4 203	4 079	4 914
Foreign controlled undertakings	669	1 624	1 166	1 392	1 116	991	983	1 822
Foreign companies (branches)	92	52	57	45	49	58	53	62
All undertakings	5 528	5 308	5 099	5 223	4 563	4 262	4 132	4 976
Net written premiums								
Domestic undertakings	112 843	122 553	107 319	102 014	116 459	141 041	144 932	131 364
Foreign controlled undertakings	34 251	35 715	31 411	27 746	33 186	43 428	44 711	42 465
Foreign companies (branches)	1 726	304	359	354	323	317	420	459
All undertakings	114 569	122 857	107 678	102 368	116 782	141 358	145 352	131 823
1.1.2 Insurance business on foreign risks, gross premiums								
Life	8 |	6	1	0	1	1	1	1
Non-life	79 |	88	60	50	53	59	54	59
Composite	1 356 |	1 554	1 608	1 935	2 044	1 904	2 016	2 070
of which:								
Life	1 020 |	1 216	1 213	1 327	1 232	1 073	1 166	1 255
Non-life	336 |	339	395	607	811	831	849	814
Total	1 442	1 648	1 670	1 984	2 098	1 963	2 071	2 130
1.1.3 Life insurance payments, by class, gross premiums								
Annuities	1 253	1 077	1 309	1 243	1 012	956	737	710
Unit linked	9 732	15 409	12 496	13 800	15 497	21 829	31 884	23 848
Other life insurance	70 130	73 627	60 064	54 597	68 501	87 639	82 220	77 596
Total life insurance	81 116	90 114	73 869	69 639	85 010	110 424	114 842	102 154
***of which:** Pension contracts*	3 548	4 026	4 116	4 296	3 825	4 873	5 492	5 848
1.1.4 Non-life insurance payments, by class, gross premiums								
Motor vehicle insurance	20 169	19 886	20 815	20 247	18 661	17 468	16 590	16 260
Marine, aviation and other transport insurance	473	461	432	366	327	334	326	417
Freight insurance	243	225	234	227	208	212	204	198
Fire and other property damage insurance	5 184	5 090	5 127	5 056	5 269	5 611	5 544	5 863
Pecuniary loss insurance	1 434	1 319	1 223	961	967	1 018	1 034	1 119
General liability insurance	3 384	3 006	2 979	2 972	2 905	2 879	2 952	3 073
Accident and health	5 428	5 281	5 306	5 151	5 144	5 221	5 415	5 868
***of which:** Health*	2 230	2 210	2 229	2 150	2 114	2 149	2 323	2 655
Other non-life insurance	922	897	944	698	1 163	988	1 082	1 217
Treaty reinsurance	227	240	275	417	0	0	0	0
Total non-life insurance	37 463	36 405	37 333	36 095	34 646	33 730	33 147	34 015

Italy
Table 1. Selected aggregates (*cont.*)

Million EUR

	2009	2010	2011	2012	2013	2014	2015	2016
1.2 Gross claims payments								
Life								
Domestic undertakings	21 489	28 862	31 179	29 764	23 754	22 852	22 955	21 169
Foreign controlled undertakings	8 319	9 213	14 849	14 078	11 058	10 413	12 229	10 866
Foreign companies (branches)	0	0	0	0	0	0	0	0
All undertakings	21 489	28 862	31 179	29 764	23 754	22 852	22 955	21 169
Non-life								
Domestic undertakings	5 736	5 907	5 191	5 084	5 061	5 016	4 931	4 776
Foreign controlled undertakings	1 892	1 767	1 748	1 802	1 758	1 853	2 005	2 008
Foreign companies (branches)	1 319	217	249	257	231	257	308	369
All undertakings	7 055	6 124	5 440	5 341	5 292	5 273	5 240	5 144
Composite								
Domestic undertakings	58 580	59 344	66 523	67 451	64 138	61 204	65 892	59 690
Foreign controlled undertakings	16 313	16 318	17 536	16 282	16 899	14 972	16 842	16 097
Foreign companies (branches)	0	0	0	0	0	0	0	0
All undertakings	58 580	59 344	66 523	67 451	64 138	61 204	65 892	59 690
of which:								
Life	36 286	37 621	45 192	47 143	44 754	43 279	48 546	43 755
Domestic undertakings	36 286	37 621	45 192	47 143	44 754	43 279	48 546	43 755
Foreign controlled undertakings	10 864	11 065	12 633	11 858	12 685	11 217	12 693	12 061
Foreign companies (branches)	0	0	0	0	0	0	0	0
All undertakings	36 286	37 621	45 192	47 143	44 754	43 279	48 546	43 755
Non-life	22 294	21 723	21 330	20 308	19 384	17 925	17 346	15 935
Domestic undertakings	22 294	21 723	21 330	20 308	19 384	17 925	17 346	15 935
Foreign controlled undertakings	5 448	217	4 903	4 424	4 215	3 754	4 149	4 037
Foreign companies (branches)	0	0	0	0	0	0	0	0
All undertakings	22 294	21 723	21 330	20 308	19 384	17 925	17 346	15 935
Total								
Domestic undertakings	85 805	94 113	102 893	102 298	92 953	89 071	93 778	85 635
Foreign controlled undertakings	26 524	27 298	34 132	32 162	29 715	27 238	31 075	28 972
Foreign companies (branches)	1 319	217	249	257	231	257	308	369
All undertakings	87 124	94 331	103 141	102 555	93 185	89 328	94 087	86 003
1.3 Commissions								
Life								
Domestic undertakings	886	988	727	601	576	650	641	626
Foreign controlled undertakings	565	607	532	405	384	430	436	449
Foreign companies (branches)	0	0	0	0	0	0	0	0
All undertakings	886	988	727	601	576	650	641	626
Non-life								
Domestic undertakings	1 777	1 932	1 721	1 620	1 576	1 656	1 706	1 748
Foreign controlled undertakings	628	655	629	560	548	608	734	767
Foreign companies (branches)	336	72	82	78	73	72	93	107
All undertakings	2 113	2 004	1 803	1 698	1 649	1 729	1 799	1 855
Composite								
Domestic undertakings	7 468	7 578	7 516	7 101	7 278	7 573	7 699	7 571
Foreign controlled undertakings	2 094	2 041	1 916	1 778	1 830	1 978	2 106	2 006
Foreign companies (branches)	0	0	0	0	0	0	0	0
All undertakings	7 468	7 578	7 516	7 101	7 278	7 573	7 699	7 571
of which:								
Life	2 313	2 384	2 187	1 868	2 088	2 273	2 447	2 306
Domestic undertakings	2 313	2 384	2 187	1 868	2 088	2 273	2 447	2 306
Foreign controlled undertakings	746	696	560	413	450	510	542	504
Foreign companies (branches)	0	0	0	0	0	0	0	0
All undertakings	2 313	2 384	2 187	1 868	2 088	2 273	2 447	2 306
Non-life	5 155	5 194	5 329	5 232	5 190	5 300	5 251	5 265
Domestic undertakings	5 155	5 194	5 329	5 232	5 190	5 300	5 251	5 265
Foreign controlled undertakings	1 348	1 346	1 356	1 366	1 380	1 468	1 564	1 502
Foreign companies (branches)	0	0	0	0	0	0	0	0
All undertakings	5 155	5 194	5 329	5 232	5 190	5 300	5 251	5 265
Total								
Domestic undertakings	10 131	10 498	9 964	9 322	9 431	9 879	10 046	9 945
Foreign controlled undertakings	3 288	3 304	3 078	2 743	2 763	3 015	3 277	3 222
Foreign companies (branches)	336	72	82	78	73	72	93	107
All undertakings	10 466	10 570	10 046	9 399	9 504	9 952	10 139	10 052

Italy
Table 1. Selected aggregates *(cont.)*

Million EUR

	2009	2010	2011	2012	2013	2014	2015	2016
1.4 Gross operating expenses								
Life								
Domestic undertakings	1 172	1 310	1 033	912	876	953	948	963
Foreign controlled undertakings	724	778	734	600	570	622	634	673
Foreign companies (branches)	0	0	0	0	0	0	0	0
All undertakings	1 172	1 310	1 033	912	876	953	948	963
Non-life								
Domestic undertakings	2 410	2 443	2 324	2 168	2 154	2 252	2 332	2 390
Foreign controlled undertakings	874	884	873	750	794	818	968	1 012
Foreign companies (branches)	512	109	119	115	112	110	144	176
All undertakings	2 922	2 552	2 442	2 283	2 266	2 362	2 476	2 565
Composite								
Domestic undertakings	9 289	9 367	9 381	9 321	9 490	9 686	9 829	9 860
Foreign controlled undertakings	2 533	2 485	2 363	2 304	2 294	2 443	2 632	2 566
Foreign companies (branches)	0	0	0	0	0	0	0	0
All undertakings	9 289	9 367	9 381	9 321	9 490	9 686	9 829	9 860
of which:								
Life	3 006	3 069	2 867	2 788	2 970	3 109	3 292	3 196
Domestic undertakings	3 006	3 069	2 867	2 788	2 970	3 109	3 292	3 196
Foreign controlled undertakings	905	857	724	635	628	696	743	708
Foreign companies (branches)	0	0	0	0	0	0	0	0
All undertakings	3 006	3 069	2 867	2 788	2 970	3 109	3 292	3 196
Non-life	6 284	6 299	6 514	6 532	6 520	6 577	6 537	6 664
Domestic undertakings	6 284	6 299	6 514	6 532	6 520	6 577	6 537	6 664
Foreign controlled undertakings	1 629	1 628	1 639	1 669	1 667	1 747	1 889	1 858
Foreign companies (branches)	0	0	0	0	0	0	0	0
All undertakings	6 284	6 299	6 514	6 532	6 520	6 577	6 537	6 664
Total								
Domestic undertakings	12 871	13 121	12 737	12 401	12 520	12 891	13 109	13 213
Foreign controlled undertakings	4 131	4 147	3 971	3 653	3 658	3 883	4 234	4 251
Foreign companies (branches)	512	109	119	115	112	110	144	176
All undertakings	13 384	13 229	12 856	12 516	12 633	13 001	13 253	13 388
1.5 Insurance business written abroad by branches, gross premiums								
Life								
Branches and agencies	0	0	0	0	0	1	1	3
Subsidaries	1 175	1 327	1 938	2 813	3 333	3 469	4 224	1 339
Total	1 175	1 327	1 938	2 813	3 333	3 469	4 226	1 342
Non-life								
Branches and agencies	28	22	24	9	12	12	9	10
Subsidaries	0	29	0	0	0	0	0	0
Total	28	51	24	9	12	12	9	10
Composite								
Branches and agencies	603	667	717	762	823	892	868	1 376
Subsidaries	57 773	58 418	56 657	57 155	56 340	54 902	58 541	57 863
Total	58 376	59 085	57 375	57 917	57 163	55 795	59 409	59 239
of which:								
Life	40 905	41 238	38 781	39 265	39 445	39 878	42 059	41 554
Branches and agencies	83	88	106	127	154	175	235	477
Subsidaries	40 821	41 151	38 675	39 138	39 291	39 703	41 824	41 077
Total	40 905	41 238	38 781	39 265	39 445	39 878	42 059	41 554
Non-life	17 471	17 847	18 593	18 652	17 718	15 917	17 350	17 685
Branches and agencies	520	579	611	634	668	718	633	899
Subsidaries	16 952	17 268	17 982	18 018	17 049	15 199	16 717	16 785
Total	17 471	17 847	18 593	18 652	17 718	15 917	17 350	17 685
Total								
Branches and agencies	631	689	741	771	835	905	878	1 390
Subsidaries	58 948	59 775	58 596	59 968	59 673	58 371	62 765	59 202
Total	59 579	60 464	59 337	60 739	60 508	59 276	63 643	60 592

| Break in series

Note: Detailed metadata at: http://metalinks.oecd.org/ins/20180621/8db0.

Disclaimer: http://oe.cd/disclaimer

Source: OECD Insurance Statistics (database)

Italy
Table 2. Number of companies and employees

	2009	2010	2011	2012	2013	2014	2015	2016
2.1 Number of companies								
Life								
Domestic undertakings	48	45	43	41	41	38	35	32
Foreign controlled undertakings	25	23	24	23	23	20	19	17
Foreign companies (branches)	16	20	21	20	17	19	20	22
All undertakings	64	65	64	61	58	57	55	54
Non-life								
Domestic undertakings	77	76	71	69	67	63	58	54
Foreign controlled undertakings	29	25	24	21	20	18	19	18
Foreign companies (branches)	53	55	59	61	65	60	65	65
All undertakings	130	131	130	130	132	123	123	119
Composite								
Domestic undertakings	31	30	28	25	23	21	21	21
Foreign controlled undertakings	10	10	11	9	8	8	9	10
Foreign companies (branches)	9	9	9	12	13	14	14	13
All undertakings	40	39	37	37	36	35	35	34
Reinsurance								
Domestic undertakings	0	0	0	0	0	0	0	0
Foreign controlled undertakings	0	0	0	0	0	0	0	0
Foreign companies (branches)	7	7	8	7	7	7	7	7
All undertakings	7	7	8	7	7	7	7	7
Total								
Domestic undertakings	156	151	142	135	131	122	114	107
Foreign controlled undertakings	64	58	59	53	51	46	47	45
Foreign companies (branches)	85	91	97	100	102	100	106	107
All undertakings	241	242	239	235	233	222	220	214
2.2 Number of employees								
Insurance undertakings	41 549	41 234	40 817	40 798	39 887	40 259	40 588	40 872
Intermediaries	220 903	221 417	226 235	220 130	227 444	220 288	220 850	212 596
Total	262 452	262 651	267 052	260 928	267 331	260 547	261 438	253 468

Note: Detailed metadata at: http://metalinks.oecd.org/ins/20180621/8db0.
Disclaimer: http://oe.cd/disclaimer
Source: OECD Insurance Statistics (database)

Japan
Table 1. Selected aggregates

Million JPY

	2009	2010	2011	2012	2013	2014	2015	2016
1.1 Insurance business written in the reporting country								
1.1.1 Insurance business, by ownership								
Gross premiums								
Domestic undertakings	41 054 599	40 592 027	41 906 428	44 184 695	42 971 395	46 031 579	46 908 456	42 615 488
Foreign controlled undertakings	4 138 808	3 937 600	4 089 357	6 746 278	6 184 716	6 724 592	7 046 820	6 617 836
Foreign companies (branches)	3 051 836	3 184 939	4 051 225	2 028 538	1 699 621	1 548 143	1 537 624	1 703 444
All undertakings	44 106 435	43 776 966	45 360 413	37 140 563	34 738 150	37 222 352	37 748 110	44 318 932
Premiums ceded								
Domestic undertakings	2 236 509	2 211 394	2 596 877	3 820 152	3 823 919	4 207 229	4 127 260	4 449 638
Foreign controlled undertakings	852 369	827 426	1 012 341	2 083 368	1 802 239	2 084 233	1 890 218	2 143 727
Foreign companies (branches)	438 803	381 244	554 339	20 507	38 391	47 768	75 917	214 477
All undertakings	2 675 312	2 592 633	3 041 779	2 188 965	1 780 848	2 129 106	2 022 086	4 664 115
Net written premiums								
Domestic undertakings	38 818 088	38 380 635	39 309 551	40 364 544	39 147 476	41 824 350	42 781 196	38 165 836
Foreign controlled undertakings	3 286 440	3 080 177	3 077 014	4 662 910	4 382 477	4 640 359	5 156 602	4 474 105
Foreign companies (branches)	2 614 781	2 804 409	3 500 605	2 008 031	1 661 230	1 500 375	1 461 707	1 488 976
All undertakings	41 432 869	41 185 044	42 322 354	34 951 598	32 957 302	35 093 246	35 726 024	39 654 812
1.1.2 Insurance business on foreign risks, gross premiums								
Life	..	..	..	..	..	..	..	..
Non-life	..	..	..	..	..	..	..	..
Composite total	..	..	..	..	..	..	..	..
Total	..	..	..	..	..	..	..	..
1.1.3 Life insurance payments, by class, gross premiums								
Annuities	..	..	..	4 374 166	4 312 468	5 154 122	4 729 892	4 340 846
Unit linked	..	..	..	..	..	..	..	..
Other life insurance	..	..	..	29 076 673	27 864 772	30 015 418	31 464 495	27 968 949
Total life insurance	34 116 113	34 454 319	35 863 385	33 450 839	32 177 240	35 169 540	36 194 387	32 309 795
***of which:** Pension contracts*	..	..	..	3 683 892	3 851 878	4 175 622	4 562 867	3 057 696
1.1.4 Non-life insurance payments, by class, gross premiums								
Motor vehicle insurance	3 642 285	3 541 931	3 650 671	5 268 338	5 632 807	5 786 949	5 916 489	6 026 253
Marine, aviation and other transport insurance	316 510	305 343	305 977	149 531	170 502	170 115	186 542	159 142
Freight insurance	76 230	64 556	67 288	217 090	242 939	248 817	242 488	230 397
Fire and other property damage insurance	1 560 319	1 619 666	1 762 054	1 787 943	1 983 049	2 104 111	2 228 178	..
Pecuniary loss insurance	..	..	..	216 797	266 835	299 082	342 570	..
General liability insurance	503 436	521 081	535 395	519 985	584 318	598 945	615 167	633 290
Accident and health	857 015	1 211 200	1 262 653	780 078	897 507	979 477	982 614	..
***of which:** Health*	..	..	..	-216	76	214	-152	..
Other non-life insurance	..	..	2 096 987	132 908	154 909	169 874	183 922	..
Treaty reinsurance	..	..	..	..	..	..	..	..
Total non-life insurance	9 049 235	7 263 777	9 730 581	9 072 670	9 932 866	10 357 370	10 697 970	10 859 799
1.2 Gross claims payments								
Life								
Domestic undertakings	33 689 120	30 677 277	29 178 265	31 012 138	33 069 327	34 214 304	31 685 988	28 227 418
Foreign controlled undertakings	3 391 509	2 821 726	2 738 842	5 218 820	6 584 738	6 428 288	5 559 928	5 107 453
Foreign companies (branches)	2 129 021	1 372 136	1 583 330	673 623	709 471	738 243	768 206	786 644
All undertakings	35 818 141	32 049 413	30 761 595	31 685 761	33 778 798	34 952 547	32 454 194	29 014 062
Non-life								
Domestic undertakings	4 235 152	4 243 987	9 249 885	6 215 207	5 904 278	5 953 809	5 917 050	6 694 135
Foreign controlled undertakings	137 240	218 720	400 264	251 245	341 353	373 601	366 795	383 518
Foreign companies (branches)	58 211	174 446	366 743	..	..	..	..	104 648
All undertakings	4 293 363	4 418 433	9 616 628	..	..	..	..	6 798 783
Composite, all undertakings	..	..	..	..	..	..	..	..
Total								
Domestic undertakings	37 924 272	34 921 264	38 428 150	37 227 345	38 973 605	40 168 113	37 603 038	34 921 553
Foreign controlled undertakings	3 528 749	3 040 446	3 139 106	5 470 065	6 926 091	6 801 889	5 926 723	5 490 971
Foreign companies (branches)	2 187 232	1 546 582	1 950 073	673 623	709 471	738 243	768 206	891 292
All undertakings	40 111 504	36 467 846	40 378 223	31 685 761	33 778 798	34 952 547	32 454 194	35 812 845

Japan
Table 1. Selected aggregates *(cont.)*

Million JPY

	2009	2010	2011	2012	2013	2014	2015	2016
1.3 Commissions								
Life								
Domestic undertakings	..	..	..	..	..	..	..	..
Foreign controlled undertakings	..	..	..	..	..	..	..	..
Foreign companies (branches)	..	..	..	..	..	..	..	..
All undertakings	..	..	..	..	..	..	..	..
Non-life								
Domestic undertakings	1 248 888	1 190 122	1 241 891	1 141 653	1 149 357	1 229 205	1 273 631	1 240 454
Foreign controlled undertakings	17 123	70 683	71 775	48 003	25 883	33 975	37 223	20 067
Foreign companies (branches)	64 076	64 395	67 079	..	..	..	..	-19 897
All undertakings	1 312 964	1 254 517	1 308 970	..	..	..	..	1 220 557
Composite, all undertakings	..	..	..	..	..	..	..	..
Total								
Domestic undertakings	1 248 888	1 190 122	1 241 891	1 141 653	1 149 357	1 229 205	1 273 631	1 240 454
Foreign controlled undertakings	17 123	70 683	71 775	48 003	25 883	33 975	37 223	20 067
Foreign companies (branches)	64 076	64 395	67 079	..	..	..	..	-19 897
All undertakings	1 312 964	1 254 517	1 308 970	..	..	..	..	1 220 557
1.4 Gross operating expenses								
Life								
Domestic undertakings	3 815 075	3 768 382	3 679 493	4 030 195	4 068 896	4 178 568	4 356 425	4 369 595
Foreign controlled undertakings	567 522	529 937	494 700	838 416	862 622	893 811	945 921	948 132
Foreign companies (branches)	509 117	537 616	565 754	319 261	320 576	320 518	349 858	357 069
All undertakings	4 324 192	4 305 998	4 245 247	4 349 456	4 389 472	4 499 086	4 706 283	4 726 664
Non-life								
Domestic undertakings	1 744 828	1 637 090	1 688 096	1 229 758	3 034 716	3 189 416	3 275 358	3 247 478
Foreign controlled undertakings	30 565	87 975	85 470	69 136	176 725	238 092	249 835	207 689
Foreign companies (branches)	112 093	114 656	124 057	..	..	..	..	34 405
All undertakings	1 856 921	1 751 746	1 812 153	..	..	..	..	3 281 883
Composite, all undertakings	..	..	..	..	..	..	..	..
Total								
Domestic undertakings	5 559 903	5 405 472	5 367 589	5 259 953	7 103 612	7 367 984	7 631 783	7 617 073
Foreign controlled undertakings	598 087	617 912	580 170	907 552	1 039 347	1 131 903	1 195 756	1 155 821
Foreign companies (branches)	621 210	652 272	689 811	319 261	320 576	320 518	349 858	391 474
All undertakings	6 181 113	6 057 744	6 057 400	4 349 456	4 389 472	4 499 086	4 706 283	8 008 547
1.5 Insurance business written abroad by branches, gross premiums								
Life								
Branches and agencies	..	..	..	..	..	..	..	..
Subsidaries	..	..	..	..	..	..	..	..
Total	..	..	..	..	..	..	..	..
Non-life								
Branches and agencies	..	..	..	..	..	..	..	..
Subsidaries	..	..	..	..	..	..	..	..
Total	..	..	..	..	..	..	..	..
Composite total	..	..	..	..	..	..	..	..
Total								
Branches and agencies	..	..	..	..	..	..	..	..
Subsidaries	..	..	..	..	..	..	..	..
Total	..	..	..	..	..	..	..	..

.. Not available

Note: Detailed metadata at: http://metalinks.oecd.org/ins/20180621/0722.

Disclaimer: http://oe.cd/disclaimer

Source: OECD Insurance Statistics (database)

Japan
Table 2. Number of companies and employees

	2009	2010	2011	2012	2013	2014	2015	2016
2.1 Number of companies								
Life								
Domestic undertakings	42	43	39	40	40	39	38	38
Foreign controlled undertakings	15	15	14	15	15	13	13	13
Foreign companies (branches)	4	4	4	3	3	3	3	3
All undertakings	46	47	43	43	43	42	41	41
Non-life								
Domestic undertakings	30	28	29	30	30	30	30	30
Foreign controlled undertakings	4	5	5	5	6	7	7	7
Foreign companies (branches)	21	22	23	23	22	22	22	21
All undertakings	51	50	52	53	52	52	52	51
Composite, all undertakings	**0**	**0**	**0**	**0**	**0**	**0**	**0**	**0**
Reinsurance								
Domestic undertakings	..	..	2	..	..	..	..	..
Foreign controlled undertakings	..	..	0	..	..	..	..	..
Foreign companies (branches)	..	..	5	..	..	..	..	..
All undertakings	..	..	7	..	..	..	..	..
Total								
Domestic undertakings	..	..	..	..	..	..	68	68
Foreign controlled undertakings	..	..	..	..	..	..	20	20
Foreign companies (branches)	..	..	..	..	..	..	25	24
All undertakings	..	..	..	..	..	..	93	92
2.2 Number of employees								
Insurance undertakings	453 584	..	..	447 435	221 675	226 043	120 353	..
Intermediaries	..	..	..	..	2 283 335	2 293 863	2 059 743	..
Total	..	..	..	..	2 505 010	2 519 906	2 080 096	..

.. Not available

Note: Detailed metadata at: http://metalinks.oecd.org/ins/20180621/0722.

Disclaimer: http://oe.cd/disclaimer

Source: OECD Insurance Statistics (database)

Korea
Table 1. Selected aggregates

Million KRW

	2009	2010	2011	2012	2013	2014	2015	2016
1.1 Insurance business written in the reporting country								
1.1.1 Insurance business, by ownership								
Gross premiums								
Domestic undertakings	122 132 179	135 405 614	148 670 607	179 792 881	180 479 019	192 380 611	205 460 047	210 800 275
Foreign controlled undertakings	14 088 283	14 764 615	15 090 753	16 543 211	15 928 630	13 324 532	15 765 302	16 670 208
Foreign companies (branches)	4 270 391	4 250 510	4 083 506	3 894 692	4 755 050	4 594 745	2 267 929	4 629 847
All undertakings	126 402 570	139 656 124	152 754 113	183 687 573	185 234 069	196 975 356	207 727 976	215 430 122
Premiums ceded								
Domestic undertakings	8 454 320	8 248 307	7 618 035	8 770 133	9 411 425	9 694 294	10 255 858	10 505 959
Foreign controlled undertakings	546 607	529 774	322 429	581 696	538 227	478 174	638 961	599 183
Foreign companies (branches)	553 407	407 499	614 890	448 135	456 049	651 726	732 347	817 712
All undertakings	9 007 727	8 655 806	8 232 925	9 218 268	9 867 474	10 346 020	10 988 205	11 323 671
Net written premiums								
Domestic undertakings	113 677 859	127 157 307	141 052 572	171 022 748	171 067 594	182 686 317	195 204 189	200 294 316
Foreign controlled undertakings	13 541 676	14 234 841	14 768 324	15 961 515	15 390 403	12 846 358	15 126 341	16 071 025
Foreign companies (branches)	3 716 984	3 843 011	3 468 616	3 446 557	4 299 001	3 943 019	1 535 582	3 812 135
All undertakings	117 394 843	131 000 318	144 521 188	174 469 305	175 366 595	186 629 336	196 739 771	204 106 451
1.1.2 Insurance business on foreign risks, gross premiums								
Life	..	..	..	..	..	..	..	..
Non-life	8 061 186	1 393 220	..	..	..	..	..	..
Composite total	..	..	..	..	..	..	..	..
Total	8 061 186	1 393 220	..	..	..	..	..	..
1.1.3 Life insurance payments, by class, gross premiums								
Annuities	14 516 005	16 493 331	17 029 899	29 118 668	25 867 249	23 905 884	24 586 649	21 347 503
Unit linked	16 767 780	18 570 246	21 278 374	21 003 522	21 073 957	20 670 949	20 643 073	19 406 180
Other life insurance	44 163 041	45 875 642	48 349 089	57 004 710	61 618 265	65 998 453	71 983 930	79 057 566
Total life insurance	75 446 826	80 939 219	86 657 362	107 126 900	108 559 471	110 575 286	117 213 652	119 811 249
***of which:** Pension contracts*	2 944 502	4 037 523	7 039 411	6 187 541	8 103 216	11 817 288	13 694 337	16 718 996
1.1.4 Non-life insurance payments, by class, gross premiums								
Motor vehicle insurance	11 513 159	12 712 741	13 714 894	13 667 642	13 692 186	14 188 378	15 635 198	16 975 333
Marine, aviation and other transport insurance	1 169 236	1 079 971	1 173 162	1 249 845	1 062 919	1 006 367	971 854	854 536
Freight insurance	..	..	..	..	0	0	..	..
Fire and other property damage insurance	481 100	343 250	433 977	509 590	515 217	484 799	472 624	471 017
Pecuniary loss insurance	1 293 541	1 367 999	1 551 994	1 697 064	1 637 782	1 601 517	1 672 799	1 693 861
General liability insurance	775 149	834 878	828 088	870 395	947 583	910 341	967 362	1 100 438
Accident and health	12 398 730	14 665 164	16 518 450	18 558 162	49 501 658	24 196 315	39 104 233	30 297 640
***of which:** Health*	4 921 216	5 877 040	6 537 864	7 171 480	83 983	10 090 810	11 740 294	13 406 917
Other non-life insurance	20 344 004	25 457 371	30 630 990	38 774 054	8 105 434	32 685 216	30 357 048	42 702 138
Treaty reinsurance	..	..	..	..	0	0	..	..
Total non-life insurance	47 974 919	56 461 374	64 851 555	75 326 752	75 462 779	85 163 744	89 181 118	94 094 963
1.2 Gross claims payments								
Life								
Domestic undertakings	46 039 241	50 304 985	50 774 694	50 571 293	51 098 146	61 070 702	65 751 692	77 155 805
Foreign controlled undertakings	5 652 840	7 571 937	7 803 732	7 981 965	8 103 569	69 035 817	6 945 034	9 505 582
Foreign companies (branches)	1 180 688	1 268 464	1 295 108	1 251 467	1 252 924	1 292 842	1 333 124	1 410 493
All undertakings	47 219 929	51 573 449	52 069 802	51 822 760	52 351 070	62 363 544	67 084 816	78 566 298
Non-life								
Domestic undertakings	18 867 283	21 683 043	23 980 095	26 319 367	22 119 519	30 233 735	30 895 053	32 747 964
Foreign controlled undertakings	580 375	664 566	620 798	833 963	516 770	844 722	843 763	802 729
Foreign companies (branches)	1 052 992	1 043 797	919 952	914 946	7 033 799	1 098 087	1 264 227	1 282 459
All undertakings	19 920 275	22 726 840	24 900 047	27 234 313	29 153 318	31 331 823	32 159 280	34 030 423
Composite, all undertakings	..	..	..	..	..	..	..	..
Total								
Domestic undertakings	64 906 524	71 988 028	74 754 789	76 890 660	73 217 665	91 304 438	96 646 745	109 903 769
Foreign controlled undertakings	6 233 215	8 236 503	8 424 530	8 815 928	8 620 339	69 880 539	7 788 797	10 308 311
Foreign companies (branches)	2 233 680	2 312 261	2 215 060	2 166 413	8 286 723	2 390 929	2 597 351	2 692 952
All undertakings	67 140 204	74 300 289	76 969 849	79 057 073	81 504 388	93 695 367	99 244 096	112 596 721
1.3 Commissions								
Life								
Domestic undertakings	8 315 606	4 774 647	..	..	..	..	..	..
Foreign controlled undertakings	1 801 392	1 125 660	..	..	..	..	..	..
Foreign companies (branches)	324 907	43 548	..	..	..	..	..	..
All undertakings	8 640 513	4 818 195	..	..	..	..	..	..
Non-life								
Domestic undertakings	4 992 487	2 242 103	..	..	..	..	..	..
Foreign controlled undertakings	1 697	162 058	..	..	..	..	..	..
Foreign companies (branches)	13 541	68 803	..	..	..	..	..	..
All undertakings	5 006 028	2 310 906	..	..	..	..	..	..
Composite, all undertakings	..	..	..	..	..	..	..	..
Total								
Domestic undertakings	13 308 093	7 016 750	..	..	..	..	..	..
Foreign controlled undertakings	1 803 089	1 287 718	..	..	..	..	..	..
Foreign companies (branches)	338 448	112 351	..	..	..	..	..	..
All undertakings	13 646 541	7 129 101	..	..	..	..	..	..

Korea
Table 1. Selected aggregates *(cont.)*

Million KRW

	2009	2010	2011	2012	2013	2014	2015	2016
1.4 Gross operating expenses								
Life								
Domestic undertakings	18 170 539	19 832 046	27 793 931	23 307 641	25 608 456	27 511 983	28 987 407	28 236 989
Foreign controlled undertakings	4 094 498	4 698 261	7 229 266	5 189 114	5 278 175	806 034	756 903	5 074 779
Foreign companies (branches)	762 857	845 704	1 024 103	734 416	770 753	4 595 483	5 009 714	760 976
All undertakings	18 933 396	20 677 750	28 818 034	24 042 057	26 379 209	32 107 466	33 997 121	28 997 965
Non-life								
Domestic undertakings	9 308 928	9 722 605	9 820 687	11 569 785	11 294 192	16 760 436	13 511 865	14 238 364
Foreign controlled undertakings	151 338	174 348	121 666	320 770	129 781	245 017	182 669	163 724
Foreign companies (branches)	492 471	479 237	428 369	331 833	1 592 503	1 116 586	405 386	411 714
All undertakings	9 801 399	10 201 842	10 249 056	11 901 618	12 886 695	17 877 022	13 917 251	14 650 078
Composite, all undertakings	..	..	..	..	..	..	..	..
Total								
Domestic undertakings	27 479 467	29 554 651	37 614 618	34 877 426	36 902 648	44 272 419	42 499 272	42 475 353
Foreign controlled undertakings	4 245 836	4 872 609	7 350 932	5 509 884	5 407 956	1 051 051	939 572	5 238 503
Foreign companies (branches)	1 255 328	1 324 941	1 452 472	1 066 249	2 363 256	5 712 069	5 415 100	1 172 690
All undertakings	28 734 795	30 879 592	39 067 090	35 943 675	39 265 904	49 984 488	47 914 372	43 648 043
1.5 Insurance business written abroad by branches, gross premiums								
Life								
Branches and agencies	..	..	..	..	..	..	..	..
Subsidaries	..	..	..	..	..	..	..	..
Total	..	..	..	..	..	..	..	..
Non-life								
Branches and agencies	..	..	..	..	..	..	..	..
Subsidaries	..	..	..	..	..	..	..	..
Total	8 061 186	1 393 220	..	..	..	..	..	..
Composite total	..	..	..	..	..	..	..	..
Total								
Branches and agencies	..	..	..	..	..	..	..	..
Subsidaries	..	..	..	..	..	..	..	..
Total	8 061 186	1 393 220	..	..	..	..	..	..

.. Not available

Note: Detailed metadata at: http://metalinks.oecd.org/ins/20180621/0432.

Disclaimer: http://oe.cd/disclaimer

Source: OECD Insurance Statistics (database)

Korea
Table 2. Number of companies and employees

	2009	2010	2011	2012	2013	2014	2015	2016
2.1 Number of companies								
Life								
Domestic undertakings	21	22	22	23	24	24	24	24
Foreign controlled undertakings	8	8	8	8	8	7	7	8
Foreign companies (branches)	1	1	1	1	1	1	1	1
All undertakings	22	23	23	24	25	25	25	25
Non-life								
Domestic undertakings	15	15	15	16	16	17	17	17
Foreign controlled undertakings	3	3	6	6	3	4	4	4
Foreign companies (branches)	8	8	8	8	8	5	5	5
All undertakings	23	23	23	24	24	22	22	22
Composite, all undertakings	**0**	**0**	**0**	**0**	**0**	**0**	**0**	**0**
Reinsurance								
Domestic undertakings	1	1	1	1	1	1	1	1
Foreign controlled undertakings	0	0	0	..	..	0	0	0
Foreign companies (branches)	6	6	6	6	6	8	8	9
All undertakings	7	7	7	7	7	9	9	10
Total								
Domestic undertakings	37	38	38	40	41	42	42	42
Foreign controlled undertakings	11	11	14	14	11	11	11	12
Foreign companies (branches)	15	15	15	15	15	14	14	15
All undertakings	52	53	53	55	56	56	56	57
2.2 Number of employees								
Insurance undertakings	53 812	55 927	57 861	62 155	63 859	61 158	59 685	58 833
Intermediaries	227 919	270 786	278 594	288 362	280 087	245 127	235 319	229 292
Total	281 731	326 713	336 455	350 517	343 946	306 285	295 004	288 125

.. Not available

Note: Detailed metadata at: http://metalinks.oecd.org/ins/20180621/0432.

Disclaimer: http://oe.cd/disclaimer

Source: OECD Insurance Statistics (database)

Latvia
Table 1. Selected aggregates

Million EUR

	2009	2010	2011	2012	2013	2014	2015	2016
1.1 Insurance business written in the reporting country								
1.1.1 Insurance business, by ownership								
Gross premiums								
Domestic undertakings	318	271	326	354	350	371	379	357
Foreign controlled undertakings	173	164	137	155	150	151	188	259
Foreign companies (branches)	50	57	73	93	121	146	152	168
All undertakings	368	328	399	447	471	517	531	525
Premiums ceded								
Domestic undertakings	31	23	24	26	17	19	22	25
Foreign controlled undertakings	12	9	6	5	4	4	7	18
Foreign companies (branches)	..	..	..	..	..	..	..	0
All undertakings	31	23	24	26	17	19	22	25
Net written premiums								
Domestic undertakings	287	248	302	328	333	352	357	332
Foreign controlled undertakings	161	155	131	150	146	147	182	241
Foreign companies (branches)	50	57	73	93	121	146	152	168
All undertakings	338	305	375	421	454	498	509	500
1.1.2 Insurance business on foreign risks, gross premiums								
Life	..	..	..	..	..	..	..	0
Non-life	..	..	..	..	..	..	..	160
Composite total	..	..	..	..	..	..	..	0
Total	..	..	..	..	..	..	..	160
1.1.3 Life insurance payments, by class, gross premiums								
Annuities	3	3	0	0	0	0	0	11
Unit linked	14	28	23	21	23	34	43	39
Other life insurance	41	44	50	57	66	73	72	68
Total life insurance	58	75	74	79	89	107	115	117
***of which:** Pension contracts*	0	0	0	0	0	0	0	..
1.1.4 Non-life insurance payments, by class, gross premiums								
Motor vehicle insurance	174	137	184	204	221	222	221	228
Marine, aviation and other transport insurance	4	2	3	3	2	2	2	4
Freight insurance	2	2	5	6	5	3	3	1
Fire and other property damage insurance	46	47	55	63	67	86	84	76
Pecuniary loss insurance	7	7	12	12	11	13	14	12
General liability insurance	10	10	15	21	17	21	21	19
Accident and health	56	36	41	50	46	52	58	55
***of which:** Health*	45	31	34	42	38	42	48	47
Other non-life insurance	11	11	9	10	12	12	13	13
Treaty reinsurance	0	0	0	0	0	0	0	0
Total non-life insurance	310	252	325	368	382	411	416	408
1.2 Gross claims payments								
Life								
Domestic undertakings	31	21	15	19	31	26	29	0
Foreign controlled undertakings	17	20	15	18	26	24	27	0
Foreign companies (branches)	9	11	26	27	31	31	34	0
All undertakings	40	32	41	46	62	57	63	0
Non-life								
Domestic undertakings	188	137	164	169	165	184	198	180
Foreign controlled undertakings	104	79	78	75	68	77	92	139
Foreign companies (branches)	19	15	18	25	38	43	50	60
All undertakings	207	152	182	194	204	226	248	240
Composite, all undertakings	..	..	..	..	..	..	..	72
Total								
Domestic undertakings	219	158	179	188	196	209	227	213
Foreign controlled undertakings	122	99	92	93	94	102	119	166
Foreign companies (branches)	28	26	44	52	69	73	83	99
All undertakings	247	184	223	240	265	283	311	312

Latvia
Table 1. Selected aggregates *(cont.)*

Million EUR

	2009	2010	2011	2012	2013	2014	2015	2016
1.3 Commissions								
Life								
Domestic undertakings	31	2	0	1	1	1	0	0
Foreign controlled undertakings	..	2	0	1	1	1	1	0
Foreign companies (branches)	1	1	4	4	5	5	6	..
All undertakings	32	3	4	5	5	6	6	0
Non-life								
Domestic undertakings	188	19	33	38	32	45	34	32
Foreign controlled undertakings	..	5	2	5	..	7	11	16
Foreign companies (branches)	2	1	2	4	10	12	13	..
All undertakings	190	20	35	41	42	58	47	32
Composite, all undertakings	..	..	..	..	..	..	..	0
Total								
Domestic undertakings	219	21	33	38	33	46	34	33
Foreign controlled undertakings	..	6	2	6	1	8	11	16
Foreign companies (branches)	3	2	6	8	15	17	19	..
All undertakings	222	23	39	46	48	64	53	33
1.4 Gross operating expenses								
Life								
Domestic undertakings	7	7	5	4	4	4	4	0
Foreign controlled undertakings	2	6	4	4	4	4	4	0
Foreign companies (branches)	..	..	..	..	..	..	..	..
All undertakings	7	7	5	4	4	4	4	0
Non-life								
Domestic undertakings	109	88	100	110	102	108	109	88
Foreign controlled undertakings	61	48	43	45	40	40	51	46
Foreign companies (branches)	..	..	..	..	..	..	..	..
All undertakings	109	88	100	110	102	108	109	88
Composite, all undertakings	..	..	..	..	..	..	..	5
Total								
Domestic undertakings	116	95	104	115	106	112	113	93
Foreign controlled undertakings	63	54	47	49	44	44	55	49
Foreign companies (branches)	..	..	..	..	..	..	..	..
All undertakings	116	95	104	115	106	112	113	93
1.5 Insurance business written abroad by branches, gross premiums								
Life								
Branches and agencies	0	0	0	0	0	0	0	0
Subsidaries	..	..	..	..	..	..	..	0
Total	0	0	0	0	0	0	0	0
Non-life								
Branches and agencies	40	56	126	143	158	168	157	158
Subsidaries	..	..	..	..	..	..	..	0
Total	40	56	126	143	158	168	157	158
Composite total	..	..	..	..	..	..	..	0
Total								
Branches and agencies	40	56	126	143	158	168	157	158
Subsidaries	..	..	..	..	..	..	..	0
Total	40	56	126	143	158	168	157	158

.. Not available

Note: Detailed metadata at: http://metalinks.oecd.org/ins/20180621/05f1.

Disclaimer: http://oe.cd/disclaimer

Source: OECD Insurance Statistics (database)

Latvia
Table 2. Number of companies and employees

	2009	2010	2011	2012	2013	2014	2015	2016
2.1 Number of companies								
Life								
Domestic undertakings	4	4	3	2	2	2	2	0
Foreign controlled undertakings	1	2	1	1	1	1	1	0
Foreign companies (branches)	5	5	5	5	5	5	4	0
All undertakings	9	9	8	7	7	7	6	0
Non-life								
Domestic undertakings	10	9	9	7	5	5	6	5
Foreign controlled undertakings	4	4	4	3	2	2	3	3
Foreign companies (branches)	6	6	5	8	7	9	10	8
All undertakings	16	15	14	15	12	14	16	13
Composite, all undertakings	**0**	..	**0**	**0**	**0**	**0**	**0**	**6**
Reinsurance								
Domestic undertakings	0	0	0	0	0	0	0	0
Foreign controlled undertakings	0	0	0	0	0	0	0	0
Foreign companies (branches)	0	0	0	0	0	0	0	0
All undertakings	0	..	0	0	0	0	0	0
Total								
Domestic undertakings	14	13	12	9	7	7	8	7
Foreign controlled undertakings	5	6	5	4	3	3	4	4
Foreign companies (branches)	11	11	10	13	12	14	14	12
All undertakings	25	24	22	22	19	21	22	19
2.2 Number of employees								
Insurance undertakings	3 030	2 876	2 873	2 749	2 300	2 121	1 047	..
Intermediaries	1 708	1 254	1 195	1 168	846	773	905	..
Total	4 738	4 130	4 068	3 917	3 146	2 894	1 952	..

.. Not available

Note: Detailed metadata at: http://metalinks.oecd.org/ins/20180621/05f1.

Disclaimer: http://oe.cd/disclaimer

Source: OECD Insurance Statistics (database)

Luxembourg
Table 1. Selected aggregates

Million EUR

	2009	2010	2011	2012	2013	2014	2015	2016
1.1 Insurance business written in the reporting country								
1.1.1 Insurance business, by ownership								
Gross premiums								
Domestic undertakings	16 437	20 584	13 626	19 445	18 410	21 712	19 100	18 259
Foreign controlled undertakings	15 490	19 165	12 583	17 930	17 036	20 356	17 075	13 690
Foreign companies (branches)	165	133	150	144	191	76	78	70
All undertakings	16 602	20 717	13 776	19 589	18 601	21 788	19 178	18 329
Premiums ceded								
Domestic undertakings	4 425	5 362	2 935	6 109	4 624	6 122	3 030	3 235
Foreign controlled undertakings	4 299	5 220	2 737	5 892	4 246	5 863	2 770	2 943
Foreign companies (branches)	34	37	37	40	37	33	26	31
All undertakings	4 459	5 399	2 973	6 149	4 661	6 155	3 056	3 267
Net written premiums								
Domestic undertakings	12 012	15 222	10 691	13 336	13 787	15 590	16 070	15 024
Foreign controlled undertakings	11 191	13 945	9 846	12 037	12 790	14 493	14 305	10 747
Foreign companies (branches)	131	96	113	104	153	43	52	39
All undertakings	12 143	15 318	10 804	13 440	13 940	15 633	16 122	15 063
1.1.2 Insurance business on foreign risks, gross premiums								
Life	14 265	18 170	11 564	17 115	15 837	18 455	16 383	15 071
Non-life	410	426	547	476	572	438	587	621
Composite	0	0	0	..	0	0	0	0
of which:								
Life	0	0	0	..	0	0	0	0
Non-life	0	0	0	..	0	0	0	0
Total	14 675	18 596	12 112	17 591	16 408	18 893	16 969	15 692
1.1.3 Life insurance payments, by class, gross premiums								
Annuities	..	..	..	..	..	..	..	..
Unit linked	11 546	13 371	8 836	11 224	10 516	11 086	12 874	11 949
Other life insurance	..	..	3 382	6 826	6 413	9 103	4 685	4 767
Total life insurance	15 464	19 392	12 218	18 050	16 929	20 190	17 559	16 716
***of which:** Pension contracts*	..	19 392	..	..	..	..	..	..
1.1.4 Non-life insurance payments, by class, gross premiums								
Motor vehicle insurance	..	..	426	..	..	..	..	..
Marine, aviation and other transport insurance	..	..	0	..	..	..	..	..
Freight insurance	..	..	30	..	..	..	..	..
Fire and other property damage insurance	..	..	271	..	..	..	..	..
Pecuniary loss insurance	..	..	321	..	..	..	..	..
General liability insurance	..	..	106	..	..	..	..	..
Accident and health	..	..	90	..	..	..	..	..
***of which:** Health*	..	..	59	..	..	..	..	..
Other non-life insurance	..	..	53	..	..	..	..	..
Treaty reinsurance	..	..	27	..	..	..	..	..
Total non-life insurance	1 124	1 184	1 325	1 300	1 501	1 339	1 476	1 554
1.2 Gross claims payments								
Life								
Domestic undertakings	5 150	6 078	7 091	11 111	11 696	10 597	9 995	11 802
Foreign controlled undertakings	5 052	5 827	6 863	10 823	11 179	10 214	9 032	11 035
Foreign companies (branches)	4	9	34	10	25	25	27	28
All undertakings	5 154	6 087	7 125	11 122	11 721	10 622	10 023	11 829
Non-life								
Domestic undertakings	496	731	606	623	1 105	809	900	860
Foreign controlled undertakings	270	411	315	348	691	428	512	766
Foreign companies (branches)	25	27	31	27	39	36	18	31
All undertakings	521	758	637	650	1 143	845	918	891
Composite								
Domestic undertakings	0	0	0	..	0	0	0	0
Foreign controlled undertakings	0	0	0	..	0	0	0	0
Foreign companies (branches)	34	32	39	38	27	133	17	8
All undertakings	34	32	39	38	27	133	17	8
of which:								
Life	16	15	19	20	15	130	17	8
Domestic undertakings	0	0	0	..	0	0	0	0
Foreign controlled undertakings	0	0	0	..	0	0	0	0
Foreign companies (branches)	16	15	19	20	15	130	17	8
All undertakings	16	15	19	20	15	130	17	8
Non-life	18	17	20	18	12	3	0	0
Domestic undertakings	0	0	0	..	0	0	0	0
Foreign controlled undertakings	0	0	0	..	0	0	0	0
Foreign companies (branches)	18	17	20	18	12	3	0	0
All undertakings	18	17	20	18	12	3	0	0
Total								
Domestic undertakings	5 646	6 809	7 697	11 734	12 801	11 406	10 896	12 661
Foreign controlled undertakings	5 322	6 238	7 178	11 171	11 869	10 642	9 544	11 802
Foreign companies (branches)	63	68	104	76	90	195	62	66
All undertakings	5 709	6 878	7 800	11 810	12 891	11 600	10 958	12 728

Luxembourg
Table 1. Selected aggregates *(cont.)*

Million EUR

	2009	2010	2011	2012	2013	2014	2015	2016
1.3 Commissions								
Life								
Domestic undertakings	313	367	353	328	327	317	326	291
Foreign controlled undertakings	299	351	..	328	309	297	289	186
Foreign companies (branches)	0	0	0	0	0	0	0	0
All undertakings	314	367	353	328	328	317	326	292
Non-life								
Domestic undertakings	382	206	217	205	217	211	237	251
Foreign controlled undertakings	307	126	..	205	119	109	122	143
Foreign companies (branches)	9	11	12	11	12	9	9	9
All undertakings	391	217	229	217	229	221	246	260
Composite								
Domestic undertakings	0	0	0	..	0	0	0	0
Foreign controlled undertakings	0	0	..	..	0	0	0	0
Foreign companies (branches)	12	12	11	12	12	3	4	4
All undertakings	12	12	11	12	12	3	4	4
of which:								
Life	4	4	5	5	5	3	4	4
Domestic undertakings	0	0	0	..	0	0	0	0
Foreign controlled undertakings	0	0	..	..	0	0	0	0
Foreign companies (branches)	4	4	5	5	5	3	4	4
All undertakings	4	4	5	5	5	3	4	4
Non-life	8	8	7	7	7	0	0	0
Domestic undertakings	0	0	0	..	0	0	0	0
Foreign controlled undertakings	0	0	..	..	0	0	0	0
Foreign companies (branches)	8	8	7	7	7	0	0	0
All undertakings	8	8	7	7	7	0	0	0
Total								
Domestic undertakings	695	573	570	533	544	528	563	542
Foreign controlled undertakings	606	477	..	533	428	406	411	329
Foreign companies (branches)	21	23	23	24	25	13	14	14
All undertakings	716	596	593	557	569	541	576	556
1.4 Gross operating expenses								
Life								
Domestic undertakings	229	243	288	656	362	376	406	417
Foreign controlled undertakings	218	231	274	622	347	358	374	352
Foreign companies (branches)	0	0	0	0	0	1	0	1
All undertakings	229	243	288	656	362	376	406	418
Non-life								
Domestic undertakings	49	54	53	270	66	72	82	81
Foreign controlled undertakings	25	30	27	270	34	41	46	78
Foreign companies (branches)	3	14	3	14	3	2	2	3
All undertakings	52	68	55	285	69	74	84	84
Composite								
Domestic undertakings	0	0	0	..	0	0	0	0
Foreign controlled undertakings	0	0	0	..	0	0	0	0
Foreign companies (branches)	5	17	6	18	7	1	1	1
All undertakings	5	17	6	18	7	1	1	1
of which:								
Life	1	6	2	7	3	1	1	1
Domestic undertakings	0	0	0	..	0	0	0	0
Foreign controlled undertakings	0	0	0	..	0	0	0	0
Foreign companies (branches)	1	6	2	7	3	1	1	1
All undertakings	1	6	2	7	3	1	1	1
Non-life	3	12	3	11	4	0	0	0
Domestic undertakings	0	0	0	..	0	0	0	0
Foreign controlled undertakings	0	0	0	..	0	0	0	0
Foreign companies (branches)	3	12	3	11	4	0	0	0
All undertakings	3	12	3	11	4	0	0	0
Total								
Domestic undertakings	278	297	341	926	429	448	488	498
Foreign controlled undertakings	243	261	302	892	381	399	421	430
Foreign companies (branches)	8	31	8	33	9	4	3	4
All undertakings	286	328	349	959	438	451	491	502

Luxembourg
Table 1. Selected aggregates *(cont.)*

Million EUR

	2009	2010	2011	2012	2013	2014	2015	2016
1.5 Insurance business written abroad by branches, gross premiums								
Life								
Branches and agencies	2 355	2 830	2 161	2 619	2 648	3 250	3 552	4 622
Subsidaries	0	0	0	0	..	..	..	..
Total	2 355	2 830	2 161	2 619	2 648	3 250	3 552	4 622
Non-life								
Branches and agencies	1 014	1 122	1 088	1 417	1 546	1 831	1 965	2 022
Subsidaries	0	0	0	0	..	..	..	..
Total	1 014	1 122	1 088	1 417	1 546	1 831	1 965	2 022
Composite								
Branches and agencies	0	0	0	..	0	0	0	0
Subsidaries	0	0	0	..	..	..	..	..
Total	0	0	0	..	0	0	0	0
of which:								
Life	0	0	0	..	0	0	0	0
Branches and agencies	0	0	0	..	0	0	0	0
Subsidaries	0	0	0	..	..	..	..	..
Total	0	0	0	..	0	0	0	0
Non-life	0	0	0	..	0	0	0	0
Branches and agencies	0	0	0	..	0	0	0	0
Subsidaries	0	0	0	..	..	..	..	..
Total	0	0	0	..	0	0	0	0
Total								
Branches and agencies	3 369	3 952	3 250	4 036	4 194	5 082	5 516	6 644
Subsidaries	0	0	0	0	..	..	..	..
Total	3 369	3 952	3 250	4 036	4 194	5 082	5 516	6 644

.. Not available; | Break in series

Note: Detailed metadata at: http://metalinks.oecd.org/ins/20180621/2ed5.

Disclaimer: http://oe.cd/disclaimer

Source: OECD Insurance Statistics (database)

Luxembourg
Table 2. Number of companies and employees

	2009	2010	2011	2012	2013	2014	2015	2016
2.1 Number of companies								
Life								
Domestic undertakings	47	46	45	43	42	44	43	40
Foreign controlled undertakings	43	42	41	39	34	39	38	34
Foreign companies (branches)	2	2	2	1	2	2	2	3
All undertakings	49	48	47	44	44	46	45	43
Non-life								
Domestic undertakings	31	29	29	31	34	34	32	33
Foreign controlled undertakings	27	25	25	27	27	8	21	24
Foreign companies (branches)	10	11	10	11	10	10	10	10
All undertakings	41	40	39	42	44	44	42	43
Composite								
Domestic undertakings	0	0	0	0	0	0	0	0
Foreign controlled undertakings	0	0	0	0	0	0	0	0
Foreign companies (branches)	3	3	3	3	3	3	3	3
All undertakings	3	3	3	3	3	3	3	3
Reinsurance								
Domestic undertakings	251	244	242	238	226	224	217	208
Foreign controlled undertakings	234	225	222	219	207	205	204	191
Foreign companies (branches)	0	8	0	0	0	0	0	0
All undertakings	251	252	242	238	226	224	217	208
Total								
Domestic undertakings	329	319	316	312	302	302	292	281
Foreign controlled undertakings	304	292	288	285	268	252	263	249
Foreign companies (branches)	15	24	15	15	15	15	15	16
All undertakings	344	343	331	327	317	317	307	297
2.2 Number of employees								
Insurance undertakings	3 710	3 956	3 967	4 326	5 692	6 057	6 484	6 484
Intermediaries	9 503	9 859	9 375	9 659	10 030	550	561	522
Total	13 213	13 815	13 342	13 985	15 722	6 607	7 045	7 006

Note: Detailed metadata at: http://metalinks.oecd.org/ins/20180621/2ed5.

Disclaimer: http://oe.cd/disclaimer

Source: OECD Insurance Statistics (database)

Mexico
Table 1. Selected aggregates

Million MXN

	2009	2010	2011	2012	2013	2014	2015	2016
1.1 Insurance business written in the reporting country								
1.1.1 Insurance business, by ownership								
Gross premiums								
Domestic undertakings	236 860	247 010	281 792	310 747	347 196	363 530	395 083	450 740
Foreign controlled undertakings	143 428	153 858	167 708	189 698	207 890	220 225	242 872	265 159
Foreign companies (branches)	..	..	..	..	..	..	..	..
All undertakings	236 860	247 010	281 792	310 747	347 196	363 530	395 083	450 740
Premiums ceded								
Domestic undertakings	42 795	36 018	49 771	50 188	60 551	58 378	67 135	70 420
Foreign controlled undertakings	18 449	19 495	21 903	24 728	26 822	29 932	40 217	40 674
Foreign companies (branches)	..	..	..	..	..	..	..	..
All undertakings	42 795	36 018	49 771	50 188	60 551	58 378	67 135	70 420
Net written premiums								
Domestic undertakings	194 065	210 991	232 021	260 559	286 645	305 152	327 947	380 320
Foreign controlled undertakings	124 979	134 363	145 805	164 970	181 068	190 293	202 655	224 485
Foreign companies (branches)	..	..	..	..	..	..	..	..
All undertakings	194 065	210 991	232 021	260 559	286 645	305 152	327 947	380 320
1.1.2 Insurance business on foreign risks, gross premiums								
Life	..	..	..	..	..	..	..	..
Non-life	..	323	349	425	402	..	..	..
Composite	..	1 463	1 553	1 787	1 692	..	..	..
of which:								
Life	407 |	..	..	..	..	..	..	..
Non-life	1 052 |	..	..	..	..	..	..	..
Total	..	1 786	1 902	2 212	2 093	..	..	..
1.1.3 Life insurance payments, by class, gross premiums								
Annuities	..	15 849	15 749	17 633	20 099	20 521	19 719	19 286
Unit linked	..	0	..	..	..	..	..	..
Other life insurance	..	97 352	109 511	125 175	138 959	148 624	162 199	189 860
Total life insurance	103 431	113 201	125 260	142 808	159 058	169 145	181 918	209 146
***of which:** Pension contracts*	8 756	0	..	..	..	..	..	..
1.1.4 Non-life insurance payments, by class, gross premiums								
Motor vehicle insurance	46 947	50 357	56 099	62 944	66 562	68 735	75 858	91 375
Marine, aviation and other transport insurance	5 951	5 765	7 049	7 691	7 851	9 356	11 007	11 312
Freight insurance	..	..	..	..	..	..	..	..
Fire and other property damage insurance	16 884	8 026	14 010	9 980	16 520	12 232	13 815	14 497
Pecuniary loss insurance	518	636	686	749	5 210	501	947	1 131
General liability insurance	5 265	5 185	5 914	6 920	7 341	7 201	9 099	9 668
Accident and health	34 511	37 557	41 814	45 526	51 189	56 686	59 550	66 512
***of which:** Health*	1 631	1 626	1 835	1 918	2 682	2 719	2 622	3 218
Other non-life insurance	22 314	24 316	30 214	33 390	32 581	38 511	42 081	45 976
Treaty reinsurance	..	..	..	..	..	..	..	..
Total non-life insurance	132 389	131 842	155 785	167 200	187 253	193 221	212 357	240 470
1.2 Gross claims payments								
Life								
Domestic undertakings	8 634 |	9 487	9 566	10 279	11 800	12 325	13 760	14 829
Foreign controlled undertakings	3 784 |	4 314	4 663	..	..	5 875	6 443	6 971
Foreign companies (branches)	..	..	..	..	..	..	..	..
All undertakings	8 634 |	9 487	9 566	10 279	11 800	12 325	13 760	14 829
Non-life								
Domestic undertakings	13 280 |	14 463	14 750	14 874	21 716	17 912	19 552	23 827
Foreign controlled undertakings	4 819 |	5 042	4 751	..	..	4 093	4 923	5 515
Foreign companies (branches)	..	..	..	..	..	..	..	..
All undertakings	13 280 |	14 463	14 750	14 874	21 716	17 912	19 552	23 827
Composite								
Domestic undertakings	96 118 |	100 430	109 005	115 041	159 315	148 932	162 803	185 481
Foreign controlled undertakings	62 564 |	67 094	70 654	..	..	104 822	109 465	125 575
Foreign companies (branches)	..	..	..	..	..	..	..	..
All undertakings	96 118 |	100 430	109 005	115 041	159 315	148 932	162 803	185 481
of which:								
Life	47 586 |	48 676	50 966	55 436	76 467	81 643	88 136	101 700
Domestic undertakings	47 586 |	48 676	50 966	55 436	76 467	81 643	88 136	101 700
Foreign controlled undertakings	35 236 |	37 971	38 918	..	..	67 866	70 802	81 020
Foreign companies (branches)	..	..	..	..	..	..	..	..
All undertakings	47 586 |	48 676	50 966	55 436	76 467	81 643	88 136	101 700
Non-life	48 531 |	51 753	58 039	59 605	82 848	67 289	74 667	83 781
Domestic undertakings	48 531 |	51 753	58 039	59 605	82 848	67 289	74 667	83 781
Foreign controlled undertakings	27 328 |	29 122	31 736	..	..	36 968	38 662	44 546
Foreign companies (branches)	..	..	..	..	..	..	..	..
All undertakings	48 531 |	51 753	58 039	59 605	82 848	67 289	74 667	83 781
Total								
Domestic undertakings	118 032	124 380	133 321	140 195	192 832	179 169	196 115	224 138
Foreign controlled undertakings	71 168	76 449	80 068	..	..	114 791	120 830	138 061
Foreign companies (branches)	..	..	..	..	..	..	..	..
All undertakings	118 032	124 380	133 321	140 195	192 832	179 169	196 115	224 138

Mexico
Table 1. Selected aggregates *(cont.)*

Million MXN

	2009	2010	2011	2012	2013	2014	2015	2016
1.3 Commissions								
Life								
Domestic undertakings	1 053	976	1 257	1 133	1 075	749	1 045	1 155
Foreign controlled undertakings	324	234	268	277	251	74	192	247
Foreign companies (branches)	..	..	..	..	..	..	..	..
All undertakings	1 053	976	1 257	1 133	1 075	749	1 045	1 155
Non-life								
Domestic undertakings	4 811	5 078	5 935	6 911	8 410	9 458	7 257	9 473
Foreign controlled undertakings	2 073	2 230	2 373	2 721	3 523	3 808	1 888	1 618
Foreign companies (branches)	..	..	..	..	..	..	..	..
All undertakings	4 811	5 078	5 935	6 911	8 410	9 458	7 257	9 473
Composite								
Domestic undertakings	31 881	34 055	38 671	44 178	46 777	49 973	48 713	56 225
Foreign controlled undertakings	20 206	21 885	24 611	28 060	29 464	31 616	30 146	33 073
Foreign companies (branches)	..	..	..	..	..	..	..	..
All undertakings	31 881	34 055	38 671	44 178	46 777	49 973	48 713	56 225
of which:								
Life	12 184	13 741	15 773	18 508	19 316	21 023	22 507	26 955
Domestic undertakings	12 184	13 741	15 773	18 508	19 316	21 023	22 507	26 955
Foreign controlled undertakings	8 294	9 518	10 807	12 501	12 940	17 514	14 838	17 151
Foreign companies (branches)	..	..	..	..	..	..	..	..
All undertakings	12 184	13 741	15 773	18 508	19 316	21 023	22 507	26 955
Non-life	19 698	20 315	22 898	25 670	27 462	28 950	26 206	29 270
Domestic undertakings	19 698	20 315	22 898	25 670	27 462	28 950	26 206	29 270
Foreign controlled undertakings	11 694	12 367	13 803	15 559	16 524	14 103	15 308	15 922
Foreign companies (branches)	..	..	..	..	..	..	..	..
All undertakings	19 698	20 315	22 898	25 670	27 462	28 950	26 206	29 270
Total								
Domestic undertakings	37 746	40 110	45 863	52 222	56 263	60 180	57 016	66 853
Foreign controlled undertakings	22 603	24 349	27 251	31 058	33 239	35 498	32 226	34 937
Foreign companies (branches)	..	..	..	..	..	..	..	..
All undertakings	37 746	40 110	45 863	52 222	56 263	60 180	57 016	66 853
1.4 Gross operating expenses								
Life								
Domestic undertakings	634	942	1 095	1 313	1 486	1 156	1 336	1 705
Foreign controlled undertakings	305	530	675	..	..	570	661	723
Foreign companies (branches)	..	..	..	..	..	..	..	..
All undertakings	634	942	1 095	1 313	1 486	1 156	1 336	1 705
Non-life								
Domestic undertakings	2 656	2 353	2 337	2 968	3 545	4 198	4 924	5 852
Foreign controlled undertakings	1 290	1 220	1 402	..	..	2 010	3 137	3 249
Foreign companies (branches)	..	..	..	..	..	..	..	..
All undertakings	2 656	2 353	2 337	2 968	3 545	4 198	4 924	5 852
Composite								
Domestic undertakings	12 630	14 102	14 115	14 382	16 389	16 621	18 736	21 447
Foreign controlled undertakings	8 263	9 018	8 627	..	..	10 470	12 270	13 297
Foreign companies (branches)	..	..	..	..	..	..	..	..
All undertakings	12 630	14 102	14 115	14 382	16 389	16 621	18 736	21 447
of which:								
Life	5 917	6 925	6 838	7 085	8 530	8 486	9 990	11 792
Domestic undertakings	5 917	6 925	6 838	7 085	8 530	8 486	9 990	11 792
Foreign controlled undertakings	4 573	5 339	5 052	..	..	6 273	7 388	8 480
Foreign companies (branches)	..	..	..	..	..	..	..	..
All undertakings	5 917	6 925	6 838	7 085	8 530	8 486	9 990	11 792
Non-life	6 714	7 178	7 277	7 298	7 859	8 135	8 746	9 655
Domestic undertakings	6 714	7 178	7 277	7 298	7 859	8 135	8 746	9 655
Foreign controlled undertakings	3 674	3 679	3 575	..	..	4 198	4 882	4 818
Foreign companies (branches)	..	..	..	..	..	..	..	..
All undertakings	6 714	7 178	7 277	7 298	7 859	8 135	8 746	9 655
Total								
Domestic undertakings	15 920	17 398	17 548	18 662	21 420	21 974	24 996	29 004
Foreign controlled undertakings	9 859	10 768	10 704	..	..	13 050	16 068	17 270
Foreign companies (branches)	..	..	..	..	..	..	..	..
All undertakings	15 920	17 398	17 548	18 662	21 420	21 974	24 996	29 004

Mexico
Table 1. Selected aggregates *(cont.)*

Million MXN

	2009	2010	2011	2012	2013	2014	2015	2016
1.5 Insurance business written abroad by branches, gross premiums								
Life								
Branches and agencies	..	..	..	..	..	..	..	..
Subsidaries	..	..	..	..	..	..	..	..
Total	..	..	..	..	..	..	..	..
Non-life								
Branches and agencies	..	..	..	..	..	..	..	..
Subsidaries	..	..	..	..	..	..	..	..
Total	..	..	..	..	..	..	..	..
Composite								
Branches and agencies	..	..	..	..	..	..	..	..
Subsidaries	..	..	..	..	..	..	..	..
Total	..	..	..	..	..	..	..	..
of which:								
Life	..	..	..	..	..	..	..	..
Branches and agencies	..	..	..	..	..	..	..	..
Subsidaries	..	..	..	..	..	..	..	..
Total	..	..	..	..	..	..	..	..
Non-life	..	..	..	..	..	..	..	..
Branches and agencies	..	..	..	..	..	..	..	..
Subsidaries	..	..	..	..	..	..	..	..
Total	..	..	..	..	..	..	..	..
Total								
Branches and agencies	..	..	..	..	..	..	..	..
Subsidaries	..	..	..	..	..	..	..	..
Total	..	..	..	..	..	..	..	..

.. Not available; | Break in series

Note: Detailed metadata at: http://metalinks.oecd.org/ins/20180621/71bc.

Disclaimer: http://oe.cd/disclaimer

Source: OECD Insurance Statistics (database)

Mexico
Table 2. Number of companies and employees

	2009	2010	2011	2012	2013	2014	2015	2016
2.1 Number of companies								
Life								
Domestic undertakings	20	21	21	20	20	16	16	17
Foreign controlled undertakings	11	12	12	11	11	9	9	10
Foreign companies (branches)	..	..	..	..	..	..	..	..
All undertakings	20	21	21	20	20	16	16	17
Non-life								
Domestic undertakings	43	42	44	47	45	49	46	44
Foreign controlled undertakings	26	25	27	27	27	26	23	22
Foreign companies (branches)	..	..	..	..	..	..	..	..
All undertakings	43	42	44	47	45	49	46	44
Composite								
Domestic undertakings	33	34	35	35	37	38	37	37
Foreign controlled undertakings	20	21	20	21	21	22	21	20
Foreign companies (branches)	..	..	..	..	..	..	..	..
All undertakings	33	34	35	35	37	38	37	37
Reinsurance								
Domestic undertakings	2	2	2	2	2	2	3	2
Foreign controlled undertakings	0	0	..	0	0	0	0	0
Foreign companies (branches)	..	..	..	..	..	..	..	..
All undertakings	2	2	2	2	2	2	3	2
Total								
Domestic undertakings	98	99	102	104	104	105	102	100
Foreign controlled undertakings	57	58	59	59	59	57	53	52
Foreign companies (branches)	..	..	..	..	..	..	..	..
All undertakings	98	99	102	104	104	105	102	100
2.2 Number of employees								
Insurance undertakings	14 064	14 133	14 487	14 491	14 500	14 799	19 168	..
Intermediaries	33 186	34 265	35 173	36 190	46 712	51 780	55 005	57 900
Total	47 250	48 398	49 660	50 681	61 212	66 579	74 173	57 900

.. Not available

Note: Detailed metadata at: http://metalinks.oecd.org/ins/20180621/71bc.

Disclaimer: http://oe.cd/disclaimer

Source: OECD Insurance Statistics (database)

Netherlands
Table 1. Selected aggregates

Million EUR

	2009	2010	2011	2012	2013	2014	2015	2016
1.1 Insurance business written in the reporting country								
1.1.1 Insurance business, by ownership								
Gross premiums								
Domestic undertakings	47 256	38 602	41 183	39 012	38 077	36 523	33 708	..
Foreign controlled undertakings	8 469	7 430	9 625	9 255	7 674	2 969	5 812	..
Foreign companies (branches)	1 093	961	955	891	430	62	0	..
All undertakings	48 349	39 564	42 138	39 903	38 507	36 585	33 708	..
Premiums ceded								
Domestic undertakings	3 619	3 407	5 720	3 109	2 951	3 880	2 814	..
Foreign controlled undertakings	1 055	995	1 701	1 706	1 484	1 615	1 365	..
Foreign companies (branches)	48	42	116	79	20	0	0	..
All undertakings	3 667	3 449	5 836	3 188	2 971	3 880	2 814	..
Net written premiums								
Domestic undertakings	43 637	35 195	35 463	35 903	35 126	32 643	30 894	..
Foreign controlled undertakings	7 414	6 434	7 923	7 549	6 190	1 354	4 447	..
Foreign companies (branches)	1 045	919	839	812	410	62	0	..
All undertakings	44 682	36 115	36 302	36 715	35 536	32 705	30 894	..
1.1.2 Insurance business on foreign risks, gross premiums								
Life	..	..	..	..	..	..	..	..
Non-life	..	..	..	..	..	..	..	..
Composite total	..	..	..	..	..	..	..	..
Total	..	..	..	..	..	..	..	..
1.1.3 Life insurance payments, by class, gross premiums								
Annuities	12 960	12 058	12 001	10 892	10 998	10 806	9 035	..
Unit linked	8 474	7 758	9 332	7 836	7 086	6 504	5 533	..
Other life insurance	398	355	329	247	188	150	122	..
Total life insurance	21 832	20 171	21 662	18 975	18 272	17 460	14 690	..
***of which:** Pension contracts*	6 410	6 941	6 887	6 034	5 810	5 552	5 208	..
1.1.4 Non-life insurance payments, by class, gross premiums								
Motor vehicle insurance	4 539	4 635	4 587	4 500	4 376	3 934	3 884	..
Marine, aviation and other transport insurance	559	543	563	596	525	435	404	..
Freight insurance	299	275	291	263	256	231	191	..
Fire and other property damage insurance	3 675	3 732	3 515	3 698	3 664	3 449	3 456	..
Pecuniary loss insurance	428	1 192	309	278	206	164	176	..
General liability insurance	1 158	1 140	1 045	1 116	1 125	1 064	1 033	..
Accident and health	8 156	8 285	8 585	8 560	8 167	7 867	7 851	..
***of which:** Health*	..	..	..	..	..	..	..	..
Other non-life insurance	2 132	1 419	2 027	1 907	1 919	1 976	2 016	..
Treaty reinsurance	..	..	..	..	..	..	..	..
Total non-life insurance	20 946	21 221	20 923	20 918	20 238	19 120	19 011	..
1.2 Gross claims payments								
Life								
Domestic undertakings	21 698	21 020	23 689	25 331	24 085	25 487	22 576	..
Foreign controlled undertakings	3 178	3 870	3 206	3 538	3 205	1 136	4 504	..
Foreign companies (branches)	74	3 281	378	401	420	0	0	..
All undertakings	21 772	24 301	24 067	25 732	24 505	25 487	22 576	..
Non-life								
Domestic undertakings	13 994	13 434	13 957	13 999	14 304	13 666	13 806	..
Foreign controlled undertakings	3 292	2 046	2 840	2 870	2 915	867	1 937	..
Foreign companies (branches)	72	305	42	41	41	149	0	..
All undertakings	14 066	13 739	13 999	14 040	14 345	13 815	13 806	..
Composite, all undertakings	..	..	..	..	..	..	..	..
Total								
Domestic undertakings	35 692	34 454	37 646	39 330	38 389	39 153	36 382	..
Foreign controlled undertakings	6 470	5 916	6 046	6 408	6 120	2 003	6 441	..
Foreign companies (branches)	146	3 586	420	442	461	149	0	..
All undertakings	35 838	38 040	38 066	39 772	38 850	39 302	36 382	..
1.3 Commissions								
Life								
Domestic undertakings	825	605	614	473	243	190	158	..
Foreign controlled undertakings	379	342	325	196	64	17	49	..
Foreign companies (branches)	3	62	14	17	12	0	0	..
All undertakings	828	667	628	490	255	190	158	..
Non-life								
Domestic undertakings	3 054	2 999	3 070	3 197	2 891	2 713	2 663	..
Foreign controlled undertakings	579	682	851	833	734	282	464	..
Foreign companies (branches)	133	24	23	22	22	21	0	..
All undertakings	3 187	3 023	3 093	3 219	2 913	2 734	2 663	..
Composite, all undertakings	..	..	..	..	..	..	..	..
Total								
Domestic undertakings	3 879	3 604	3 684	3 670	3 134	2 903	2 821	..
Foreign controlled undertakings	958	1 024	1 176	1 029	798	299	513	..
Foreign companies (branches)	136	86	37	39	34	21	0	..
All undertakings	4 015	3 690	3 721	3 709	3 168	2 924	2 821	..

Netherlands
Table 1. Selected aggregates *(cont.)*

Million EUR

	2009	2010	2011	2012	2013	2014	2015	2016
1.4 Gross operating expenses								
Life								
Domestic undertakings	3 461	2 642	2 768	2 827	2 266	2 497	2 072	..
Foreign controlled undertakings	473	646	349	342	297	113	378	..
Foreign companies (branches)	8	488	59	37	44	0	0	..
All undertakings	3 469	3 130	2 827	2 864	2 310	2 497	2 072	..
Non-life								
Domestic undertakings	5 278	4 775	4 863	4 933	4 809	4 635	4 485	..
Foreign controlled undertakings	690	845	1 244	1 181	1 136	373	771	..
Foreign companies (branches)	146	26	25	24	25	23	0	..
All undertakings	5 424	4 801	4 888	4 957	4 834	4 658	4 485	..
Composite, all undertakings	..	..	..	..	..	..	..	..
Total								
Domestic undertakings	8 739	7 417	7 631	7 759	7 075	7 132	6 557	..
Foreign controlled undertakings	1 163	1 491	1 593	1 523	1 433	486	1 149	..
Foreign companies (branches)	154	514	84	61	69	23	0	..
All undertakings	8 893	7 931	7 715	7 820	7 144	7 155	6 557	..
1.5 Insurance business written abroad by branches, gross premiums								
Life								
Branches and agencies	..	621	662	540	370	276	..	..
Subsidaries	..	..	..	..	..	..	..	..
Total	..	621	662	540	370	276	267	..
Non-life								
Branches and agencies	1 684	1 789	1 067	1 276	1 132	1 289	..	..
Subsidaries	..	..	..	..	..	..	..	..
Total	..	1 789	1 067	1 276	1 132	1 289	1 487	..
Composite total	..	..	..	..	..	..	..	..
Total								
Branches and agencies	1 684	2 410	1 729	1 816	1 502	1 565	..	..
Subsidaries	..	..	..	..	..	..	..	..
Total	..	2 410	1 729	1 816	1 502	1 565	1 754	..

.. Not available

Note: Detailed metadata at: http://metalinks.oecd.org/ins/20180621/155b.

Disclaimer: http://oe.cd/disclaimer

Source: OECD Insurance Statistics (database)

Netherlands
Table 2. Number of companies and employees

	2009	2010	2011	2012	2013	2014	2015	2016
2.1 Number of companies								
Life								
Domestic undertakings	64	49	52	41	36	38	..	..
Foreign controlled undertakings	12	8	8	6	6	7	..	..
Foreign companies (branches)	1	1	1	4	4	0	..	..
All undertakings	65	50	53	45	40	38	..	..
Non-life								
Domestic undertakings	205	193	174	158	316	136	..	..
Foreign controlled undertakings	17	14	5	15	14	8	..	..
Foreign companies (branches)	6	4	4	2	1	2	..	..
All undertakings	211	197	178	160	317	138	..	..
Composite, all undertakings	**0**	**0**	**0**	**0**	**0**	**0**	**0**	**0**
Reinsurance								
Domestic undertakings	6	14	16	15	11	10	..	..
Foreign controlled undertakings	0	2	1	1	0	0	..	..
Foreign companies (branches)	..	..	..	0	0	0	..	..
All undertakings	6	14	16	15	11	10	..	..
Total								
Domestic undertakings	275	256	242	214	363	184	..	..
Foreign controlled undertakings	29	24	14	22	20	15	..	..
Foreign companies (branches)	7	5	5	6	5	2	..	..
All undertakings	282	261	247	220	368	186	..	..
2.2 Number of employees								
Insurance undertakings	..	..	..	..	..	..	..	..
Intermediaries	..	..	..	..	..	..	..	..
Total	..	..	..	..	..	..	..	..

.. Not available

Note: Detailed metadata at: http://metalinks.oecd.org/ins/20180621/155b.

Disclaimer: http://oe.cd/disclaimer

Source: OECD Insurance Statistics (database)

New Zealand
Table 1. Selected aggregates

Million NZD

	2009	2010	2011	2012	2013	2014	2015	2016
1.1 Insurance business written in the reporting country								
1.1.1 Insurance business, by ownership								
Gross premiums								
Domestic undertakings	..	..	..	..	..	..	..	..
Foreign controlled undertakings	..	..	..	..	..	..	..	..
Foreign companies (branches)	..	..	..	..	..	..	..	..
All undertakings	4 719	4 680	..	5 665	6 266	6 460	6 678	6 828
Premiums ceded								
Domestic undertakings	..	..	..	..	..	..	..	..
Foreign controlled undertakings	..	..	..	..	..	..	..	..
Foreign companies (branches)	..	..	..	..	..	..	..	..
All undertakings	610	610	..	1 207	1 412	1 292	1 305	1 789
Net written premiums								
Domestic undertakings	..	..	..	..	..	..	..	..
Foreign controlled undertakings	..	..	..	..	..	..	..	..
Foreign companies (branches)	..	..	..	..	..	..	..	..
All undertakings	5 365	5 730	..	6 365	6 758	7 186	7 523	7 303
1.1.2 Insurance business on foreign risks, gross premiums								
Life	..	..	..	..	..	..	..	..
Non-life	..	..	..	..	..	..	..	..
Composite	..	..	..	..	..	..	..	..
of which:								
Life	..	..	..	..	..	..	..	..
Non-life	..	..	..	..	..	..	..	..
Total	..	..	..	..	..	..	..	..
1.1.3 Life insurance payments, by class, gross premiums								
Annuities	..	..	..	..	..	..	..	..
Unit linked	..	..	..	..	..	..	..	..
Other life insurance	..	..	..	..	..	..	..	..
Total life insurance	..	..	..	..	..	..	..	..
of which: *Pension contracts*	..	..	..	..	..	..	..	..
1.1.4 Non-life insurance payments, by class, gross premiums								
Motor vehicle insurance	..	..	..	..	..	..	..	..
Marine, aviation and other transport insurance	..	..	..	..	..	..	..	..
Freight insurance	..	..	..	..	..	..	..	..
Fire and other property damage insurance	..	..	..	..	..	..	..	..
Pecuniary loss insurance	..	..	..	..	..	..	..	..
General liability insurance	..	..	..	..	..	..	..	..
Accident and health	..	..	..	..	..	..	..	..
of which: *Health*	..	..	..	..	..	..	..	..
Other non-life insurance	..	..	..	..	..	..	..	..
Treaty reinsurance	..	..	..	..	..	..	..	..
Total non-life insurance	4 719	4 680	..	5 665	6 266	6 460	6 678	6 828

New Zealand
Table 1. Selected aggregates *(cont.)*

Million NZD

	2009	2010	2011	2012	2013	2014	2015	2016
1.2 Gross claims payments								
Life								
Domestic undertakings	..	..	..	..	..	..	..	..
Foreign controlled undertakings	..	..	..	..	..	..	..	..
Foreign companies (branches)	..	..	..	..	..	..	..	..
All undertakings	895	1 437	..	1 360	1 303	1 399	1 544	1 598
Non-life								
Domestic undertakings	..	..	..	..	..	..	..	..
Foreign controlled undertakings	..	..	..	..	..	..	..	..
Foreign companies (branches)	..	..	..	..	..	..	..	..
All undertakings	2 925	2 802	..	9 531	4 539	5 642	6 302	4 864
Composite								
Domestic undertakings	..	..	..	..	..	..	..	..
Foreign controlled undertakings	..	..	..	..	..	..	..	..
Foreign companies (branches)	..	..	..	..	..	..	..	..
All undertakings	..	..	..	..	..	..	..	..
of which:								
Life	..	..	..	..	..	..	..	..
Domestic undertakings	..	..	..	..	..	..	..	..
Foreign controlled undertakings	..	..	..	..	..	..	..	..
Foreign companies (branches)	..	..	..	..	..	..	..	..
All undertakings	..	..	..	..	..	..	..	..
Non-life	..	..	..	..	..	..	..	..
Domestic undertakings	..	..	..	..	..	..	..	..
Foreign controlled undertakings	..	..	..	..	..	..	..	..
Foreign companies (branches)	..	..	..	..	..	..	..	..
All undertakings	..	..	..	..	..	..	..	..
Total								
Domestic undertakings	..	..	..	..	..	..	..	..
Foreign controlled undertakings	..	..	..	..	..	..	..	..
Foreign companies (branches)	..	..	..	..	..	..	..	..
All undertakings	3 820	4 239	..	10 891	5 842	7 041	7 846	6 462
1.3 Commissions								
Life								
Domestic undertakings	..	..	..	..	..	..	..	..
Foreign controlled undertakings	..	..	..	..	..	..	..	..
Foreign companies (branches)	..	..	..	..	..	..	..	..
All undertakings	..	..	..	..	..	..	..	..
Non-life								
Domestic undertakings	..	..	..	..	..	..	..	..
Foreign controlled undertakings	..	..	..	..	..	..	..	..
Foreign companies (branches)	..	..	..	..	..	..	..	..
All undertakings	..	..	..	..	..	..	..	..
Composite								
Domestic undertakings	..	..	..	..	..	..	..	..
Foreign controlled undertakings	..	..	..	..	..	..	..	..
Foreign companies (branches)	..	..	..	..	..	..	..	..
All undertakings	..	..	..	..	..	..	..	..
of which:								
Life	..	..	..	..	..	..	..	..
Domestic undertakings	..	..	..	..	..	..	..	..
Foreign controlled undertakings	..	..	..	..	..	..	..	..
Foreign companies (branches)	..	..	..	..	..	..	..	..
All undertakings	..	..	..	..	..	..	..	..
Non-life	..	..	..	..	..	..	..	..
Domestic undertakings	..	..	..	..	..	..	..	..
Foreign controlled undertakings	..	..	..	..	..	..	..	..
Foreign companies (branches)	..	..	..	..	..	..	..	..
All undertakings	..	..	..	..	..	..	..	..
Total								
Domestic undertakings	..	..	..	..	..	..	..	..
Foreign controlled undertakings	..	..	..	..	..	..	..	..
Foreign companies (branches)	..	..	..	..	..	..	..	..
All undertakings	..	..	..	..	..	..	..	..

New Zealand
Table 1. Selected aggregates *(cont.)*

Million NZD

	2009	2010	2011	2012	2013	2014	2015	2016
1.4 Gross operating expenses								
Life								
Domestic undertakings	..	..	..	..	..	..	..	..
Foreign controlled undertakings	..	..	..	..	..	..	..	..
Foreign companies (branches)	..	..	..	..	..	..	..	..
All undertakings	2 161	2 403	..	2 169	2 151	2 384	2 323	2 489
Non-life								
Domestic undertakings	..	..	..	..	..	..	..	..
Foreign controlled undertakings	..	..	..	..	..	..	..	..
Foreign companies (branches)	..	..	..	..	..	..	..	..
All undertakings	4 202	4 213	..	12 070	6 102	7 490	8 472	6 875
Composite								
Domestic undertakings	..	..	..	..	..	..	..	..
Foreign controlled undertakings	..	..	..	..	..	..	..	..
Foreign companies (branches)	..	..	..	..	..	..	..	..
All undertakings	..	..	..	..	..	..	..	..
of which:								
Life	..	..	..	..	..	..	..	..
Domestic undertakings	..	..	..	..	..	..	..	..
Foreign controlled undertakings	..	..	..	..	..	..	..	..
Foreign companies (branches)	..	..	..	..	..	..	..	..
All undertakings	..	..	..	..	..	..	..	..
Non-life	..	..	..	..	..	..	..	..
Domestic undertakings	..	..	..	..	..	..	..	..
Foreign controlled undertakings	..	..	..	..	..	..	..	..
Foreign companies (branches)	..	..	..	..	..	..	..	..
All undertakings	..	..	..	..	..	..	..	..
Total								
Domestic undertakings	..	..	..	..	..	..	..	..
Foreign controlled undertakings	..	..	..	..	..	..	..	..
Foreign companies (branches)	..	..	..	..	..	..	..	..
All undertakings	6 364	6 616	..	14 239	8 253	9 874	10 795	9 364
1.5 Insurance business written abroad by branches, gross premiums								
Life								
Branches and agencies	..	..	..	..	..	..	..	..
Subsidaries	..	..	..	..	..	..	..	..
Total	..	..	..	..	..	..	..	..
Non-life								
Branches and agencies	..	..	..	..	..	..	..	..
Subsidaries	..	..	..	..	..	..	..	..
Total	..	..	..	..	..	..	..	..
Composite								
Branches and agencies	..	..	..	..	..	..	..	..
Subsidaries	..	..	..	..	..	..	..	..
Total	..	..	..	..	..	..	..	..
of which:								
Life	..	..	..	..	..	..	..	..
Branches and agencies	..	..	..	..	..	..	..	..
Subsidaries	..	..	..	..	..	..	..	..
Total	..	..	..	..	..	..	..	..
Non-life	..	..	..	..	..	..	..	..
Branches and agencies	..	..	..	..	..	..	..	..
Subsidaries	..	..	..	..	..	..	..	..
Total	..	..	..	..	..	..	..	..
Total								
Branches and agencies	..	..	..	..	..	..	..	..
Subsidaries	..	..	..	..	..	..	..	..
Total	..	..	..	..	..	..	..	..

.. Not available

Note: Detailed metadata at: http://metalinks.oecd.org/ins/20180621/8e23.

Disclaimer: http://oe.cd/disclaimer

Source: OECD Insurance Statistics (database)

New Zealand
Table 2. Number of companies and employees

	2009	2010	2011	2012	2013	2014	2015	2016
2.1 Number of companies								
Life								
Domestic undertakings	..	..	..	..	..	..	..	..
Foreign controlled undertakings	..	..	..	..	..	..	..	..
Foreign companies (branches)	..	..	..	..	..	..	..	..
All undertakings	42	42	..	43	37	43	30	30
Non-life								
Domestic undertakings	..	..	..	..	..	..	..	..
Foreign controlled undertakings	..	..	..	..	..	..	..	..
Foreign companies (branches)	..	..	..	..	..	..	..	..
All undertakings	152	147	..	142	130	145	102	90
Composite								
Domestic undertakings	..	..	..	..	..	..	..	..
Foreign controlled undertakings	..	..	..	..	..	..	..	..
Foreign companies (branches)	..	..	..	..	..	..	..	..
All undertakings	..	..	..	..	..	..	..	..
Reinsurance								
Domestic undertakings	..	..	..	..	..	..	..	..
Foreign controlled undertakings	..	..	..	..	..	..	..	..
Foreign companies (branches)	..	..	..	..	..	..	..	..
All undertakings	..	..	..	..	..	..	..	..
Total								
Domestic undertakings	..	..	..	..	..	..	..	..
Foreign controlled undertakings	..	..	..	..	..	..	..	..
Foreign companies (branches)	..	..	..	..	..	..	..	..
All undertakings	194	189	..	185	167	188	132	120
2.2 Number of employees								
Insurance undertakings	..	..	..	..	10 780	10 720	10 680	..
Intermediaries	..	..	..	..	..	..	..	..
Total	9 550	9 650	..	10 640	10 780	..	..	..

.. Not available

Note: Detailed metadata at: http://metalinks.oecd.org/ins/20180621/8e23.

Disclaimer: http://oe.cd/disclaimer

Source: OECD Insurance Statistics (database)

Norway
Table 1. Selected aggregates

Million NOK

	2009	2010	2011	2012	2013	2014	2015	2016
1.1 Insurance business written in the reporting country								
1.1.1 Insurance business, by ownership								
Gross premiums								
Domestic undertakings	34 066	99 610	106 973	119 751	119 149	134 884	135 864	138 612
Foreign controlled undertakings	943	6 299	6 388	8 589	8 948	11 029	13 195	..
Foreign companies (branches)	24 349	24 719	26 383	30 039	30 872	31 867	30 638	31 150
All undertakings	58 415	124 329	133 356	149 790	150 021	166 751	166 502	169 762
Premiums ceded								
Domestic undertakings	6 897	..	..	6 252	6 396	6 891	7 973	7 053
Foreign controlled undertakings	170	..	..	316	173	198	218	..
Foreign companies (branches)	1 647	..	..	4 290	4 219	4 653	4 976	5 362
All undertakings	8 544	..	..	10 542	10 614	11 544	12 950	12 415
Net written premiums								
Domestic undertakings	27 169	..	..	113 499	112 754	127 993	127 890	131 559
Foreign controlled undertakings	774	..	..	8 273	8 775	10 832	12 978	..
Foreign companies (branches)	22 702	..	..	25 749	26 653	27 213	25 662	25 788
All undertakings	49 871	..	..	139 248	139 407	155 206	153 552	157 347
1.1.2 Insurance business on foreign risks, gross premiums								
Life	..	..	..	31	..	..	9	7
Non-life	3 711	2 779	1 556	7 352	6 202	11 468	11 250	10 855
Composite total	..	..	..	..	..	..	..	..
Total	3 711	2 779	1 556	7 383	6 202	11 468	11 260	10 862
1.1.3 Life insurance payments, by class, gross premiums								
Annuities	..	..	..	..	..	..	..	..
Unit linked	..	..	..	..	..	..	..	..
Other life insurance	..	..	..	..	..	..	..	..
Total life insurance	75 256	66 586	71 577	81 742	81 299	92 185	91 794	94 093
***of which:** Pension contracts*	..	..	..	69 652	66 873	..	..	..
1.1.4 Non-life insurance payments, by class, gross premiums								
Motor vehicle insurance	8 855	10 409	10 787	19 403	..	20 378	20 706	21 040
Marine, aviation and other transport insurance	8 752	3 974	4 009	9 581	..	6 574	5 201	10 808
Freight insurance	..	..	..	..	..	..	..	..
Fire and other property damage insurance	7 903	9 470	10 811	17 738	..	18 195	19 041	23 325
Pecuniary loss insurance	72	119	125	585	..	127	97	433
General liability insurance	578	647	686	1 755	..	1 695	1 637	2 099
Accident and health	3 084	3 205	3 229	6 111	..	5 608	5 553	10 782
***of which:** Health*	..	..	..	..	..	..	..	..
Other non-life insurance	2 988	5 993	5 967	12 875	..	21 989	13 048	7 183
Treaty reinsurance	2 988	..	..	..	..	..	..	..
Total non-life insurance	..	33 817	35 615	68 048	..	74 566	65 283	75 669
1.2 Gross claims payments								
Life								
Domestic undertakings	45 863	40 443	40 252	45 033	45 143	45 742	49 007	51 548
Foreign controlled undertakings	3 530	3 309	2 723	3 120	3 186	3 150	4 796	.. c
Foreign companies (branches)	671	405	494	482	692	476	235	288
All undertakings	46 534	40 848	40 746	45 515	45 835	46 218	49 242	51 836
Non-life								
Domestic undertakings	21 538	21 364	26 292	28 356	23 486	30 742	34 587	28 914
Foreign controlled undertakings	931	441	342	542	.. c	.. c	.. c	.. c
Foreign companies (branches)	16 567	16 445	17 552	24 549	20 026	22 287	21 584	6 961
All undertakings	38 105	37 809	43 844	52 905	43 512	53 030	56 170	35 875
Composite, all undertakings	..	..	..	..	..	..	..	..
Total								
Domestic undertakings	67 401	61 807	66 544	73 389	68 629	76 485	83 593	80 462
Foreign controlled undertakings	4 461	3 750	3 065	3 662	3 186	3 150	4 796	..
Foreign companies (branches)	17 238	16 850	18 046	25 031	20 718	22 763	21 819	7 249
All undertakings	84 639	78 657	84 590	98 420	89 347	99 248	105 413	87 711

Norway
Table 1. Selected aggregates (*cont.*)

Million NOK

	2009	2010	2011	2012	2013	2014	2015	2016
1.3 Commissions								
Life								
Domestic undertakings	..	..	..	692	774	839	916	890
Foreign controlled undertakings	..	..	..	152	179	202	227	.. c
Foreign companies (branches)	..	..	..	0	0	0	..	..
All undertakings	..	..	..	692	774	839	916	890
Non-life								
Domestic undertakings	..	..	..	1 507	1 536	2 204	2 119	1 956
Foreign controlled undertakings	..	..	..	35	.. c	.. c	..	.. c
Foreign companies (branches)	..	..	..	1 101	1 084	1 099	1 107	950
All undertakings	..	..	..	2 608	2 619	3 303	3 226	2 906
Composite, all undertakings	..	..	..	..	..	..	..	..
Total								
Domestic undertakings	..	..	..	2 199	2 310	3 043	3 035	2 846
Foreign controlled undertakings	..	..	..	187	179	202	227	..
Foreign companies (branches)	..	..	..	1 101	1 084	1 099	1 107	950
All undertakings	..	..	..	3 300	3 393	4 142	4 142	3 797
1.4 Gross operating expenses								
Life								
Domestic undertakings	6 636	6 839	5 818	7 019	6 688	7 205	7 383	7 750
Foreign controlled undertakings	622	646	688	692	185	807	765	.. c
Foreign companies (branches)	132	151	144	0	126	162	..	157
All undertakings	6 768	6 990	5 962	7 019	6 814	7 367	7 383	7 907
Non-life								
Domestic undertakings	5 501	5 703	6 155	5 527	5 925	6 585	6 138	6 139
Foreign controlled undertakings	149	141	76	48	.. c	.. c	.. c	.. c
Foreign companies (branches)	5 495	5 451	5 121	4 765	4 203	5 318	5 574	5 465
All undertakings	10 996	11 154	11 276	10 292	10 128	11 903	11 712	11 605
Composite, all undertakings	..	..	..	..	..	..	..	..
Total								
Domestic undertakings	12 137	12 542	11 973	12 546	12 613	13 790	13 521	13 889
Foreign controlled undertakings	771	787	764	740	185	807	765	..
Foreign companies (branches)	5 627	5 602	5 265	4 765	4 329	5 480	5 574	5 623
All undertakings	17 764	18 144	17 238	17 311	16 942	19 270	19 095	19 512
1.5 Insurance business written abroad by branches, gross premiums								
Life								
Branches and agencies	..	89	..	..	.. c	..	..	..
Subsidaries	..	..	..	..	..	..	..	..
Total	..	89	..	..	.. c	..	..	..
Non-life								
Branches and agencies	2 446	2 977	2 476	2 454	1 134	4 636	1 569	7 141
Subsidaries	..	..	..	..	.. c	.. c	..	..
Total	2 446	2 977	2 476	2 454	1 134	4 636	1 569	7 141
Composite total	..	..	..	..	..	..	..	..
Total								
Branches and agencies	2 446	3 066	2 476	2 454	1 134	4 636	1 569	7 141
Subsidaries	..	..	..	..	..	..	..	..
Total	2 446	3 066	2 476	2 454	1 134	4 636	1 569	7 141

.. Not available; c Confidential data

Note: Detailed metadata at: http://metalinks.oecd.org/ins/20180621/ba46.

Disclaimer: http://oe.cd/disclaimer

Source: OECD Insurance Statistics (database)

Norway
Table 2. Number of companies and employees

	2009	2010	2011	2012	2013	2014	2015	2016
2.1 Number of companies								
Life								
Domestic undertakings	..	12	12	10	12	10	10	10
Foreign controlled undertakings	..	2	2	2	2	2	2	2
Foreign companies (branches)	..	10	10	9	9	7	7	7
All undertakings	..	22	22	19	21	17	17	17
Non-life								
Domestic undertakings	78	77	76	63	59	59	58	59
Foreign controlled undertakings	2	1	1	1	1	1	2	2
Foreign companies (branches)	28	24	21	25	25	22	21	23
All undertakings	106	101	97	88	84	81	79	82
Composite, all undertakings	**0**	**0**	**0**	**0**	**0**	**0**	**0**	**0**
Reinsurance								
Domestic undertakings	1	..	..	..	..	..	..	..
Foreign controlled undertakings	0	..	..	..	..	..	..	..
Foreign companies (branches)	0	..	..	..	..	..	..	..
All undertakings	1	..	..	..	..	..	..	..
Total								
Domestic undertakings	..	89	88	73	71	69	68	69
Foreign controlled undertakings	..	3	3	3	3	3	4	4
Foreign companies (branches)	..	34	31	34	34	29	28	30
All undertakings	..	123	119	107	105	98	96	99
2.2 Number of employees								
Insurance undertakings	..	9 753	..	..	..	..	..	..
Intermediaries	..	..	..	..	..	..	..	..
Total	..	9 753	..	..	..	..	..	..

.. Not available

Note: Detailed metadata at: http://metalinks.oecd.org/ins/20180621/ba46.

Disclaimer: http://oe.cd/disclaimer

Source: OECD Insurance Statistics (database)

Poland
Table 1. Selected aggregates

Million PLN

	2009	2010	2011	2012	2013	2014	2015	2016
1.1 Insurance business written in the reporting country								
1.1.1 Insurance business, by ownership								
Gross premiums								
Domestic undertakings	51 343	54 164	57 151	62 627	57 863	54 927	54 804	56 039
Foreign controlled undertakings	26 758	29 135	31 683	35 100	31 562	30 425	30 801	31 961
Foreign companies (branches)	62	..	..	..	..	..	..	..
All undertakings	51 405	54 164	57 151	62 627	57 863	54 927	54 804	56 039
Premiums ceded								
Domestic undertakings	2 406	3 393	3 852	4 598	4 214	4 170	5 197	6 765
Foreign controlled undertakings	1 687	2 043	4 647	4 224	3 664	3 533	4 355	4 798
Foreign companies (branches)	0	..	..	..	..	..	..	..
All undertakings	2 406	3 393	3 852	4 598	4 214	4 170	5 197	6 765
Net written premiums								
Domestic undertakings	48 937	50 771	53 299	58 029	53 649	50 757	49 606	49 274
Foreign controlled undertakings	25 071	27 092	27 036	30 876	27 898	26 892	26 446	27 163
Foreign companies (branches)	62	..	..	..	..	..	..	..
All undertakings	48 999	50 771	53 299	58 029	53 649	50 757	49 606	49 274
1.1.2 Insurance business on foreign risks, gross premiums								
Life	..	0	..	..	..	..	..	..
Non-life	..	202	..	..	..	..	..	..
Composite total	..	..	..	..	..	..	..	..
Total	..	203	..	..	..	..	..	..
1.1.3 Life insurance payments, by class, gross premiums								
Annuities	71	83	98	99	107	114	131	138
Unit linked	6 458	8 120	10 307	12 046	13 052	12 600	12 996	10 325
Other life insurance	23 685	23 150	21 415	24 203	18 082	15 933	14 377	13 370
Total life insurance	30 214	31 354	31 820	36 348	31 241	28 646	27 505	23 833
***of which:** Pension contracts*	294	329	376	371	396	356	356	..
1.1.4 Non-life insurance payments, by class, gross premiums								
Motor vehicle insurance	12 209	12 932	14 543	14 780	13 945	13 397	13 910	18 744
Marine, aviation and other transport insurance	171	163	232	256	267	275	210	185
Freight insurance	92	96	107	119	117	126	116	120
Fire and other property damage insurance	3 892	4 334	5 056	5 441	5 973	5 715	5 938	6 246
Pecuniary loss insurance	1 617	1 593	1 631	1 526	1 858	2 149	1 893	1 805
General liability insurance	1 129	1 302	1 459	1 773	1 891	1 964	2 134	1 915
Accident and health	1 510	1 621	1 688	1 801	1 926	2 007	2 273	2 222
***of which:** Health*	279	1 269	1 245	513	612	656	613	618
Other non-life insurance	452	698	575	554	622	627	804	947
Treaty reinsurance	0	0	..	..	..	..	..	..
Total non-life insurance	21 073	22 739	25 291	26 250	26 599	26 260	27 278	32 182
1.2 Gross claims payments								
Life								
Domestic undertakings	27 702	22 585	26 069	25 917	23 087	20 360	19 358	18 284
Foreign controlled undertakings	12 880	10 545	12 116	13 331	10 927	9 783	8 795	9 543
Foreign companies (branches)	0	..	..	..	..	..	..	..
All undertakings	27 702	22 585	26 069	25 917	23 087	20 360	19 358	18 284
Non-life								
Domestic undertakings	12 471	14 169	13 738	14 046	13 711	13 811	15 488	18 393
Foreign controlled undertakings	6 690	8 017	8 128	8 890	8 434	8 579	9 515	10 911
Foreign companies (branches)	37	..	..	..	..	..	..	..
All undertakings	12 508	14 169	13 738	14 046	13 711	13 811	15 488	18 393
Composite, all undertakings	..	..	..	..	..	..	..	..
Total								
Domestic undertakings	40 172	36 754	39 807	39 963	36 798	34 171	34 846	36 677
Foreign controlled undertakings	19 570	18 562	20 244	22 221	19 362	18 363	18 310	20 454
Foreign companies (branches)	37	..	..	..	..	..	..	..
All undertakings	40 209	36 754	39 807	39 963	36 798	34 171	34 846	36 677
1.3 Commissions								
Life								
Domestic undertakings	44	3 006	3 245	70	93	203	231	222
Foreign controlled undertakings	48	2 485	2 591	69	70	191	223	218
Foreign companies (branches)	0	..	..	..	..	..	..	..
All undertakings	44	3 006	3 245	70	93	203	231	222
Non-life								
Domestic undertakings	434	3 490	4 015	657	740	651	719	1 115
Foreign controlled undertakings	347	2 202	2 659	648	606	594	657	929
Foreign companies (branches)	0	..	..	..	..	..	..	..
All undertakings	434	3 490	4 015	657	740	651	719	1 115
Composite, all undertakings	..	..	..	..	..	..	..	..
Total								
Domestic undertakings	478	6 496	7 260	727	833	854	950	1 337
Foreign controlled undertakings	395	4 688	5 250	717	676	785	880	1 147
Foreign companies (branches)	0	..	..	..	..	..	..	..
All undertakings	478	6 496	7 260	727	833	854	950	1 337

Poland
Table 1. Selected aggregates *(cont.)*

Million PLN

	2009	2010	2011	2012	2013	2014	2015	2016
1.4 Gross operating expenses								
Life								
Domestic undertakings	6 554	5 295	5 605	6 416	6 146	6 588	6 476	5 647
Foreign controlled undertakings	4 669	3 777	3 944	4 244	3 831	4 369	4 182	3 797
Foreign companies (branches)	0	..	..	..	..	..	..	..
All undertakings	6 554	5 295	5 605	6 416	6 146	6 588	6 476	5 647
Non-life								
Domestic undertakings	8 816	6 791	7 276	7 733	7 775	8 018	8 335	9 104
Foreign controlled undertakings	4 874	3 958	4 549	5 225	5 090	5 135	5 569	5 978
Foreign companies (branches)	27	..	..	..	..	..	..	..
All undertakings	8 843	6 791	7 276	7 733	7 775	8 018	8 335	9 104
Composite, all undertakings	..	..	..	..	..	..	..	..
Total								
Domestic undertakings	15 369	12 086	12 882	14 149	13 921	14 606	14 811	14 751
Foreign controlled undertakings	9 543	7 734	8 493	9 469	8 921	9 504	9 751	9 776
Foreign companies (branches)	27	..	..	..	..	..	..	..
All undertakings	15 397	12 086	12 882	14 149	13 921	14 606	14 811	14 751
1.5 Insurance business written abroad by branches, gross premiums								
Life								
Branches and agencies	..	14	19	26	..	79	92	..
Subsidaries	..	..	..	..	..	..	..	..
Total	..	14	19	26	..	79	92	..
Non-life								
Branches and agencies	..	14	62	53	..	98	116	..
Subsidaries	..	..	49	..	..	..	..	..
Total	..	14	111	53	..	98	116	..
Composite total	..	..	..	..	..	..	..	..
Total								
Branches and agencies	..	29	82	79	..	177	208	..
Subsidaries	..	..	49	..	..	..	..	..
Total	..	29	130	79	..	177	208	..

.. Not available

Note: Detailed metadata at: http://metalinks.oecd.org/ins/20180621/bc50.

Disclaimer: http://oe.cd/disclaimer

Source: OECD Insurance Statistics (database)

Poland
Table 2. Number of companies and employees

	2009	2010	2011	2012	2013	2014	2015	2016
2.1 Number of companies								
Life								
Domestic undertakings	31	30	28	28	27	26	28	27
Foreign controlled undertakings	22	23	22	23	21	19	21	21
Foreign companies (branches)	0	..	2	..	..	..	..	..
All undertakings	31	30	30	28	27	26	28	27
Non-life								
Domestic undertakings	33	32	32	30	30	30	32	33
Foreign controlled undertakings	22	21	22	21	19	19	22	20
Foreign companies (branches)	1	..	11	..	..	..	..	..
All undertakings	34	32	43	30	30	30	32	33
Composite, all undertakings	**0**	**0**	**0**	**0**	**0**	**0**	**0**	**0**
Reinsurance								
Domestic undertakings	1	1	1	1	1	1	1	1
Foreign controlled undertakings	0	1	1	1	1	1	1	1
Foreign companies (branches)	0	..	..	..	..	..	..	..
All undertakings	1	1	1	1	1	1	1	1
Total								
Domestic undertakings	65	63	61	59	58	57	61	61
Foreign controlled undertakings	44	45	45	45	41	39	44	42
Foreign companies (branches)	1	..	13	..	..	..	..	..
All undertakings	66	63	74	59	58	57	61	61
2.2 Number of employees								
Insurance undertakings	36 877	35 803	37 239	37 205	37 187	35 922	35 282	..
Intermediaries	60 789	62 347	68 168	58 879	69 621	58 004	49 126	..
Total	97 666	98 150	105 407	96 083	106 808	93 926	84 408	..

.. Not available

Note: Detailed metadata at: http://metalinks.oecd.org/ins/20180621/bc50.

Disclaimer: http://oe.cd/disclaimer

Source: OECD Insurance Statistics (database)

Portugal
Table 1. Selected aggregates

Million EUR

	2009	2010	2011	2012	2013	2014	2015	2016
1.1 Insurance business written in the reporting country								
1.1.1 Insurance business, by ownership								
Gross premiums								
Domestic undertakings	14 111	15 816	11 165	10 553	12 802	14 051	12 568	10 913
Foreign controlled undertakings	2 067	1 758	1 676	1 553	1 617	8 737	8 890	9 048
Foreign companies (branches)	89	75	73	0	0	0	0	0
All undertakings	14 200	15 891	11 238	10 553	12 802	14 051	12 568	10 913
Premiums ceded								
Domestic undertakings	992	1 013	982	1 096	1 144	1 118	1 194	1 214
Foreign controlled undertakings	189	80	153	130	140	836	924	992
Foreign companies (branches)	28	26	23	0	0	0	0	0
All undertakings	1 020	1 039	1 005	1 096	1 144	1 118	1 194	1 214
Net written premiums								
Domestic undertakings	7 184	14 802	10 183	9 457	11 658	12 933	11 374	9 698
Foreign controlled undertakings	1 806	1 678	1 523	1 423	1 477	7 902	7 966	8 056
Foreign companies (branches)	61	49	50	0	0	0	0	0
All undertakings	7 245	14 851	10 232	9 457	11 658	12 933	11 374	9 698
1.1.2 Insurance business on foreign risks, gross premiums								
Life	5	0	0	2	3	13	8	11
Non-life	5	1	2	15	14	13	13	4
Composite	76	0	0	54	64	92	107	127
of which:								
Life	38	0	0	27	27	53	63	70
Non-life	38	0	0	27	38	39	44	57
Total	85	1	2	72	81	118	129	142
1.1.3 Life insurance payments, by class, gross premiums								
Annuities	37	33	19	46	79	64	109	142
Unit linked	2 908	2 389	1 954	1 999	1 851	1 966	2 119	1 655
Other life insurance	7 094	9 414	5 240	4 633	7 094	8 220	6 254	4 708
Total life insurance	10 039	11 835	7 213	6 678	9 023	10 249	8 481	6 504
***of which:** Pension contracts*	..	..	..	..	..	..	..	..
1.1.4 Non-life insurance payments, by class, gross premiums								
Motor vehicle insurance	1 563	1 454	1 447	1 353	1 277	1 256	1 316	1 399
Marine, aviation and other transport insurance	44	37	35	35	33	29	28	25
Freight insurance	26	26	26	25	25	24	23	22
Fire and other property damage insurance	684	657	686	702	700	699	745	771
Pecuniary loss insurance	66	53	54	63	69	70	73	84
General liability insurance	95	93	90	89	84	87	94	99
Accident and health	1 522	1 504	1 480	1 430	1 413	1 452	1 602	1 783
***of which:** Health*	756	806	820	838	862	896	973	1 084
Other non-life insurance	150	165	170	177	178	183	205	225
Treaty reinsurance	0	0	0	0	0	0	0	0
Total non-life insurance	4 149	3 988	3 988	3 874	3 778	3 802	4 086	4 408

Portugal
Table 1. Selected aggregates *(cont.)*

Million EUR

	2009	2010	2011	2012	2013	2014	2015	2016
1.2 Gross claims payments								
Life								
Domestic undertakings	4 687	3 782	6 935	4 875	4 518	5 254	6 133	6 568
Foreign controlled undertakings	410	457	505	461	374	2 667	2 724	2 252
Foreign companies (branches)	0	0	0	0	0	0	0	0
All undertakings	4 687	3 782	6 935	4 875	4 518	5 254	6 133	6 568
Non-life								
Domestic undertakings	1 636	1 628	1 588	1 471	1 446	1 407	1 520	1 336
Foreign controlled undertakings	678	518	424	385	376	1 174	1 278	1 070
Foreign companies (branches)	15	0	0	0	0	0	0	0
All undertakings	1 652	1 628	1 588	1 471	1 446	1 407	1 520	1 336
Composite								
Domestic undertakings	4 859	7 074	7 987	5 927	5 427	5 201	5 128	4 554
Foreign controlled undertakings	415	474	517	541	562	3 991	3 922	4 501
Foreign companies (branches)	57	43	43	0	0	0	0	0
All undertakings	4 916	7 116	8 030	5 927	5 427	5 201	5 128	4 554
of which:								
Life	3 598	5 828	6 661	4 616	4 067	3 895	3 840	2 867
Domestic undertakings	3 542	5 787	6 621	4 616	4 067	3 895	3 840	2 867
Foreign controlled undertakings	129	151	173	184	167	2 904	2 839	2 815
Foreign companies (branches)	55	41	41	0	0	0	0	0
All undertakings	3 598	5 828	6 661	4 616	4 067	3 895	3 840	2 867
Non-life	1 319	1 288	1 369	1 311	1 360	1 306	1 288	1 687
Domestic undertakings	1 317	1 286	1 367	1 311	1 360	1 306	1 288	1 687
Foreign controlled undertakings	286	323	344	357	395	1 087	1 083	1 686
Foreign companies (branches)	2	2	2	0	0	0	0	0
All undertakings	1 319	1 288	1 369	1 311	1 360	1 306	1 288	1 687
Total								
Domestic undertakings	11 183	12 485	16 510	12 274	11 391	11 861	12 782	12 458
Foreign controlled undertakings	1 503	1 449	1 446	1 387	1 312	7 832	7 923	7 822
Foreign companies (branches)	72	43	43	0	0	0	0	0
All undertakings	11 255	12 527	16 553	12 274	11 391	11 861	12 782	12 458
1.3 Commissions								
Life								
Domestic undertakings	61	69	38	47	144	40	77	105
Foreign controlled undertakings	11	9	9	7	7	15	41	42
Foreign companies (branches)	0	0	0	0	0	0	0	0
All undertakings	61	69	38	47	144	40	77	105
Non-life								
Domestic undertakings	188	179	155	157	156	153	178	164
Foreign controlled undertakings	91	58	44	40	38	117	133	98
Foreign companies (branches)	0	0	0	0	0	0	0	0
All undertakings	188	179	155	157	156	153	178	164
Composite								
Domestic undertakings	259	256	273	272	291	301	295	286
Foreign controlled undertakings	57	63	76	81	99	208	222	283
Foreign companies (branches)	23	22	20	0	0	0	0	0
All undertakings	282	277	293	272	291	301	295	286
of which:								
Life	124	119	114	87	98	100	82	49
Domestic undertakings	103	99	96	87	98	100	82	49
Foreign controlled undertakings	20	19	20	21	28	42	44	47
Foreign companies (branches)	22	20	18	0	0	0	0	0
All undertakings	124	119	114	87	98	100	82	49
Non-life	158	158	179	185	193	201	214	237
Domestic undertakings	156	157	177	185	193	201	214	237
Foreign controlled undertakings	37	44	56	60	71	165	178	236
Foreign companies (branches)	2	2	2	0	0	0	0	0
All undertakings	158	158	179	185	193	201	214	237
Total								
Domestic undertakings	508	504	466	476	591	493	550	554
Foreign controlled undertakings	159	131	130	128	144	339	396	423
Foreign companies (branches)	23	22	20	0	0	0	0	0
All undertakings	532	525	486	476	591	493	550	554

Portugal
Table 1. Selected aggregates *(cont.)*

Million EUR

	2009	2010	2011	2012	2013	2014	2015	2016
1.4 Gross operating expenses								
Life								
Domestic undertakings	241 |	234	202	206	314	212	244	300
Foreign controlled undertakings	32 |	37	37	36	33	136	163	168
Foreign companies (branches)	0 |	0	0	0	0	0	0	0
All undertakings	241 |	234	202	206	314	212	244	300
Non-life								
Domestic undertakings	568 |	555	528	511	496	495	550	467
Foreign controlled undertakings	253 |	179	155	144	133	398	441	357
Foreign companies (branches)	2 |	0	0	0	0	0	0	0
All undertakings	570 |	555	528	511	496	495	550	467
Composite								
Domestic undertakings	739 |	689	710	723	715	717	720	711
Foreign controlled undertakings	185 |	163	190	200	198	541	571	702
Foreign companies (branches)	36 |	38	39	0	0	0	0	0
All undertakings	775 |	727	750	723	715	717	720	711
of which:								
Life	271 |	270	258	221	234	230	222	148
Domestic undertakings	240 |	238	226	221	234	230	222	148
Foreign controlled undertakings	49 |	45	48	49	48	125	145	140
Foreign companies (branches)	31 |	32	32	0	0	0	0	0
All undertakings	271 |	270	258	221	234	230	222	148
Non-life	504 |	457	492	502	481	487	497	562
Domestic undertakings	499 |	451	484	502	481	487	497	562
Foreign controlled undertakings	136 |	118	142	151	151	416	427	562
Foreign companies (branches)	5 |	6	7	0	0	0	0	0
All undertakings	504 |	457	492	502	481	487	497	562
Total								
Domestic undertakings	1 547	1 478	1 440	1 440	1 525	1 425	1 513	1 478
Foreign controlled undertakings	471	379	381	380	364	1 076	1 176	1 227
Foreign companies (branches)	39	38	39	0	0	0	0	0
All undertakings	1 586	1 516	1 480	1 440	1 525	1 425	1 513	1 478
1.5 Insurance business written abroad by branches, gross premiums								
Life								
Branches and agencies	5 |	4	6	2	3	13	8	11
Subsidaries	0	0	0	0	0	0	0	0
Total	5 |	4	6	2	3	13	8	11
Non-life								
Branches and agencies	5 |	7	8	14	12	12	12	1
Subsidaries	0	0	0	0	0	0	0	0
Total	5 |	7	8	14	12	12	12	1
Composite								
Branches and agencies	76 |	79	55	54	64	92	107	127
Subsidaries	0	0	0	0	0	0	0	0
Total	76 |	79	55	54	64	92	107	127
of which:								
Life	38 |	40	28	27	27	53	63	70
Branches and agencies	38 |	40	28	27	27	53	63	70
Subsidaries	0	0	0	0	0	0	0	0
Total	38 |	40	28	27	27	53	63	70
Non-life	38 |	39	27	27	38	39	44	57
Branches and agencies	38 |	39	27	27	38	39	44	57
Subsidaries	0	0	0	0	0	0	0	0
Total	38 |	39	27	27	38	39	44	57
Total								
Branches and agencies	85	89	69	70	79	117	128	138
Subsidaries	0	0	0	0	0	0	0	0
Total	85	89	69	70	79	117	128	138

.. Not available; | Break in series

Note: Detailed metadata at: http://metalinks.oecd.org/ins/20180621/40f8.

Disclaimer: http://oe.cd/disclaimer

Source: OECD Insurance Statistics (database)

Portugal
Table 2. Number of companies and employees

	2009	2010	2011	2012	2013	2014	2015	2016
2.1 Number of companies								
Life								
Domestic undertakings	15	15	14	14	14	16	16	14
Foreign controlled undertakings	5	6	5	5	5	10	10	9
Foreign companies (branches)	6	6	6	6	5	5	5	4
All undertakings	21	21	20	20	19	21	21	18
Non-life								
Domestic undertakings	24	23	21	21	21	21	24	23
Foreign controlled undertakings	7	6	5	4	4	15	16	15
Foreign companies (branches)	27	26	24	25	24	23	21	19
All undertakings	51	49	45	46	45	44	45	42
Composite								
Domestic undertakings	6	7	7	6	6	5	5	5
Foreign controlled undertakings	2	2	2	2	2	3	3	4
Foreign companies (branches)	7	5	5	5	6	6	7	7
All undertakings	13	12	12	11	12	11	12	12
Reinsurance								
Domestic undertakings	1	1	1	1	1	1	1	1
Foreign controlled undertakings	0	0	0	0	0	1	1	1
Foreign companies (branches)	0	0	0	0	0	0	0	0
All undertakings	1	1	1	1	1	1	1	1
Total								
Domestic undertakings	46	46	43	42	42	43	46	43
Foreign controlled undertakings	14	14	12	11	11	29	30	29
Foreign companies (branches)	40	37	35	36	35	34	33	30
All undertakings	86	83	78	78	77	77	79	73
2.2 Number of employees								
Insurance undertakings	10 300	10 565	10 937	8 807	9 224	9 252	9 441	9 387
Intermediaries	27 139	25 897	25 397	24 624	24 207	23 465	22 738	21 426
Total	37 439	36 462	36 334	33 431	33 431	32 717	32 179	30 813

Note: Detailed metadata at: http://metalinks.oecd.org/ins/20180621/40f8.
Disclaimer: http://oe.cd/disclaimer
Source: OECD Insurance Statistics (database)

Slovak Republic
Table 1. Selected aggregates

Million EUR

	2009	2010	2011	2012	2013	2014	2015	2016
1.1 Insurance business written in the reporting country								
1.1.1 Insurance business, by ownership								
Gross premiums								
Domestic undertakings	1 985	2 015	2 040	2 036	2 082	2 106	2 020	..
Foreign controlled undertakings	1 846	1 861	1 875	1 863	1 901	1 918	1 827	..
Foreign companies (branches)	93	109	114	121	146	142	143	..
All undertakings	2 078	2 124	2 154	2 157	2 228	2 248	2 163	..
Premiums ceded								
Domestic undertakings	244	263	294	294	298	314	319	..
Foreign controlled undertakings	228	241	268	267	268	283	287	..
Foreign companies (branches)	15	16	17	17	19	17	17	..
All undertakings	259	279	312	311	316	331	336	..
Net written premiums								
Domestic undertakings	1 741	1 752	1 746	1 742	1 785	1 792	1 701	..
Foreign controlled undertakings	1 618	1 607	1 606	1 596	1 633	1 635	1 540	..
Foreign companies (branches)	78	93	96	104	127	126	126	..
All undertakings	1 819	1 845	1 842	1 846	1 912	1 917	1 827	..
1.1.2 Insurance business on foreign risks, gross premiums								
Life	..	..	..	..	..	..	..	..
Non-life	..	..	..	..	..	..	..	..
Composite	..	..	..	..	..	..	..	..
of which:								
Life	..	..	..	..	..	..	..	..
Non-life	..	..	..	..	..	..	..	..
Total	..	..	..	..	..	..	..	..
1.1.3 Life insurance payments, by class, gross premiums								
Annuities	623	637	619	607	649	623	586	..
Unit linked	284	315	338	409	423	417	351	..
Other life insurance	122	128	137	146	164	180	171	..
Total life insurance	1 029	1 079	1 094	1 162	1 236	1 220	1 108	..
***of which:** Pension contracts*	19	16	15	13	12	12	12	..
1.1.4 Non-life insurance payments, by class, gross premiums								
Motor vehicle insurance	578	579	568	548	528	532	547	..
Marine, aviation and other transport insurance	6	6	6	7	6	6	6	..
Freight insurance	9	8	8	8	8	8	8	..
Fire and other property damage insurance	227	235	248	247	250	257	257	..
Pecuniary loss insurance	13	23	25	24	27	33	34	..
General liability insurance	52	67	65	68	73	78	78	..
Accident and health	32	40	38	40	45	49	44	..
***of which:** Health*	2	2	2	2	2	2	3	..
Other non-life insurance	27	29	31	32	34	35	39	..
Treaty reinsurance	12	12	19	21	21	32	42	..
Total non-life insurance	956	997	1 009	996	992	1 028	1 055	..

Slovak Republic
Table 1. Selected aggregates *(cont.)*

Million EUR

	2009	2010	2011	2012	2013	2014	2015	2016
1.2 Gross claims payments								
Life								
Domestic undertakings	73	84	97	93	91	107	98	186
Foreign controlled undertakings	73	84	97	93	91	107	98	..
Foreign companies (branches)	2	1	0	0	0	0	2	..
All undertakings	75	85	97	93	91	108	100	..
Non-life								
Domestic undertakings	4	5	5	1	0	0	0	..
Foreign controlled undertakings	4	5	5	1	0	0	0	..
Foreign companies (branches)	15	27	24	44	27	29	32	..
All undertakings	19	32	29	45	27	29	32	..
Composite								
Domestic undertakings	957	1 043	1 075	1 083	1 117	1 084	1 057	2 291
Foreign controlled undertakings	850	922	945	948	979	948	911	1 909
Foreign companies (branches)	3	3	5	12	14	16	16	..
All undertakings	959	1 046	1 079	1 094	1 131	1 099	1 073	..
of which:								
Life	480	528	566	640	658	646	575	..
Domestic undertakings	478	525	562	632	647	634	563	1 794
Foreign controlled undertakings	400	431	463	527	544	533	457	1 459
Foreign companies (branches)	1	3	4	8	11	12	12	..
All undertakings	480	528	566	640	658	646	575	..
Non-life	480	518	513	455	473	453	497	..
Domestic undertakings	479	518	513	451	470	450	494	497
Foreign controlled undertakings	449	490	483	421	435	415	454	450
Foreign companies (branches)	1	0	0	4	4	3	3	..
All undertakings	480	518	513	455	473	453	497	..
Total								
Domestic undertakings	1 034	1 132	1 177	1 176	1 208	1 191	1 155	2 477
Foreign controlled undertakings	927	1 010	1 047	1 042	1 070	1 055	1 010	1 909
Foreign companies (branches)	20	30	30	55	42	44	49	..
All undertakings	1 054	1 162	1 206	1 232	1 249	1 236	1 205	..
1.3 Commissions								
Life								
Domestic undertakings	25	22	26	28	29	33	37	..
Foreign controlled undertakings	25	22	26	28	29	33	37	..
Foreign companies (branches)	0	0	1	1	1	1	2	..
All undertakings	25	22	27	29	30	34	39	..
Non-life								
Domestic undertakings	1	1	2	1	0	0	0	..
Foreign controlled undertakings	1	1	2	1	0	0	0	..
Foreign companies (branches)	6	9	9	11	13	15	18	..
All undertakings	8	10	11	12	13	15	18	..
Composite								
Domestic undertakings	218	221	230	238	251	259	250	..
Foreign controlled undertakings	210	210	219	225	238	244	233	..
Foreign companies (branches)	21	18	17	17	18	4	16	..
All undertakings	238	239	247	255	269	264	266	..
of which:								
Life	107	98	97	102	107	95	89	..
Domestic undertakings	86	80	82	86	93	95	77	..
Foreign controlled undertakings	85	77	79	81	90	91	73	..
Foreign companies (branches)	20	17	16	16	14	0	12	..
All undertakings	107	98	97	102	107	95	89	..
Non-life	132	141	149	154	162	168	177	..
Domestic undertakings	131	141	149	152	158	164	173	..
Foreign controlled undertakings	125	133	141	143	149	153	160	..
Foreign companies (branches)	1	1	1	2	4	4	5	..
All undertakings	132	141	149	154	162	168	177	..
Total								
Domestic undertakings	244	244	258	266	279	292	287	..
Foreign controlled undertakings	236	233	247	253	267	277	270	..
Foreign companies (branches)	27	27	27	30	32	21	36	..
All undertakings	271	271	285	296	311	313	323	..

Slovak Republic
Table 1. Selected aggregates *(cont.)*

Million EUR

	2009	2010	2011	2012	2013	2014	2015	2016
1.4 Gross operating expenses								
Life								
Domestic undertakings	52 |	50	58	58	57	63	72	..
Foreign controlled undertakings	52 |	50	58	58	57	63	72	..
Foreign companies (branches)	1	1	2	3	2	2	3	..
All undertakings	53 |	51	60	60	59	65	75	..
Non-life								
Domestic undertakings	6 |	6	6	2	0	0	0	..
Foreign controlled undertakings	6 |	6	6	2	0	0	0	..
Foreign companies (branches)	18	20	23	26	30	31	32	..
All undertakings	24 |	26	29	28	30	31	32	..
Composite								
Domestic undertakings	488 |	488	492	510	522	529	505	..
Foreign controlled undertakings	468 |	463	465	481	492	498	472	..
Foreign companies (branches)	27	45	23	29	28	7	25	..
All undertakings	515 |	532	515	539	549	536	531	..
of which:								
Life	230 |	219	212	231	228	212	187	..
Domestic undertakings	205 |	196	190	207	207	212	170	..
Foreign controlled undertakings	199 |	184	180	195	197	202	160	..
Foreign companies (branches)	25	24	22	24	21	1	17	..
All undertakings	230 |	219	212	231	228	212	187	..
Non-life	285 |	313	302	308	321	324	344	..
Domestic undertakings	283 |	292	301	303	314	317	336	..
Foreign controlled undertakings	269 |	279	285	286	295	295	312	..
Foreign companies (branches)	2	21	1	5	7	6	8	..
All undertakings	285 |	313	302	308	321	324	344	..
Total								
Domestic undertakings	546	543	555	569	578	592	578	..
Foreign controlled undertakings	526	518	529	541	549	561	544	..
Foreign companies (branches)	46	66	48	57	60	40	60	..
All undertakings	592	610	603	627	639	632	638	..
1.5 Insurance business written abroad by branches, gross premiums								
Life								
Branches and agencies	0 |	0	0	0	0	0	1	..
Subsidaries	0 |	0	0	0	0	1	5	..
Total	0 |	0	0	0	0	1	6	..
Non-life								
Branches and agencies	0 |	0	0	0	0	0	0	..
Subsidaries	0 |	0	0	0	0	0	0	..
Total	0 |	0	0	0	0	0	0	..
Composite								
Branches and agencies	1 |	0	0	1	1	2	2	..
Subsidaries	4 |	4	4	3	3	4	6	..
Total	4 |	4	4	4	5	6	8	..
of which:								
Life	0 |	0	0	0	0	0	0	..
Branches and agencies	0 |	0	0	0	0	0	0	..
Subsidaries	0 |	0	0	0	0	0	0	..
Total	0 |	0	0	0	0	0	0	..
Non-life	4 |	4	4	4	5	6	8	..
Branches and agencies	1 |	0	0	1	1	2	2	..
Subsidaries	4 |	4	4	3	3	4	6	..
Total	4 |	4	4	4	5	6	8	..
Total								
Branches and agencies	1	0	0	1	1	2	3	..
Subsidaries	4	4	4	3	3	5	10	..
Total	4	4	4	4	5	7	14	..

.. Not available; | Break in series

Note: Detailed metadata at: http://metalinks.oecd.org/ins/20180621/cffd.

Disclaimer: http://oe.cd/disclaimer

Source: OECD Insurance Statistics (database)

Slovak Republic
Table 2. Number of companies and employees

	2009	2010	2011	2012	2013	2014	2015	2016
2.1 Number of companies								
Life								
Domestic undertakings	6	6	6	5	5	5	5	3
Foreign controlled undertakings	6	6	6	5	5	5	5	3
Foreign companies (branches)	2	2	2	1	1	1	1	2
All undertakings	8	8	8	6	6	6	6	5
Non-life								
Domestic undertakings	2	2	2	1	0	0	0	0
Foreign controlled undertakings	2	2	2	1	0	0	0	0
Foreign companies (branches)	10	12	13	16	17	17	17	19
All undertakings	12	14	15	17	17	17	17	19
Composite								
Domestic undertakings	12	12	12	12	12	12	12	12
Foreign controlled undertakings	10	10	10	10	10	10	10	12
Foreign companies (branches)	2	1	2	2	2	2	2	18
All undertakings	14	13	14	14	14	14	14	30
Reinsurance								
Domestic undertakings	0	0	0	0	0	0	0	0
Foreign controlled undertakings	0	0	0	0	0	0	0	0
Foreign companies (branches)	0	1	1	1	1	1	1	0
All undertakings	0	1	1	1	1	1	1	0
Total								
Domestic undertakings	20	20	20	18	17	17	17	15
Foreign controlled undertakings	18	18	18	16	15	15	15	15
Foreign companies (branches)	14	16	18	20	21	21	21	39
All undertakings	34	36	38	38	38	38	38	54
2.2 Number of employees								
Insurance undertakings	6 359	6 213	6 087	5 878	5 778	5 937	..	..
Intermediaries	1 268	962	1 020	1 373	..	1 358	..	..
Total	7 627	7 175	7 107	7 251	..	7 295	..	..

.. Not available

Note: Detailed metadata at: http://metalinks.oecd.org/ins/20180621/cffd.

Disclaimer: http://oe.cd/disclaimer

Source: OECD Insurance Statistics (database)

Slovenia
Table 1. Selected aggregates

Million EUR

	2009	2010	2011	2012	2013	2014	2015	2016
1.1 Insurance business written in the reporting country								
1.1.1 Insurance business, by ownership								
Gross premiums								
Domestic undertakings	2 174	2 178	2 184	2 192	2 114	2 095	2 150	2 182
Foreign controlled undertakings	151	164	169	166	166	166	172	180
Foreign companies (branches)	..	..	..	..	..	..	..	..
All undertakings	2 174	2 178	2 184	2 192	2 114	2 095	2 150	2 182
Premiums ceded								
Domestic undertakings	294	277	279	283	258	274	256	269
Foreign controlled undertakings	36	41	40	27	27	28	33	39
Foreign companies (branches)	..	..	..	..	..	..	..	..
All undertakings	294	277	279	283	258	274	256	269
Net written premiums								
Domestic undertakings	1 880	1 901	1 905	1 909	1 856	1 821	1 894	1 914
Foreign controlled undertakings	115	123	128	139	140	137	139	141
Foreign companies (branches)	..	..	..	..	..	..	..	..
All undertakings	1 880	1 901	1 905	1 909	1 856	1 821	1 894	1 914
1.1.2 Insurance business on foreign risks, gross premiums								
Life	1	0	0	0	..	..	..	..
Non-life	0	..	..	..	0	0	0	..
Composite	1	0	0	2	2	1	1	..
of which:								
Life	0	..	..	..	0	0	1	..
Non-life	1	0	0	2	1	1	0	..
Total	1	1	0	2	2	2	2	..
1.1.3 Life insurance payments, by class, gross premiums								
Annuities	..	..	..	..	..	..	..	..
Unit linked	219	231	228	219	201	195	215	213
Other life insurance	258	254	252	266	273	284	283	279
Total life insurance	477	485	479	485	473	479	498	492
***of which:** Pension contracts*	120	52	51	65	45	37	37	39
1.1.4 Non-life insurance payments, by class, gross premiums								
Motor vehicle insurance	646	627	601	559	513	495	484	499
Marine, aviation and other transport insurance	15	14	15	18	15	16	18	18
Freight insurance	13	15	15	15	14	13	15	16
Fire and other property damage insurance	366	377	389	396	370	372	393	405
Pecuniary loss insurance	43	51	50	48	49	56	62	62
General liability insurance	54	54	58	61	63	65	64	72
Accident and health	538	528	544	580	585	574	591	591
***of which:** Health*	415	409	428	467	480	470	484	489
Other non-life insurance	22	25	32	30	31	24	25	28
Treaty reinsurance	..	0	0	0	..	0	0	0
Total non-life insurance	1 697	1 691	1 704	1 706	1 641	1 616	1 652	1 690

Slovenia
Table 1. Selected aggregates (cont.)

Million EUR

	2009	2010	2011	2012	2013	2014	2015	2016
1.2 Gross claims payments								
Life								
Domestic undertakings	15 |	22	35	40	31	36	52	50
Foreign controlled undertakings	0 |	0	0	0	0	1	0	2
Foreign companies (branches)	..	..	..	..	..	..	..	..
All undertakings	15 |	22	35	40	31	36	52	50
Non-life								
Domestic undertakings	452 |	456	443	463	482	449	499	491
Foreign controlled undertakings	0 |	0	0	..	..	..	1	0
Foreign companies (branches)	..	..	..	..	..	..	..	..
All undertakings	452 |	456	443	463	482	449	499	491
Composite								
Domestic undertakings	942 |	889	878	902	951	941	911	903
Foreign controlled undertakings	62 |	72	77	84	93	90	91	95
Foreign companies (branches)	..	..	..	..	..	..	..	..
All undertakings	942 |	889	878	902	951	941	911	903
of which:								
Life	148 |	186	229	259	299	304	305	314
Domestic undertakings	148 |	186	229	259	299	304	305	314
Foreign controlled undertakings	28 |	35	41	47	51	50	51	50
Foreign companies (branches)	..	..	..	..	..	..	..	..
All undertakings	148 |	186	229	259	299	304	305	314
Non-life	794 |	704	649	642	651	637	606	590
Domestic undertakings	794 |	704	649	642	651	637	606	590
Foreign controlled undertakings	35 |	37	36	38	42	41	40	45
Foreign companies (branches)	..	..	..	..	..	..	..	..
All undertakings	794 |	704	649	642	651	637	606	590
Total								
Domestic undertakings	1 408	1 368	1 355	1 404	1 464	1 426	1 461	1 445
Foreign controlled undertakings	63	72	78	85	93	91	91	97
Foreign companies (branches)	..	..	..	..	..	..	..	..
All undertakings	1 408	1 368	1 355	1 404	1 464	1 426	1 461	1 445
1.3 Commissions								
Life								
Domestic undertakings	11 |	8	7	6	3	3	3	3
Foreign controlled undertakings	0 |	0	0	0	0	0	0	0
Foreign companies (branches)	..	..	..	..	..	..	..	..
All undertakings	11 |	8	7	6	3	3	3	3
Non-life								
Domestic undertakings	2 |	2	2	2	4	7	8	7
Foreign controlled undertakings	0 |	0	0	..	..	..	0	0
Foreign companies (branches)	..	..	..	..	..	..	..	..
All undertakings	2 |	2	2	2	4	7	8	7
Composite								
Domestic undertakings	63 |	70	90	80	84	86	89	86
Foreign controlled undertakings	15 |	17	19	19	19	20	21	28
Foreign companies (branches)	..	..	..	..	..	..	..	..
All undertakings	63 |	70	90	80	84	86	89	86
of which:								
Life	22 |	26	36	27	32	32	34	32
Domestic undertakings	22 |	26	36	27	32	32	34	32
Foreign controlled undertakings	8 |	8	9	10	10	10	10	15
Foreign companies (branches)	..	..	..	..	..	..	..	..
All undertakings	22 |	26	36	27	32	32	34	32
Non-life	42 |	44	53	53	52	54	56	54
Domestic undertakings	42 |	44	53	53	52	54	56	54
Foreign controlled undertakings	7 |	9	9	9	9	10	11	13
Foreign companies (branches)	..	..	..	..	..	..	..	..
All undertakings	42 |	44	53	53	52	54	56	54
Total								
Domestic undertakings	76	80	99	89	91	96	100	96
Foreign controlled undertakings	16	17	19	20	19	20	21	28
Foreign companies (branches)	..	..	..	..	..	..	..	..
All undertakings	76	80	99	89	91	96	100	96

Slovenia
Table 1. Selected aggregates *(cont.)*

Million EUR

	2009	2010	2011	2012	2013	2014	2015	2016
1.4 Gross operating expenses								
Life								
Domestic undertakings	31 |	27	26	28	14	15	16	12
Foreign controlled undertakings	1 |	2	1	2	2	1	1	1
Foreign companies (branches)	..	..	..	..	..	..	..	..
All undertakings	31 |	27	26	28	14	15	16	12
Non-life								
Domestic undertakings	84 |	80	74	80	81	86	90	97
Foreign controlled undertakings	1 |	1	1	..	..	..	0	1
Foreign companies (branches)	..	..	..	..	..	..	..	..
All undertakings	84 |	80	74	80	81	86	90	97
Composite								
Domestic undertakings	302 |	354	356	361	366	362	368	378
Foreign controlled undertakings	44 |	31	52	56	47	57	60	60
Foreign companies (branches)	..	..	..	..	..	..	..	..
All undertakings	302 |	354	356	361	366	362	368	378
of which:								
Life	47 |	86	91	93	104	99	100	99
Domestic undertakings	47 |	86	91	93	104	99	100	99
Foreign controlled undertakings	23 |	20	26	28	26	27	28	26
Foreign companies (branches)	..	..	..	..	..	..	..	..
All undertakings	47 |	86	91	93	104	99	100	99
Non-life	256 |	267	265	269	263	263	268	279
Domestic undertakings	256 |	267	265	269	263	263	268	279
Foreign controlled undertakings	20 |	11	26	28	21	30	32	33
Foreign companies (branches)	..	..	..	..	..	..	..	..
All undertakings	256 |	267	265	269	263	263	268	279
Total								
Domestic undertakings	417	460	456	469	461	462	474	487
Foreign controlled undertakings	46	34	55	57	49	59	62	62
Foreign companies (branches)	..	..	..	..	..	..	..	..
All undertakings	417	460	456	469	461	462	474	487
1.5 Insurance business written abroad by branches, gross premiums								
Life								
Branches and agencies	1 |	0	0	..	..	..	..	..
Subsidaries	0	..	..	..	..	..	..	..
Total	1 |	0	0	..	..	..	..	..
Non-life								
Branches and agencies	..	..	..	..	..	..	..	..
Subsidaries	0	..	..	..	..	..	..	..
Total	..	..	..	..	..	..	..	..
Composite								
Branches and agencies	1 |	0	0	..	..	..	2	..
Subsidaries	0	..	..	..	..	..	..	..
Total	1 |	0	0	..	..	..	2	..
of which:								
Life	..	..	..	..	..	..	2	..
Branches and agencies	..	..	..	..	..	..	2	..
Subsidaries	0	..	..	..	..	..	..	..
Total	..	..	..	..	..	..	2	..
Non-life	1 |	0	0	..	..	..	0	..
Branches and agencies	1 |	0	0	..	..	..	0	..
Subsidaries	0	..	..	..	..	..	..	..
Total	1 |	0	0	..	..	..	0	..
Total								
Branches and agencies	1	0	0	..	..	..	2	..
Subsidaries	0	..	..	..	..	..	..	..
Total	1	0	0	..	..	..	2	..

.. Not available; | Break in series

Note: Detailed metadata at: http://metalinks.oecd.org/ins/20180621/9457.

Disclaimer: http://oe.cd/disclaimer

Source: OECD Insurance Statistics (database)

Slovenia
Table 2. Number of companies and employees

	2009	2010	2011	2012	2013	2014	2015	2016
2.1 Number of companies								
Life								
Domestic undertakings	3	3	4	4	3	3	3	3
Foreign controlled undertakings	1	1	1	1	1	1	1	1
Foreign companies (branches)	0	0	0	0	0	0	0	0
All undertakings	3	3	4	4	3	3	3	3
Non-life								
Domestic undertakings	4	4	4	3	3	3	4	4
Foreign controlled undertakings	1	1	1	0	0	0	0	0
Foreign companies (branches)	1	1	1	3	4	4	4	4
All undertakings	5	5	5	6	7	7	8	8
Composite								
Domestic undertakings	8	8	8	8	8	8	8	7
Foreign controlled undertakings	3	3	3	3	3	3	3	3
Foreign companies (branches)	2	2	2	2	2	2	2	2
All undertakings	10	10	10	10	10	10	10	9
Reinsurance								
Domestic undertakings	2	2	2	2	2	2	2	2
Foreign controlled undertakings	0	0	0	0	0	0	0	0
Foreign companies (branches)	0	0	0	0	0	0	0	0
All undertakings	2	2	2	2	2	2	2	2
Total								
Domestic undertakings	17	17	18	17	16	16	17	16
Foreign controlled undertakings	5	5	5	4	4	4	4	4
Foreign companies (branches)	3	3	3	5	6	6	6	6
All undertakings	20	20	21	22	22	22	23	22
2.2 Number of employees								
Insurance undertakings	6 306	..	..	..	..	..	..	..
Intermediaries	6 230	..	..	..	..	..	..	..
Total	12 536	..	..	..	..	..	..	..

.. Not available

Note: Detailed metadata at: http://metalinks.oecd.org/ins/20180621/9457.

Disclaimer: http://oe.cd/disclaimer

Source: OECD Insurance Statistics (database)

Spain
Table 1. Selected aggregates

Million EUR

	2009	2010	2011	2012	2013	2014	2015	2016
1.1 Insurance business written in the reporting country								
1.1.1 Insurance business, by ownership								
Gross premiums								
Domestic undertakings	61 178	57 485	61 922	56 608	58 110	57 662	59 048	66 541
Foreign controlled undertakings	9 940	8 322	8 045	14 689	12 578	12 542	11 038	..
Foreign companies (branches)	127	135	133	117	0	0	0	..
All undertakings	61 305	57 620	62 055	56 725	58 110	57 662	59 048	66 541
Premiums ceded								
Domestic undertakings	4 886	4 333	4 305	4 235	5 831	5 019	5 161	6 014
Foreign controlled undertakings	1 590	482	793	1 094	1 058	923	736	..
Foreign companies (branches)	42	44	44	42	0	0	0	..
All undertakings	4 928	4 377	4 349	4 277	5 831	5 019	5 161	6 014
Net written premiums								
Domestic undertakings	56 292	53 154	57 617	52 373	52 279	52 643	53 886	60 527
Foreign controlled undertakings	8 349	7 576	7 252	13 594	11 520	11 620	10 301	..
Foreign companies (branches)	86	91	89	75	0	0	0	..
All undertakings	56 377	53 245	57 706	52 448	52 279	52 643	53 886	60 527
1.1.2 Insurance business on foreign risks, gross premiums								
Life	..	..	1	16	22	7	11	13
Non-life	..	..	73	138	79	73	59	45
Composite	..	..	79	54	52	44	61	49
of which:								
Life	..	..	42	39	42	34	46	35
Non-life	..	..	36	16	10	9	15	14
Total	..	..	153	209	153	123	130	107
1.1.3 Life insurance payments, by class, gross premiums								
Annuities	0	6 097	8 992	7 052	7 946	6 406	5 881	8 746
Unit linked	4 340	4 760	4 077	3 748	3 062	2 816	2 721	2 981
Other life insurance	24 811	16 510	16 704	15 828	14 865	16 021	17 128	19 330
Total life insurance	29 151	27 367	29 773	26 629	25 873	25 244	25 730	31 056
of which: *Pension contracts*	0	..	..	..	..	..	..	..
1.1.4 Non-life insurance payments, by class, gross premiums								
Motor vehicle insurance	11 451	10 731	10 698	9 961	9 610	9 445	9 695	10 451
Marine, aviation and other transport insurance	389	356	480	329	390	361	369	369
Freight insurance	216	194	268	194	294	268	261	270
Fire and other property damage insurance	1 298	1 147	2 701	913	2 246	2 315	2 610	2 895
Pecuniary loss insurance	338	298	359	311	175	178	208	283
General liability insurance	1 623	1 283	1 274	1 096	1 077	1 009	1 011	1 049
Accident and health	7 003	6 501	7 630	7 629	7 888	8 227	8 449	8 879
of which: *Health*	6 034	5 611	6 650	6 777	7 031	7 356	7 536	7 902
Other non-life insurance	9 789	9 709	10 410	10 502	10 531	10 558	10 729	11 001
Treaty reinsurance	..	..	0	0	0	0	0	0
Total non-life insurance	32 107	30 219	33 820	30 933	32 211	32 362	33 332	35 197

Spain
Table 1. Selected aggregates (*cont.*)

Million EUR

	2009	2010	2011	2012	2013	2014	2015	2016
1.2 Gross claims payments								
Life								
Domestic undertakings	6 202 |	6 082	12 763	15 189	14 147	16 777	18 872	3 070
Foreign controlled undertakings	1 425 |	1 414	1 996	2 127	1 814	1 688	1 582	..
Foreign companies (branches)	0 |	0	0	0	0	0	0	..
All undertakings	6 202 |	6 082	12 763	15 189	14 147	16 777	18 872	3 070
Non-life								
Domestic undertakings	10 761 |	7 982	9 573	9 489	9 463	9 250	9 593	9 453
Foreign controlled undertakings	2 988 |	1 406	4 025	3 926	3 947	3 890	2 592	..
Foreign companies (branches)	0 |	0	0	0	0	0	0	..
All undertakings	10 761 |	7 982	9 573	9 489	9 463	9 250	9 593	9 453
Composite								
Domestic undertakings	30 439 |	32 008	23 611	22 204	21 477	21 596	20 659	32 425
Foreign controlled undertakings	3 594 |	3 607	5 663	6 495	5 208	5 230	5 136	..
Foreign companies (branches)	52 |	55	63	49	0	0	0	..
All undertakings	30 491 |	32 063	23 674	22 252	21 477	21 596	20 659	32 425
of which:								
Life	18 600 |	19 737	11 327	11 547	9 702	9 986	8 948	20 670
Domestic undertakings	18 559 |	19 702	11 288	11 511	9 702	9 986	8 948	20 670
Foreign controlled undertakings	1 255 |	1 286	2 437	3 836	2 320	2 497	2 292	..
Foreign companies (branches)	41 |	35	38	36	0	0	0	..
All undertakings	18 600 |	19 737	11 327	11 547	9 702	9 986	8 948	20 670
Non-life	11 890 |	12 326	12 347	10 705	11 775	11 610	11 711	11 755
Domestic undertakings	11 880 |	12 306	12 323	10 693	11 775	11 610	11 711	11 755
Foreign controlled undertakings	2 339 |	1 321	3 226	2 659	2 888	2 733	2 843	..
Foreign companies (branches)	10 |	20	24	12	0	0	0	..
All undertakings	11 890 |	12 326	12 347	10 705	11 775	11 610	11 711	11 755
Total								
Domestic undertakings	47 402	46 072	45 947	46 882	45 088	47 622	49 125	44 947
Foreign controlled undertakings	8 007	6 427	11 684	12 548	10 968	10 809	9 310	..
Foreign companies (branches)	52	55	63	49	0	0	0	..
All undertakings	47 454	46 127	46 009	46 930	45 088	47 622	49 125	44 947
1.3 Commissions								
Life								
Domestic undertakings	..	..	..	..	..	660	712	234
Foreign controlled undertakings	..	..	..	..	..	86	71	..
Foreign companies (branches)	..	..	..	..	..	0	0	..
All undertakings	..	..	..	..	..	660	712	234
Non-life								
Domestic undertakings	..	..	..	..	..	1 472	1 436	1 433
Foreign controlled undertakings	..	..	..	..	..	642	517	..
Foreign companies (branches)	..	..	..	..	..	0	0	..
All undertakings	..	..	..	..	..	1 472	1 436	1 433
Composite								
Domestic undertakings	..	..	..	..	..	2 270	2 635	3 328
Foreign controlled undertakings	..	..	..	..	..	669	710	..
Foreign companies (branches)	..	..	..	..	..	0	0	..
All undertakings	..	..	..	..	..	2 270	2 635	3 328
of which:								
Life	..	..	..	..	..	418	379	979
Domestic undertakings	..	..	..	..	..	418	379	979
Foreign controlled undertakings	..	..	..	..	..	94	103	..
Foreign companies (branches)	..	..	..	..	..	0	0	..
All undertakings	..	..	..	..	..	418	379	979
Non-life	..	..	..	..	..	1 852	2 255	2 349
Domestic undertakings	..	..	..	..	..	1 852	2 255	2 349
Foreign controlled undertakings	..	..	..	..	..	576	607	..
Foreign companies (branches)	..	..	..	..	..	0	0	..
All undertakings	..	..	..	..	..	1 852	2 255	2 349
Total								
Domestic undertakings	..	..	..	..	..	4 403	4 782	4 995
Foreign controlled undertakings	..	..	..	..	..	1 398	1 298	..
Foreign companies (branches)	..	..	..	..	..	0	0	..
All undertakings	..	..	..	..	..	4 403	4 782	4 995

Spain
Table 1. Selected aggregates *(cont.)*

Million EUR

	2009	2010	2011	2012	2013	2014	2015	2016
1.4 Gross operating expenses								
Life								
Domestic undertakings	473 |	1 778	171	220	968	994	1 075	425
Foreign controlled undertakings	185 |	207	42	39	201	190	192	..
Foreign companies (branches)	0 |	31	0	0	0	..	..	..
All undertakings	473 |	1 809	171	220	968	994	1 075	425
Non-life								
Domestic undertakings	3 441 |	6 317	487	491	3 046	2 880	2 832	2 876
Foreign controlled undertakings	1 024 |	517	254	242	1 272	1 289	947	..
Foreign companies (branches)	1 |	41	0	0	0	..	..	..
All undertakings	3 442 |	6 358	487	491	3 046	2 880	2 832	2 876
Composite								
Domestic undertakings	16 805 |	..	622	564	5 322	5 034	5 250	6 332
Foreign controlled undertakings	3 132 |	..	140	120	1 152	1 070	1 100	..
Foreign companies (branches)	39 |	..	6	5	1	..	4	..
All undertakings	16 844 |	..	628	569	5 323	5 034	5 254	6 332
of which:								
Life	1 380 |	..	119	87	809	797	729	1 489
Domestic undertakings	1 354 |	..	117	85	809	797	729	1 489
Foreign controlled undertakings	122 |	..	25	26	162	178	186	..
Foreign companies (branches)	26 |	..	2	2	0	..	..	..
All undertakings	1 380 |	..	119	87	809	797	729	1 489
Non-life	15 464 |	..	509	482	4 515	4 237	4 525	4 843
Domestic undertakings	15 451 |	..	506	479	4 514	4 237	4 521	4 843
Foreign controlled undertakings	3 010 |	..	116	94	990	892	913	..
Foreign companies (branches)	13 |	..	4	3	1	0	4	..
All undertakings	15 464 |	..	509	482	4 515	4 237	4 525	4 843
Total								
Domestic undertakings	20 719	8 095	1 280	1 275	9 337	8 907	9 157	9 633
Foreign controlled undertakings	4 341	724	436	401	2 625	2 549	2 239	..
Foreign companies (branches)	40	72	6	5	1	..	4	..
All undertakings	20 759	8 167	1 286	1 280	9 338	8 907	9 161	9 633
1.5 Insurance business written abroad by branches, gross premiums								
Life								
Branches and agencies	..	..	938	323	274	0	0	0
Subsidaries	..	..	..	..	..	..	..	..
Total	..	..	..	..	..	..	..	0
Non-life								
Branches and agencies	..	..	296	419	592	654	701	1 694
Subsidaries	..	..	..	..	..	..	..	..
Total	..	..	..	..	..	..	..	1 694
Composite								
Branches and agencies	..	..	759	135	885	1 286	1 361	1 262
Subsidaries	..	..	..	..	..	..	..	..
Total	..	..	..	..	..	..	..	1 262
of which:								
Life	..	..	..	..	..	..	..	518
Branches and agencies	..	..	157	23	212	559	694	518
Subsidaries	..	..	..	..	..	..	..	..
Total	..	..	..	..	..	..	..	518
Non-life	..	..	..	..	..	..	..	744
Branches and agencies	..	..	602	113	673	728	667	744
Subsidaries	..	..	..	..	..	..	..	..
Total	..	..	..	..	..	..	..	744
Total								
Branches and agencies	..	..	1 994	878	1 751	1 940	2 062	2 955
Subsidaries	..	..	..	..	..	..	..	..
Total	..	..	..	..	..	..	..	2 955

.. Not available; | Break in series

Note: Detailed metadata at: http://metalinks.oecd.org/ins/20180621/cbc2.

Disclaimer: http://oe.cd/disclaimer

Source: OECD Insurance Statistics (database)

Spain
Table 2. Number of companies and employees

	2009	2010	2011	2012	2013	2014	2015	2016
2.1 Number of companies								
Life								
Domestic undertakings	89	93	89	84	83	79	78	32
Foreign controlled undertakings	7	6	11	10	10	9	8	..
Foreign companies (branches)	0	0	0	0	0	0	0	..
All undertakings	89	93	89	84	83	79	78	32
Non-life								
Domestic undertakings	149	141	140	136	132	127	118	121
Foreign controlled undertakings	15	14	19	18	19	19	17	..
Foreign companies (branches)	0	1	0	0	0	0	1	..
All undertakings	149	142	140	136	132	127	119	121
Composite								
Domestic undertakings	56	51	47	46	47	45	41	75
Foreign controlled undertakings	9	8	10	10	8	8	8	..
Foreign companies (branches)	2	1	2	2	1	1	0	..
All undertakings	58	52	49	48	48	46	41	75
Reinsurance								
Domestic undertakings	0	0	2	2	2	3	3	3
Foreign controlled undertakings	0	0	..	0	0	0	0	..
Foreign companies (branches)	0	0	0	0	0	0	0	..
All undertakings	0	0	2	2	2	3	3	3
Total								
Domestic undertakings	294	285	278	268	264	254	240	231
Foreign controlled undertakings	31	28	40	38	37	36	33	..
Foreign companies (branches)	2	2	2	2	1	1	1	..
All undertakings	296	287	280	270	265	255	241	231
2.2 Number of employees								
Insurance undertakings	48 203	48 116	46 557	46 439	46 324	45 535	45 218	47 453
Intermediaries	3 015	3 006	..	..	121 427	129 549	..	..
Total	51 218	51 122	..	..	167 751	175 084	..	..

.. Not available

Note: Detailed metadata at: http://metalinks.oecd.org/ins/20180621/cbc2.

Disclaimer: http://oe.cd/disclaimer

Source: OECD Insurance Statistics (database)

Sweden
Table 1. Selected aggregates

Million SEK

	2009	2010	2011	2012	2013	2014	2015	2016
1.1 Insurance business written in the reporting country								
1.1.1 Insurance business, by ownership								
Gross premiums								
Domestic undertakings	194 904	184 684	182 225	167 132	177 197	332 028	339 533	334 834
Foreign controlled undertakings	65 563	65 344	63 298	65 752	66 854	66 041	62 537	67 208
Foreign companies (branches)	..	..	..	..	..	10 260	..	..
All undertakings	194 904	184 684	182 225	167 132	177 197	342 288	339 533	334 834
Premiums ceded								
Domestic undertakings	14 966	13 654	12 870	13 068	12 967	15 157	10 306	9 139
Foreign controlled undertakings	5 382	4 475	4 583	5 428	4 727	3 870	4 441	4 296
Foreign companies (branches)	..	..	..	..	..	..	..	..
All undertakings	14 966	13 654	12 870	13 068	12 967	15 157	10 306	9 139
Net written premiums								
Domestic undertakings	179 938	171 029	169 355	154 064	164 230	316 871	329 227	325 695
Foreign controlled undertakings	60 181	60 869	58 715	60 324	62 127	62 171	58 096	62 912
Foreign companies (branches)	..	..	..	..	..	10 260	..	..
All undertakings	179 938	171 029	169 355	154 064	164 230	327 131	329 227	325 695
1.1.2 Insurance business on foreign risks, gross premiums								
Life	..	..	..	..	..	581	667	60
Non-life	..	..	..	..	..	28 134	27 121	26 941
Composite total	..	..	..	..	..	..	..	..
Total	..	..	..	..	..	28 715	27 788	27 001
1.1.3 Life insurance payments, by class, gross premiums								
Annuities	79 771	70 960	72 263	73 378	73 377	205 927	169 626	94 037
Unit linked	5 642	5 742	3 790	1 708	1 188	2 366	75 221	85 696
Other life insurance	12 579	12 610	13 615	13 229	13 591	29 900	3 957	71 084
Total life insurance	97 992	89 312	89 668	88 315	88 156	238 192	248 804	250 817
***of which:** Pension contracts*	..	..	..	..	..	..	..	..
1.1.4 Non-life insurance payments, by class, gross premiums								
Motor vehicle insurance	..	..	..	..	..	30 360	21 348	..
Marine, aviation and other transport insurance	..	..	..	..	..	2 627	749	..
Freight insurance	..	..	..	..	..	..	..	..
Fire and other property damage insurance	..	..	..	..	..	29 146	36 720	..
Pecuniary loss insurance	..	..	..	..	..	459	1 070	..
General liability insurance	..	..	..	..	..	4 045	4 119	..
Accident and health	..	..	..	..	..	5 674	5 155	..
***of which:** Health*	..	..	..	..	..	..	..	..
Other non-life insurance	..	..	..	..	..	9 165	21 483	..
Treaty reinsurance	..	..	..	..	..	13 811	..	..
Total non-life insurance	95 932	94 518	91 819	76 947	84 766	95 287	90 644	83 954
1.2 Gross claims payments								
Life								
Domestic undertakings	51 762	50 681	53 464	58 780	64 657	60 930	64 815	76 869
Foreign controlled undertakings	9 493	7 837	7 533	3 499	6 337	6 055	5 719	5 852
Foreign companies (branches)	..	..	..	..	..	5 999	..	..
All undertakings	61 255	50 681	53 464	58 780	64 657	66 929	64 815	76 869
Non-life								
Domestic undertakings	69 046	67 685	68 400	69 882	69 100	75 805	64 537	65 941
Foreign controlled undertakings	31 968	31 815	31 370	31 639	31 398	31 024	23 701	22 495
Foreign companies (branches)	..	..	..	..	..	5 328	..	..
All undertakings	..	67 685	68 400	69 882	69 100	81 133	64 537	65 941
Composite, all undertakings	..	..	..	..	..	..	..	..
Total								
Domestic undertakings	120 808	118 366	121 864	128 662	133 757	136 735	129 352	142 810
Foreign controlled undertakings	41 461	39 652	38 903	35 138	37 735	37 079	29 420	28 347
Foreign companies (branches)	..	..	..	..	..	11 327	..	..
All undertakings	61 255	118 366	121 864	128 662	133 757	148 062	129 352	142 810

Sweden
Table 1. Selected aggregates *(cont.)*

Million SEK

	2009	2010	2011	2012	2013	2014	2015	2016
1.3 Commissions								
Life								
Domestic undertakings	..	..	..	..	..	4 167	3 782	3 063
Foreign controlled undertakings	..	..	..	..	..	1 302	610	274
Foreign companies (branches)	..	..	..	..	..	121	..	..
All undertakings	..	..	..	..	..	4 288	3 782	3 063
Non-life								
Domestic undertakings	..	..	..	..	..	4 168	4 264	3 848
Foreign controlled undertakings	..	..	..	..	..	2 049	2 589	2 362
Foreign companies (branches)	..	..	..	..	..	786	..	..
All undertakings	..	..	..	..	..	4 954	4 264	3 848
Composite, all undertakings	..	..	..	..	..	..	..	..
Total								
Domestic undertakings	..	..	..	..	..	8 335	8 046	6 911
Foreign controlled undertakings	..	..	..	..	..	3 351	3 199	2 636
Foreign companies (branches)	..	..	..	..	..	907	..	..
All undertakings	..	..	..	..	..	9 242	8 046	6 911
1.4 Gross operating expenses								
Life								
Domestic undertakings	10 158	10 514	10 785	11 509	12 115	12 738	13 573	12 617
Foreign controlled undertakings	2 736	3 264	3 488	3 557	3 630	3 639	2 122	1 297
Foreign companies (branches)	..	..	..	..	..	..	..	..
All undertakings	12 894	10 514	10 785	11 509	12 115	12 738	13 573	12 617
Non-life								
Domestic undertakings	15 208	15 117	14 468	14 989	15 004	16 878	16 854	15 781
Foreign controlled undertakings	8 235	8 189	7 262	7 138	7 248	8 238	7 704	7 205
Foreign companies (branches)	..	..	..	..	..	..	..	..
All undertakings	23 443	15 117	14 468	14 989	15 004	16 878	16 854	15 781
Composite, all undertakings	..	..	..	..	..	..	..	..
Total								
Domestic undertakings	25 366	25 631	25 253	26 498	27 119	29 616	30 427	28 398
Foreign controlled undertakings	10 971	11 453	10 750	10 695	10 878	11 877	9 826	8 502
Foreign companies (branches)	..	..	..	..	..	..	..	..
All undertakings	36 337	25 631	25 253	26 498	27 119	29 616	30 427	28 398
1.5 Insurance business written abroad by branches, gross premiums								
Life								
Branches and agencies	435	315	108	234	..	243	279	284
Subsidaries	..	..	..	..	..	..	..	..
Total	..	..	108	234	..	243	279	284
Non-life								
Branches and agencies	19 022	19 011	18 526	18 948	..	18 630	18 207	18 337
Subsidaries	..	..	..	..	..	..	..	..
Total	..	..	18 526	18 948	..	18 630	18 207	18 337
Composite total	..	..	..	..	..	..	..	..
Total								
Branches and agencies	19 457	19 326	18 634	19 182	..	18 873	18 486	18 621
Subsidaries	..	..	..	..	..	..	..	..
Total	..	..	18 634	19 182	..	18 873	18 486	18 621

.. Not available

Note: Detailed metadata at: http://metalinks.oecd.org/ins/20180621/81db.

Disclaimer: http://oe.cd/disclaimer

Source: OECD Insurance Statistics (database)

Sweden
Table 2. Number of companies and employees

	2009	2010	2011	2012	2013	2014	2015	2016
2.1 Number of companies								
Life								
Domestic undertakings	45	39	39	39	39	39	38	37
Foreign controlled undertakings	9	7	8	9	8	8	8	6
Foreign companies (branches)	9	9	5	5	5	6	8	6
All undertakings	54	48	44	44	44	45	46	43
Non-life								
Domestic undertakings	149	150	139	131	130	130	127	120
Foreign controlled undertakings	17	18	18	46	44	34	24	14
Foreign companies (branches)	37	39	31	32	32	28	33	31
All undertakings	186	189	170	163	162	158	160	151
Composite, all undertakings	**0**	**0**	**0**	**0**	**0**	**0**	**0**	**0**
Reinsurance								
Domestic undertakings	5	3	3	2	1	1	1	0
Foreign controlled undertakings	1	1	2	0	0	0	1	0
Foreign companies (branches)	0	..	..	0	..	0	0	..
All undertakings	5	3	3	2	1	1	1	..
Total								
Domestic undertakings	199	192	181	172	170	170	166	157
Foreign controlled undertakings	27	26	28	55	52	42	33	20
Foreign companies (branches)	46	48	36	37	37	34	41	37
All undertakings	245	240	217	209	207	204	207	194
2.2 Number of employees								
Insurance undertakings	19 940	19 017	18 848	19 158	19 059	19 573	18 792	20 600
Intermediaries	2 000	2 000	2 000	2 000	2 000	3 849	3 235	3 540
Total	21 940	21 017	20 848	21 158	21 059	23 422	22 027	..

.. Not available

Note: Detailed metadata at: http://metalinks.oecd.org/ins/20180621/81db.

Disclaimer: http://oe.cd/disclaimer

Source: OECD Insurance Statistics (database)

Switzerland
Table 1. Selected aggregates

Million CHF

	2009	2010	2011	2012	2013	2014	2015	2016
1.1 Insurance business written in the reporting country								
1.1.1 Insurance business, by ownership								
Gross premiums								
Domestic undertakings	60 259	61 448	61 417	63 507	66 569	66 312	65 628	63 975
Foreign controlled undertakings	..	13 162	13 600	14 322	15 423	14 214	13 846	12 578
Foreign companies (branches)	1 973	2 834	2 062	2 331	2 267	1 923	2 091	2 522
All undertakings	62 232	64 282	63 479	65 838	68 836	68 235	67 720	66 497
Premiums ceded								
Domestic undertakings	3 872	4 802	4 000	4 479	4 536	4 346	4 141	3 363
Foreign controlled undertakings	..	1 289	1 024	1 219	963	831	731	506
Foreign companies (branches)	380	442	467	487	532	533	553	813
All undertakings	4 252	5 244	4 467	4 965	5 068	4 879	4 694	4 176
Net written premiums								
Domestic undertakings	56 387	56 646	57 417	59 028	62 033	61 966	61 487	60 612
Foreign controlled undertakings	..	11 873	12 577	13 102	14 460	13 383	13 115	12 072
Foreign companies (branches)	1 593	2 392	1 595	1 845	1 735	1 390	1 539	1 709
All undertakings	57 980	59 038	59 012	60 873	63 768	63 356	63 026	62 321
1.1.2 Insurance business on foreign risks, gross premiums								
Life	..	..	..	..	..	..	..	..
Non-life	..	..	..	..	..	..	..	..
Composite total	..	..	..	..	..	..	..	..
Total	..	..	..	..	..	..	..	..
1.1.3 Life insurance payments, by class, gross premiums								
Annuities	1 254	873	737	677	564	441	495	428
Unit linked	2 797	3 052	2 423	2 037	2 403	1 730	1 755	1 738
Other life insurance	25 378	26 239	27 397	27 841	29 707	30 478	30 359	28 518
Total life insurance	29 429	30 164	30 557	31 155	32 675	32 649	32 609	30 684
***of which:** Pension contracts*	19 748	..	..	..	..	..	..	..
1.1.4 Non-life insurance payments, by class, gross premiums								
Motor vehicle insurance	9 480	6 357	6 382	6 526	6 556	6 580	6 595	6 598
Marine, aviation and other transport insurance	3 379	964	804	968	1 060	876	732	657
Freight insurance	..	..	..	..	..	..	..	..
Fire and other property damage insurance	15 102	7 335	7 457	8 150	8 206	8 123	7 909	7 411
Pecuniary loss insurance	1 293	885	832	932	1 042	1 096	897	1 095
General liability insurance	6 360	3 550	3 243	3 514	3 558	3 658	3 562	3 293
Accident and health	12 789	12 540	12 551	13 093	13 889	13 414	13 387	14 585
***of which:** Health*	9 019	9 182	9 383	9 656	9 911	9 934	10 266	10 606
Other non-life insurance	1 032	1 073	1 036	1 151	1 351	1 378	1 525	1 649
Treaty reinsurance	4 816	..	..	..	..	..	..	..
Total non-life insurance	54 251	32 704	32 306	34 334	35 661	35 125	34 607	35 288
1.2 Gross claims payments								
Life								
Domestic undertakings	28 255	25 420	27 182	25 817	27 624	27 943	27 794	29 083
Foreign controlled undertakings	..	7 127	7 354	7 060	8 854	7 917	8 123	8 578
Foreign companies (branches)	19	44	104	186	306	3	3	3
All undertakings	28 274	25 464	27 286	26 003	27 930	27 946	27 797	29 086
Non-life								
Domestic undertakings	15 676	15 122	15 548	20 279	19 735	20 149	20 621	20 498
Foreign controlled undertakings	..	1 962	1 974	2 292	2 171	2 281	2 671	2 471
Foreign companies (branches)	518	85	404	667	798	874	902	1 105
All undertakings	16 194	15 207	15 952	20 946	20 533	21 023	21 523	21 603
Composite, all undertakings	..	..	..	..	..	..	..	..
Total								
Domestic undertakings	43 931	40 542	42 730	46 096	47 359	48 092	48 415	49 581
Foreign controlled undertakings	..	9 090	9 328	9 352	11 025	10 198	10 794	11 049
Foreign companies (branches)	537	129	509	853	1 104	877	905	1 108
All undertakings	44 468	40 671	43 238	46 949	48 463	48 969	49 320	50 689
1.3 Commissions								
Life								
Domestic undertakings	947	906	848	875	904	920	856	856
Foreign controlled undertakings	..	109	107	103	148	114	169	169
Foreign companies (branches)	3	9	8	8	11	0	0	1
All undertakings	950	915	856	883	915	920	856	857
Non-life								
Domestic undertakings	2 005	2 052	1 886	1 955	2 067	1 597	2 188	2 289
Foreign controlled undertakings	..	471	450	442	372	381	441	450
Foreign companies (branches)	49	76	85	88	95	91	78	65
All undertakings	2 054	2 128	1 970	2 043	2 162	1 688	2 266	2 354
Composite, all undertakings	..	..	..	..	..	..	..	..
Total								
Domestic undertakings	2 952	2 958	2 734	2 830	2 971	2 517	3 044	3 145
Foreign controlled undertakings	..	581	557	545	520	495	610	619
Foreign companies (branches)	52	85	92	96	106	91	78	66
All undertakings	3 004	3 043	2 826	2 926	3 077	2 608	3 122	3 211

Switzerland
Table 1. Selected aggregates *(cont.)*

Million CHF

	2009	2010	2011	2012	2013	2014	2015	2016
1.4 Gross operating expenses								
Life								
Domestic undertakings	2 505	2 382	2 444	1 390	1 289	1 364	1 078	1 085
Foreign controlled undertakings	366	395	450	239	176	209	156	156
Foreign companies (branches)	6	12	11	4	4	2	1	1
All undertakings	2 518	2 394	2 455	1 394	1 293	1 366	1 079	1 086
Non-life								
Domestic undertakings	7 943	7 677	7 179	3 835	3 745	5 520	2 975	2 981
Foreign controlled undertakings	1 088	1 063	1 039	371	416	420	341	310
Foreign companies (branches)	162	459	408	80	100	108	103	215
All undertakings	8 267	8 136	7 588	3 915	3 845	5 628	3 078	3 196
Composite, all undertakings	..	..	..	..	..	..	..	..
Total								
Domestic undertakings	10 448	10 059	9 624	5 225	5 034	6 884	4 053	4 066
Foreign controlled undertakings	1 454	1 458	1 489	610	592	629	497	466
Foreign companies (branches)	168	471	419	84	104	110	104	216
All undertakings	10 785	10 530	10 043	5 309	5 138	6 994	4 157	4 282
1.5 Insurance business written abroad by branches, gross premiums								
Life								
Branches and agencies	2 668	2 219	2 036	2 006	1 967	1 794	1 604	1 567
Subsidaries	..	..	..	..	..	..	..	..
Total	2 668	2 219	2 036	2 006	1 967	1 794	1 604	1 567
Non-life								
Branches and agencies	18 286	16 881	13 446	15 417	15 563	15 331	14 100	12 578
Subsidaries	..	..	..	..	..	..	..	..
Total	18 286	16 881	13 446	15 417	15 563	15 331	14 100	12 578
Composite total	..	..	..	..	..	..	..	..
Total								
Branches and agencies	20 954	19 100	15 482	17 423	17 531	17 125	15 704	14 145
Subsidaries	..	..	..	..	..	..	..	..
Total	20 954	19 100	15 482	17 423	17 531	17 125	15 704	14 145

.. Not available

Note: Detailed metadata at: http://metalinks.oecd.org/ins/20180621/b5fd.

Disclaimer: http://oe.cd/disclaimer

Source: OECD Insurance Statistics (database)

Switzerland
Table 2. Number of companies and employees

	2009	2010	2011	2012	2013	2014	2015	2016
2.1 Number of companies								
Life								
Domestic undertakings	21	21	20	19	19	18	17	16
Foreign controlled undertakings	..	1	1	1	1	1	1	1
Foreign companies (branches)	4	4	4	4	4	3	3	3
All undertakings	25	25	24	23	23	21	20	19
Non-life								
Domestic undertakings	79	79	79	81	80	79	76	74
Foreign controlled undertakings	..	6	6	6	6	6	6	5
Foreign companies (branches)	46	47	45	42	44	48	46	46
All undertakings	125	126	124	123	124	127	122	120
Composite, all undertakings	**0**	**0**	**0**	**0**	**0**	**0**	**0**	**0**
Reinsurance								
Domestic undertakings	68	62	62	61	62	62	59	55
Foreign controlled undertakings	..	8	7	7	7	7	7	7
Foreign companies (branches)	..	..	..	..	..	..	..	..
All undertakings	68	62	62	61	62	62	59	55
Total								
Domestic undertakings	168	162	161	161	161	159	152	145
Foreign controlled undertakings	..	15	14	14	14	14	14	13
Foreign companies (branches)	50	51	49	46	48	51	49	49
All undertakings	218	213	210	207	209	210	201	194
2.2 Number of employees								
Insurance undertakings	41 130	..	..	..	..	..	..	..
Intermediaries	..	..	..	..	..	..	..	..
Total	41 130	..	..	..	..	..	..	..

.. Not available

Note: Detailed metadata at: http://metalinks.oecd.org/ins/20180621/b5fd.

Disclaimer: http://oe.cd/disclaimer

Source: OECD Insurance Statistics (database)

Turkey
Table 1. Selected aggregates

Million TRY

	2009	2010	2011	2012	2013	2014	2015	2016
1.1 Insurance business written in the reporting country								
1.1.1 Insurance business, by ownership								
Gross premiums								
Domestic undertakings	13 097	14 958	17 131	20 427	25 084	26 872	31 903	41 280
Foreign controlled undertakings	6 828	7 525	8 956	10 122	14 981	15 528	20 981	25 640
Foreign companies (branches)	8	27	32	46	68	77	126	152
All undertakings	13 105	14 985	17 164	20 473	25 152	26 949	32 029	41 431
Premiums ceded								
Domestic undertakings	3 412	3 443	4 287	4 483	6 077	6 686	7 984	9 816
Foreign controlled undertakings	1 822	1 834	2 229	2 192	3 458	3 510	4 773	5 482
Foreign companies (branches)	6	21	22	33	49	57	74	76
All undertakings	3 418	3 464	4 309	4 516	6 126	6 743	8 059	9 892
Net written premiums								
Domestic undertakings	9 685	11 515	12 845	15 944	19 006	20 186	23 919	31 464
Foreign controlled undertakings	5 006	5 691	6 728	7 931	11 522	12 018	16 208	20 158
Foreign companies (branches)	2	6	10	13	20	20	52	76
All undertakings	9 687	11 521	12 854	15 957	19 026	20 206	23 971	31 540
1.1.2 Insurance business on foreign risks, gross premiums								
Life	..	..	..	..	..	3 280	..	6 166
Non-life	..	..	..	..	..	22 711	..	34 322
Composite	..	..	..	..	..	958	..	943
of which:								
Life	..	..	..	..	..	24	..	19
Non-life	..	..	..	..	..	934	..	924
Total	..	..	..	..	..	26 948	..	41 431
1.1.3 Life insurance payments, by class, gross premiums								
Annuities	..	..	..	..	..	..	..	..
Unit linked	..	..	..	..	..	..	..	..
Other life insurance	..	..	..	..	..	..	..	..
Total life insurance	..	2 576	3 087	3 107	3 354	3 895	3 720	5 916
***of which:** Pension contracts*	..	..	..	..	..	..	..	..
1.1.4 Non-life insurance payments, by class, gross premiums								
Motor vehicle insurance	5 058	5 867	6 761	8 091	10 411	10 648	13 102	19 156
Marine, aviation and other transport insurance	245	185	268	263	253	321	423	455
Freight insurance	286	327	359	378	416	530	580	585
Fire and other property damage insurance	3 236	3 401	3 783	4 390	5 512	6 992	8 105	9 032
Pecuniary loss insurance	112	135	204	228	302	318	443	439
General liability insurance	265	407	386	420	508	679	811	863
Accident and health	2 040	2 413	2 657	2 897	3 352	4 010	4 685	4 582
***of which:** Health*	1 499	1 810	1 999	2 227	2 472	0	0	..
Other non-life insurance	37	44	77	61	74	147	99	134
Treaty reinsurance	..	..	..	..	..	..	0	..
Total non-life insurance	11 280	12 778	14 496	16 727	20 828	23 645	28 249	35 246

Turkey
Table 1. Selected aggregates *(cont.)*

Million TRY

	2009	2010	2011	2012	2013	2014	2015	2016
1.2 Gross claims payments								
Life								
Domestic undertakings	1 787	1 787	1 935	2 037	2 355	2 085	2 557	2 957
Foreign controlled undertakings	817	817	582	483	1 128	760	1 194	1 485
Foreign companies (branches)	0	0	..	..	..	..	..	0
All undertakings	1 787	1 787	1 935	2 037	2 355	2 085	2 557	2 957
Non-life								
Domestic undertakings	5 960	6 142	7 968	9 163	9 440	11 314	13 322	15 041
Foreign controlled undertakings	3 705	3 978	4 786	5 327	6 301	7 496	8 700	-9 940
Foreign companies (branches)	10	0	2	3	11	10	34	128
All undertakings	5 970	6 143	7 969	9 166	9 451	11 325	13 356	15 168
Composite								
Domestic undertakings	1 334	1 344	..	..	619	592	664	572
Foreign controlled undertakings	69	82	..	..	..	..	..	..
Foreign companies (branches)	0	0	..	..	..	..	..	..
All undertakings	1 334	1 344	0	721	619	592	664	572
of which:								
Life	7	10	0	6	7	11	6	9
Domestic undertakings	7	10	..	..	7	11	6	9
Foreign controlled undertakings	0	0	..	..	..	..	..	..
Foreign companies (branches)	0	0	..	..	..	..	..	..
All undertakings	7	10	0	6	7	11	6	9
Non-life	1 328	1 334	0	715	612	581	657	564
Domestic undertakings	1 328	1 334	..	..	612	581	657	564
Foreign controlled undertakings	69	82	..	..	..	..	..	..
Foreign companies (branches)	0	0	..	..	..	..	..	..
All undertakings	1 328	1 334	0	715	612	581	657	564
Total								
Domestic undertakings	9 081	9 273	9 903	11 200	12 413	13 991	16 543	18 570
Foreign controlled undertakings	4 591	4 877	5 369	5 810	7 429	8 256	9 894	-8 455
Foreign companies (branches)	10	0	2	3	11	10	34	128
All undertakings	9 092	9 273	9 905	11 924	12 425	14 001	16 578	18 698
1.3 Commissions								
Life								
Domestic undertakings	..	..	..	..	..	..	..	..
Foreign controlled undertakings	..	..	..	..	..	..	..	..
Foreign companies (branches)	..	..	..	..	..	..	..	..
All undertakings	..	..	..	..	..	..	..	..
Non-life								
Domestic undertakings	..	..	..	..	..	..	..	..
Foreign controlled undertakings	..	..	..	..	..	..	..	..
Foreign companies (branches)	..	..	..	..	..	..	..	..
All undertakings	..	..	..	..	..	..	..	..
Composite								
Domestic undertakings	..	..	..	..	..	..	..	..
Foreign controlled undertakings	..	..	..	..	..	..	..	..
Foreign companies (branches)	..	..	..	..	..	..	..	..
All undertakings	..	..	..	..	..	..	..	..
of which:								
Life	..	..	..	..	..	..	..	..
Domestic undertakings	..	..	..	..	..	..	..	..
Foreign controlled undertakings	..	..	..	..	..	..	..	..
Foreign companies (branches)	..	..	..	..	..	..	..	..
All undertakings	..	..	..	..	..	..	..	..
Non-life	..	..	..	..	..	..	..	..
Domestic undertakings	..	..	..	..	..	..	..	..
Foreign controlled undertakings	..	..	..	..	..	..	..	..
Foreign companies (branches)	..	..	..	..	..	..	..	..
All undertakings	..	..	..	..	..	..	..	..
Total								
Domestic undertakings	..	..	..	..	..	..	..	..
Foreign controlled undertakings	..	..	..	..	..	..	..	..
Foreign companies (branches)	..	..	..	..	..	..	..	..
All undertakings	..	..	..	..	..	..	..	..

Turkey
Table 1. Selected aggregates (cont.)

Million TRY

	2009	2010	2011	2012	2013	2014	2015	2016
1.4 Gross operating expenses								
Life								
Domestic undertakings	586 |	717	836	978	2 009	1 198	1 595	1 970
Foreign controlled undertakings	273 |	287	361	422	1 242	765	1 033	1 241
Foreign companies (branches)	0	0	..	..	..	..	..	..
All undertakings	586 |	717	836	978	2 009	1 198	1 595	1 970
Non-life								
Domestic undertakings	1 975 |	2 336	2 859	3 230	3 726	4 309	4 648	5 579
Foreign controlled undertakings	1 290 |	1 585	1 827	1 976	2 564	2 944	3 110	3 847
Foreign companies (branches)	4	4	8	12	19	20	24	26
All undertakings	1 979 |	2 340	2 867	3 242	3 745	4 329	4 672	5 604
Composite								
Domestic undertakings	391 |	421	..	..	..	..	309	316
Foreign controlled undertakings	19 |	16	..	..	..	..	..	5
Foreign companies (branches)	0	0	..	..	..	..	..	..
All undertakings	391 |	421	0	285	294	289	309	316
of which:								
Life	6 |	7	0	8	10	8	10	10
Domestic undertakings	6 |	7	..	..	..	..	10	10
Foreign controlled undertakings	0 |	0	..	..	..	..	..	..
Foreign companies (branches)	0	0	..	..	..	..	..	..
All undertakings	6 |	7	0	8	10	8	10	10
Non-life	385 |	414	0	277	284	281	299	306
Domestic undertakings	385 |	414	..	..	..	..	299	306
Foreign controlled undertakings	19 |	16	..	..	..	..	..	5
Foreign companies (branches)	0	0	..	..	..	..	..	..
All undertakings	385 |	414	0	277	284	281	299	306
Total								
Domestic undertakings	2 952	3 473	3 694	4 209	5 735	5 507	6 552	7 865
Foreign controlled undertakings	1 582	1 888	2 188	2 399	3 806	3 708	4 143	5 092
Foreign companies (branches)	4	4	8	12	19	20	24	26
All undertakings	2 956	3 478	3 702	4 506	6 048	5 816	6 576	7 890
1.5 Insurance business written abroad by branches, gross premiums								
Life								
Branches and agencies	..	..	..	..	..	..	..	..
Subsidaries	..	..	..	..	..	..	..	..
Total	..	..	..	..	..	..	..	..
Non-life								
Branches and agencies	..	..	..	..	..	..	..	..
Subsidaries	..	..	..	..	..	..	..	..
Total	..	..	..	..	..	..	..	..
Composite								
Branches and agencies	..	..	..	..	..	..	..	..
Subsidaries	..	..	..	..	..	..	..	..
Total	..	..	..	..	..	..	..	..
of which:								
Life	..	..	..	..	..	..	..	..
Branches and agencies	..	..	..	..	..	..	..	..
Subsidaries	..	..	..	..	..	..	..	..
Total	..	..	..	..	..	..	..	..
Non-life	..	..	..	..	..	..	..	..
Branches and agencies	..	..	..	..	..	..	..	..
Subsidaries	..	..	..	..	..	..	..	..
Total	..	..	..	..	..	..	..	..
Total								
Branches and agencies	..	..	..	..	..	..	..	..
Subsidaries	..	..	..	..	..	..	..	..
Total	..	..	..	..	..	..	..	..

.. Not available; | Break in series

Note: Detailed metadata at: http://metalinks.oecd.org/ins/20180621/8fc0.

Disclaimer: http://oe.cd/disclaimer

Source: OECD Insurance Statistics (database)

Turkey
Table 2. Number of companies and employees

	2009	2010	2011	2012	2013	2014	2015	2016
2.1 Number of companies								
Life								
Domestic undertakings	21	23	24	23	24	25	23	22
Foreign controlled undertakings	13	14	14	13	16	16	15	15
Foreign companies (branches)	0	0	..	0	..	0	..	0
All undertakings	21	23	24	23	24	25	23	22
Non-life								
Domestic undertakings	27	29	33	33	34	36	36	35
Foreign controlled undertakings	17	19	23	22	22	24	22	23
Foreign companies (branches)	2	2	2	2	2	2	2	2
All undertakings	29	31	35	35	36	38	38	37
Composite								
Domestic undertakings	3	3	..	0	..	0	..	0
Foreign controlled undertakings	1	1	..	0	..	0	..	0
Foreign companies (branches)	0	0	..	0	..	0	..	0
All undertakings	3	3	..	0	..	0	..	0
Reinsurance								
Domestic undertakings	1	1	2	1	1	1	1	2
Foreign controlled undertakings	0	0	..	0	..	0	..	1
Foreign companies (branches)	0	0	..	0	..	0	..	0
All undertakings	1	1	2	1	1	1	1	2
Total								
Domestic undertakings	52	56	59	57	59	62	60	59
Foreign controlled undertakings	31	34	37	35	38	40	37	39
Foreign companies (branches)	2	2	2	2	2	2	2	2
All undertakings	54	58	61	59	61	64	62	61
2.2 Number of employees								
Insurance undertakings	15 610	15 412	10 123	17 304	18 297	19 305	19 274	19 240
Intermediaries	26 567	16 282	16 706	16 994	15 603	15 587	18 931	35 992
Total	42 177	31 694	26 829	34 298	33 900	34 892	38 205	55 232

.. Not available

Note: Detailed metadata at: http://metalinks.oecd.org/ins/20180621/8fc0.

Disclaimer: http://oe.cd/disclaimer

Source: OECD Insurance Statistics (database)

United Kingdom
Table 1. Selected aggregates

Million GBP

	2009	2010	2011	2012	2013	2014	2015	2016
1.1 Insurance business written in the reporting country								
1.1.1 Insurance business, by ownership								
Gross premiums								
Domestic undertakings	216 268	206 167	208 608	230 559	215 494	219 832	217 673	287 883
Foreign controlled undertakings	59 431	54 294	60 570	75 289	69 361	57 959	58 471	..
Foreign companies (branches)	3 659	4 258	3 204	2 735	2 237	2 407	2 741	485
All undertakings	219 927	210 425	211 811	233 294	217 731	222 239	220 414	288 368
Premiums ceded								
Domestic undertakings	20 851	21 397	24 305	28 545	27 456	33 780	24 299	69 739
Foreign controlled undertakings	7 612	7 143	7 946	8 285	9 270	11 048	10 801	..
Foreign companies (branches)	407	403	356	179	53	47	52	167
All undertakings	21 259	21 800	24 661	28 724	27 509	33 827	24 351	69 906
Net written premiums								
Domestic undertakings	195 417	184 770	184 303	202 014	188 038	186 052	193 374	218 144
Foreign controlled undertakings	51 820	47 151	52 623	67 004	60 091	46 911	47 670	..
Foreign companies (branches)	3 252	3 855	2 847	2 555	2 184	2 361	2 689	318
All undertakings	198 669	188 625	187 150	204 570	190 222	188 412	196 062	218 462
1.1.2 Insurance business on foreign risks, gross premiums								
Life	..	..	..	..	..	..	..	..
Non-life	..	..	..	..	..	..	..	..
Composite	..	..	..	..	..	..	..	..
of which:								
Life	..	..	..	..	..	..	..	..
Non-life	..	..	..	..	..	..	..	..
Total	..	..	..	..	..	..	..	..
1.1.3 Life insurance payments, by class, gross premiums								
Annuities	36 105	33 344	31 964	..	20 899	22 295	17 278	..
Unit linked	106 589	99 537	98 203	..	112 727	114 296	117 452	..
Other life insurance	19 124	16 864	14 777	..	9 393	11 834	10 622	..
Total life insurance	161 818	149 745	144 943	163 481	143 018	148 425	145 353	107 693
***of which:** Pension contracts*	135 559	126 173	125 482	143 813	104 333	132 542	128 601	..
1.1.4 Non-life insurance payments, by class, gross premiums								
Motor vehicle insurance	10 929	12 112	12 786	12 643	12 133	12 069	12 883	12 711
Marine, aviation and other transport insurance	3 049	3 351	3 513	3 634	3 805	3 098	2 604	9 167
Freight insurance	706	674	718	778	942	885	808	..
Fire and other property damage insurance	15 008	15 322	15 413	16 087	16 500	15 969	15 544	26 026
Pecuniary loss insurance	4 737	5 512	5 498	5 707	5 717	5 966	5 791	7 318
General liability insurance	8 732	8 747	8 561	8 750	10 218	10 593	10 308	16 223
Accident and health	7 156	7 244	6 907	7 287	7 895	7 662	7 821	16 424
***of which:** Health*	..	..	..	..	..	..	..	..
Other non-life insurance	2 523	2 486	2 815	2 442	2 859	2 962	3 177	715
Treaty reinsurance	..	..	..	..	..	..	..	8 419
Total non-life insurance	52 840	55 448	56 212	57 328	60 070	59 206	58 936	94 481

United Kingdom
Table 1. Selected aggregates *(cont.)*

Million GBP

	2009	2010	2011	2012	2013	2014	2015	2016
1.2 Gross claims payments								
Life								
Domestic undertakings	160 384	156 626	162 040	166 655	166 084	161 503	172 514	122 430
Foreign controlled undertakings	39 273	35 287	36 240	51 269	42 535	26 653	29 078	..
Foreign companies (branches)	3	3	5	4	-1	4	5	..
All undertakings	160 387	156 629	162 044	166 658	166 083	161 507	172 518	122 430
Non-life								
Domestic undertakings	29 473	30 795	31 223	30 566	33 152	32 079	30 897	31 384
Foreign controlled undertakings	12 349	14 747	15 499	16 160	17 593	17 062	16 387	..
Foreign companies (branches)	1 572	1 764	2 082	1 785	1 405	1 469	1 871	..
All undertakings	31 045	32 560	33 305	32 351	34 557	33 548	32 768	31 384
Composite								
Domestic undertakings	18 478	18 662	19 413	20 735	21 625	22 527	23 077	50 512
Foreign controlled undertakings	1 937	1 293	1 006	615	754	2 170	2 734	..
Foreign companies (branches)	2 979	2 272	880	1 729	0	0	0	..
All undertakings	21 457	20 934	20 293	22 464	21 625	22 527	23 077	50 512
of which:								
Life	20 265	19 734	19 063	21 386	20 366	21 254	21 794	23 630
Domestic undertakings	17 330	17 499	18 219	19 657	20 366	21 254	21 794	23 630
Foreign controlled undertakings	1 666	1 040	721	342	326	1 876	2 413	..
Foreign companies (branches)	2 935	2 235	845	1 729	0	0	0	..
All undertakings	20 265	19 734	19 063	21 386	20 366	21 254	21 794	23 630
Non-life	1 192	1 200	1 229	1 077	1 259	1 273	1 283	26 882
Domestic undertakings	1 148	1 164	1 194	1 077	1 259	1 273	1 283	26 882
Foreign controlled undertakings	272	253	281	273	428	294	321	..
Foreign companies (branches)	44	36	35	0	0	0	0	..
All undertakings	1 192	1 200	1 229	1 077	1 259	1 273	1 283	26 882
Total								
Domestic undertakings	208 335	206 083	212 675	217 956	220 861	216 108	226 488	204 326
Foreign controlled undertakings	53 560	51 327	52 744	68 043	60 882	45 885	48 198	..
Foreign companies (branches)	4 553	4 039	2 967	3 517	1 404	1 474	1 875	..
All undertakings	212 889	210 122	215 642	221 473	222 265	217 582	228 363	204 326
1.3 Commissions								
Life								
Domestic undertakings	..	..	..	..	..	..	..	..
Foreign controlled undertakings	..	..	..	..	..	..	..	..
Foreign companies (branches)	..	..	..	..	..	..	..	..
All undertakings	..	..	..	..	..	..	..	..
Non-life								
Domestic undertakings	..	..	..	..	..	..	..	..
Foreign controlled undertakings	..	..	..	..	..	..	..	..
Foreign companies (branches)	..	..	..	..	..	..	..	..
All undertakings	..	..	..	..	..	..	..	..
Composite								
Domestic undertakings	..	..	..	..	..	..	..	..
Foreign controlled undertakings	..	..	..	..	..	..	..	..
Foreign companies (branches)	..	..	..	..	..	..	..	..
All undertakings	..	..	..	..	..	..	..	..
of which:								
Life	..	..	..	..	..	..	..	..
Domestic undertakings	..	..	..	..	..	..	..	..
Foreign controlled undertakings	..	..	..	..	..	..	..	..
Foreign companies (branches)	..	..	..	..	..	..	..	..
All undertakings	..	..	..	..	..	..	..	..
Non-life	..	..	..	..	..	..	..	..
Domestic undertakings	..	..	..	..	..	..	..	..
Foreign controlled undertakings	..	..	..	..	..	..	..	..
Foreign companies (branches)	..	..	..	..	..	..	..	..
All undertakings	..	..	..	..	..	..	..	..
Total								
Domestic undertakings	..	..	..	..	..	..	..	..
Foreign controlled undertakings	..	..	..	..	..	..	..	..
Foreign companies (branches)	..	..	..	..	..	..	..	..
All undertakings	..	..	..	..	..	..	..	..

United Kingdom
Table 1. Selected aggregates *(cont.)*

Million GBP

	2009	2010	2011	2012	2013	2014	2015	2016
1.4 Gross operating expenses								
Life								
Domestic undertakings	6 397	6 464	6 488	6 511	6 453	6 694	6 794	16 642
Foreign controlled undertakings	748	740	989	961	976	929	850	..
Foreign companies (branches)	1	1	1	1	0	1	1	..
All undertakings	6 398	6 466	6 489	6 512	6 453	6 695	6 795	16 642
Non-life								
Domestic undertakings	5 894	5 985	6 110	6 843	7 125	6 782	6 639	17 885
Foreign controlled undertakings	2 702	2 892	2 921	3 168	3 589	3 549	3 562	..
Foreign companies (branches)	128	152	152	200	167	174	186	..
All undertakings	6 022	6 137	6 262	7 044	7 292	6 956	6 825	17 885
Composite								
Domestic undertakings	1 644	1 701	1 936	1 856	1 978	2 127	2 325	22 264
Foreign controlled undertakings	198	262	261	195	172	277	328	..
Foreign companies (branches)	73	77	79	22	0	0	0	..
All undertakings	1 717	1 778	2 015	1 877	1 978	2 127	2 325	22 264
of which:								
Life	1 549	1 542	1 751	1 637	1 736	1 874	2 038	6 514
Domestic undertakings	1 507	1 501	1 709	1 616	1 736	1 874	2 038	6 514
Foreign controlled undertakings	164	163	156	102	91	185	211	..
Foreign companies (branches)	42	41	42	22	0	0	0	..
All undertakings	1 549	1 542	1 751	1 637	1 736	1 874	2 038	6 514
Non-life	168	236	264	240	242	252	287	14 316
Domestic undertakings	137	200	227	240	242	252	287	14 316
Foreign controlled undertakings	34	98	105	94	82	92	117	..
Foreign companies (branches)	31	36	37	0	0	0	0	..
All undertakings	168	236	264	240	242	252	287	14 316
Total								
Domestic undertakings	13 934	14 150	14 534	15 209	15 556	15 602	15 759	56 791
Foreign controlled undertakings	3 648	3 893	4 171	4 324	4 737	4 754	4 740	..
Foreign companies (branches)	202	230	233	224	167	175	187	..
All undertakings	14 137	14 381	14 767	15 433	15 723	15 777	15 946	56 791
1.5 Insurance business written abroad by branches, gross premiums								
Life								
Branches and agencies	..	..	..	..	..	..	..	..
Subsidaries	..	..	..	..	..	..	..	..
Total	..	..	..	..	..	..	..	..
Non-life								
Branches and agencies	..	..	..	..	..	..	..	..
Subsidaries	..	..	..	..	..	..	..	..
Total	..	..	..	..	..	..	..	..
Composite								
Branches and agencies	..	..	..	..	..	..	..	..
Subsidaries	..	..	..	..	..	..	..	..
Total	..	..	..	..	..	..	..	..
of which:								
Life	..	..	..	..	..	..	..	..
Branches and agencies	..	..	..	..	..	..	..	..
Subsidaries	..	..	..	..	..	..	..	..
Total	..	..	..	..	..	..	..	..
Non-life	..	..	..	..	..	..	..	..
Branches and agencies	..	..	..	..	..	..	..	..
Subsidaries	..	..	..	..	..	..	..	..
Total	..	..	..	..	..	..	..	..
Total								
Branches and agencies	..	..	..	..	..	..	..	..
Subsidaries	..	..	..	..	..	..	..	..
Total	..	..	..	..	..	..	..	..

.. Not available

Note: Detailed metadata at: http://metalinks.oecd.org/ins/20180621/d700.

Disclaimer: http://oe.cd/disclaimer

Source: OECD Insurance Statistics (database)

United Kingdom
Table 2. Number of companies and employees

	2009	2010	2011	2012	2013	2014	2015	2016
2.1 Number of companies								
Life								
Domestic undertakings	184	184	184	184	183	181	181	85
Foreign controlled undertakings	15	15	15	15	15	14	14	..
Foreign companies (branches)	1	1	1	1	1	1	1	1
All undertakings	185	185	185	185	184	182	182	86
Non-life								
Domestic undertakings	257	245	242	234	227	214	209	187
Foreign controlled undertakings	106	106	107	104	99	92	89	..
Foreign companies (branches)	18	16	16	15	10	12	7	25
All undertakings	275	261	258	249	237	226	216	212
Composite								
Domestic undertakings	21	21	21	21	21	25	25	17
Foreign controlled undertakings	7	7	7	7	7	8	8	..
Foreign companies (branches)	2	2	2	2	2	2	2	0
All undertakings	23	23	23	23	23	27	27	17
Reinsurance								
Domestic undertakings	34	32	31	31	30	29	26	9
Foreign controlled undertakings	20	20	20	19	18	16	13	..
Foreign companies (branches)	2	2	2	2	2	2	3	4
All undertakings	36	34	33	33	32	31	29	13
Total								
Domestic undertakings	496	482	478	470	461	449	441	298
Foreign controlled undertakings	148	148	149	145	139	130	124	..
Foreign companies (branches)	23	21	21	20	15	17	13	30
All undertakings	519	503	499	490	476	466	454	328
2.2 Number of employees								
Insurance undertakings	..	..	..	..	..	..	..	..
Intermediaries	..	..	..	..	..	..	..	..
Total	..	..	..	..	..	..	..	..

.. Not available

Note: Detailed metadata at: http://metalinks.oecd.org/ins/20180621/d700.

Disclaimer: http://oe.cd/disclaimer

Source: OECD Insurance Statistics (database)

United States
Table 1. Selected aggregates

Million USD

	2009	2010	2011	2012	2013	2014	2015	2016
1.1 Insurance business written in the reporting country								
1.1.1 Insurance business, by ownership								
Gross premiums								
Domestic undertakings	2 028 861	2 034 932	2 154 120	2 278 908	2 289 259	2 430 627	2 619 954	2 702 786
Foreign controlled undertakings	431 708	335 832	349 856	317 074	321 246	330 660	324 083	393 449
Foreign companies (branches)	643	629	731	909	662	696	1 129	1 007
All undertakings	2 029 504	2 035 562	2 154 851	2 279 817	2 289 921	2 431 323	2 621 083	2 703 793
Premiums ceded								
Domestic undertakings	604 210	531 114	560 386	601 133	657 662	609 531	713 961	743 307
Foreign controlled undertakings	208 658	163 993	170 330	140 316	175 424	134 223	139 675	195 708
Foreign companies (branches)	244	244	254	298	275	287	252	260
All undertakings	604 454	531 358	560 640	601 431	657 937	609 818	714 213	743 567
Net written premiums								
Domestic undertakings	1 424 661	1 503 818	1 593 733	1 677 776	1 631 597	1 821 096	1 905 993	1 959 479
Foreign controlled undertakings	223 050	171 839	179 526	176 758	145 822	196 437	184 408	197 742
Foreign companies (branches)	399	386	478	611	387	409	877	747
All undertakings	1 425 050	1 504 204	1 594 211	1 678 387	1 631 984	1 821 505	1 906 870	1 960 226
1.1.2 Insurance business on foreign risks, gross premiums								
Life	27 652	34 018	..	38 347	22 113	..	..	..
Non-life	22 055	..	..	..	..	..	..	..
Composite total	..	..	..	..	..	..	..	..
Total	49 707	34 018	..	38 347	22 113	..	..	..
1.1.3 Life insurance payments, by class, gross premiums								
Annuities	249 674	237 782	255 059	272 564	248 568	261 327	264 944	254 313
Unit linked	161 885	..	..	..	..	..	..	..
Other life insurance	765 602	762 172	811 561	557 259	533 515	527 280	561 674	581 948
Total life insurance	1 015 276	999 954	1 066 620	829 823	782 083	788 607	826 618	836 261
***of which:** Pension contracts*	880	..	..	..	..	..	..	..
1.1.4 Non-life insurance payments, by class, gross premiums								
Motor vehicle insurance	312 719	312 705	315 167	329 520	342 548	379 889	393 897	422 808
Marine, aviation and other transport insurance	3 667	3 452	3 337	3 545	3 245	3 070	2 911	4 815
Freight insurance	28 429	27 363	28 836	31 107	33 819	36 319	39 175	41 305
Fire and other property damage insurance	197 856	200 755	215 618	224 336	232 328	243 389	248 174	250 765
Pecuniary loss insurance	39 109	35 251	34 165	34 967	35 133	33 690	36 271	38 699
General liability insurance	173 097	170 571	172 997	183 263	191 562	204 069	208 722	211 362
Accident and health	471 470	482 830	516 841	550 291	566 173	646 938	714 394	761 509
***of which:** Health*	..	..	..	..	..	..	..	..
Other non-life insurance	4 328	3 532	3 018	3 179	3 505	3 780	3 728	3 921
Treaty reinsurance	..	..	0	..	..	0	0	0
Total non-life insurance	1 230 674	1 236 459	1 289 979	1 360 207	1 408 312	1 551 144	1 647 272	1 735 184
1.2 Gross claims payments								
Life								
Domestic undertakings	318 554	330 925	345 963	356 040	369 618	357 201	376 240	396 611
Foreign controlled undertakings	67 878	60 398	61 430	66 275	66 267	69 748	68 967	79 082
Foreign companies (branches)	2 319	2 293	0	0	0	0	0	0
All undertakings	320 873	333 218	345 963	356 040	369 618	357 201	376 240	396 611
Non-life								
Domestic undertakings	838 670	827 860	3 355 889	920 214	917 856	980 750	1 077 317	1 145 423
Foreign controlled undertakings	145 857	94 274	539 753	80 801	84 201	76 540	79 309	84 878
Foreign companies (branches)	416	309	2 253	723	234	240	359	504
All undertakings	839 086	828 168	3 358 142	920 937	918 090	980 990	1 077 676	1 145 927
Composite, all undertakings	..	..	..	..	..	..	..	..
Total								
Domestic undertakings	1 157 224	1 158 785	3 701 852	1 276 254	1 287 474	1 337 951	1 453 557	1 542 034
Foreign controlled undertakings	213 735	154 672	601 184	147 076	150 468	146 288	148 276	163 960
Foreign companies (branches)	2 735	2 602	2 253	723	234	240	359	504
All undertakings	1 159 959	1 161 386	3 704 105	1 276 977	1 287 708	1 338 191	1 453 916	1 542 538

United States
Table 1. Selected aggregates *(cont.)*

Million USD

	2009	2010	2011	2012	2013	2014	2015	2016
1.3 Commissions								
Life								
Domestic undertakings	39 925	..	..	..	..	53 082	56 784	67 963
Foreign controlled undertakings	9 784	..	..	..	..	11 165	10 339	10 639
Foreign companies (branches)	0	..	..	..	..	0	0	0
All undertakings	39 925	..	..	..	..	53 082	56 784	67 963
Non-life								
Domestic undertakings	99 023	..	..	..	..	..	..	..
Foreign controlled undertakings	9 858	..	..	..	..	..	..	..
Foreign companies (branches)	1	..	..	..	..	..	..	..
All undertakings	99 024	..	..	..	..	..	..	..
Composite, all undertakings	..	..	..	..	..	..	..	..
Total								
Domestic undertakings	138 948	..	..	..	..	53 082	56 784	67 963
Foreign controlled undertakings	19 642	..	..	..	..	11 165	10 339	10 639
Foreign companies (branches)	1	..	..	..	..	0	0	0
All undertakings	138 949	..	..	..	..	53 082	56 784	67 963
1.4 Gross operating expenses								
Life								
Domestic undertakings	71 693	74 311	66 258	67 534	65 424	67 225	68 488	69 722
Foreign controlled undertakings	15 873	12 817	9 782	9 962	9 814	10 285	9 952	11 175
Foreign companies (branches)	578	565	0	0	0	0	0	..
All undertakings	72 271	74 876	66 258	67 534	65 424	67 225	68 488	69 722
Non-life								
Domestic undertakings	231 186	233 969	239 829	250 270	261 844	281 766	298 911	308 839
Foreign controlled undertakings	33 838	27 537	28 759	22 153	23 185	23 274	23 035	26 711
Foreign companies (branches)	237	238	283	312	165	194	410	354
All undertakings	231 423	234 207	240 112	250 582	262 009	281 960	299 321	309 193
Composite, all undertakings	..	..	..	..	..	..	..	..
Total								
Domestic undertakings	302 879	308 279	306 087	317 804	327 268	348 991	367 399	378 561
Foreign controlled undertakings	49 711	40 354	38 542	32 115	32 999	33 559	32 987	37 886
Foreign companies (branches)	815	803	283	312	165	194	410	354
All undertakings	303 694	309 083	306 370	318 116	327 433	349 185	367 809	378 915
1.5 Insurance business written abroad by branches, gross premiums								
Life								
Branches and agencies	0	0	..	..	..	..	..	..
Subsidaries	27 652	0	..	..	..	..	..	..
Total	27 652	0	..	..	..	..	..	..
Non-life								
Branches and agencies	0	..	..	..	..	..	..	..
Subsidaries	22 055	..	..	..	..	..	..	..
Total	22 055	..	..	..	..	..	..	..
Composite total	..	..	..	..	..	..	..	..
Total								
Branches and agencies	0	0	..	..	..	..	..	..
Subsidaries	49 707	0	..	..	..	..	..	..
Total	49 707	0	..	..	..	..	..	..

.. Not available

Note: Detailed metadata at: http://metalinks.oecd.org/ins/20180621/e803.

Disclaimer: http://oe.cd/disclaimer

Source: OECD Insurance Statistics (database)

United States
Table 2. Number of companies and employees

	2009	2010	2011	2012	2013	2014	2015	2016
2.1 Number of companies								
Life								
Domestic undertakings	944	902	904	904	995	1 031	1 030	738
Foreign controlled undertakings	103	166	168	162	156	158	158	168
Foreign companies (branches)	2	0	..	..	..	..	..	..
All undertakings	946	902	904	904	995	1 031	1 030	738
Non-life								
Domestic undertakings	3 479	3 441	3 426	3 428	3 425	3 404	3 185	3 205
Foreign controlled undertakings	344	373	388	407	403	404	390	418
Foreign companies (branches)	19	7	8	9	11	9	13	19
All undertakings	3 498	3 448	3 434	3 437	3 436	3 413	3 198	3 224
Composite, all undertakings	**0**	**0**	**0**	**0**	**0**	**0**	**0**	**0**
Reinsurance								
Domestic undertakings	266	257	251	250	247	234	354	221
Foreign controlled undertakings	81	84	73	62	65	64	76	52
Foreign companies (branches)	1	2	1	1	1	1	4	2
All undertakings	267	259	252	251	248	235	358	223
Total								
Domestic undertakings	4 689	4 600	4 581	4 582	4 667	4 669	4 569	4 164
Foreign controlled undertakings	528	623	629	631	624	626	624	638
Foreign companies (branches)	22	9	9	10	12	10	17	21
All undertakings	4 711	4 609	4 590	4 592	4 679	4 679	4 586	4 185
2.2 Number of employees								
Insurance undertakings	..	..	..	..	..	..	..	..
Intermediaries	..	..	..	..	..	..	..	..
Total	..	..	..	..	..	..	..	..

.. Not available

Note: Detailed metadata at: http://metalinks.oecd.org/ins/20180621/e803.

Disclaimer: http://oe.cd/disclaimer

Source: OECD Insurance Statistics (database)

ORGANISATION FOR ECONOMIC CO-OPERATION AND DEVELOPMENT

The OECD is a unique forum where governments work together to address the economic, social and environmental challenges of globalisation. The OECD is also at the forefront of efforts to understand and to help governments respond to new developments and concerns, such as corporate governance, the information economy and the challenges of an ageing population. The Organisation provides a setting where governments can compare policy experiences, seek answers to common problems, identify good practice and work to co-ordinate domestic and international policies.

The OECD member countries are: Australia, Austria, Belgium, Canada, Chile, the Czech Republic, Denmark, Estonia, Finland, France, Germany, Greece, Hungary, Iceland, Ireland, Israel, Italy, Japan, Korea, Latvia, Lithuania, Luxembourg, Mexico, the Netherlands, New Zealand, Norway, Poland, Portugal, the Slovak Republic, Slovenia, Spain, Sweden, Switzerland, Turkey, the United Kingdom and the United States. The European Union takes part in the work of the OECD.

OECD Publishing disseminates widely the results of the Organisation's statistics gathering and research on economic, social and environmental issues, as well as the conventions, guidelines and standards agreed by its members.

OECD PUBLISHING, 2, rue André-Pascal, 75775 PARIS CEDEX 16
(21 2018 03 1 P) ISBN 978-92-64-30342-3 – 2018

www.ingramcontent.com/pod-product-compliance
Lightning Source LLC
Chambersburg PA
CBHW061215240926
51846CB00006B/1234
* 9 7 8 9 2 6 4 3 0 3 4 2 3 *